WORK AND WELFARE

Volume 99, Sage Library of Social Research

SAGE LIBRARY OF SOCIAL RESEARCH

Work and Welfare

The Unholy Alliance

David Macarov

Volume 99
SAGE LIBRARY OF
SOCIAL RESEARCH

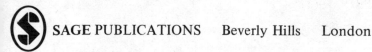

SAGE PUBLICATIONS   Beverly Hills   London

For information address:

SAGE Publications, Inc.
275 South Beverly Drive
Beverly Hills, California 90212

SAGE Publications Ltd
28 Banner Street
London EC1Y 8QE, England

Printed in the United States of America

Library of Congress Cataloging in Publication Data

Macarov, David.
  Work and welfare.

  (Sage library of social science research ; v. 99)
  Bibliography: p.
  Includes index.
  1. Public welfare. 2. Work. 3. Social ethics.
4. Poverty. I. Title.
HV31.M24   361.6   79-25740
ISBN 0-8039-1408-3
ISBN 0-8039-1409-1 pbk.

FIRST PRINTING

CONTENTS

To the memory of my mother,
whose life consisted of hard work.
She deserved better.

PREFACE

In writing this book, as in writing my previous ones, I have had the encouragement, help, and support of many people. These include my colleagues at the Paul Baerwald School of Social Work who participated in two colloquia on the subject; the participants in a seminar, "The Right to Treatment—Welfare as a Right," held in Jerusalem, and those who participated in the seminar "Molding Leisure Policies," also in Jerusalem, at both of which I broached some of the ideas contained in this book; and the organizers of the NATO Conference "Changes in the Nature and Quality of Working Life," who permitted me to attend even though Israel is not a member of NATO.

A number of individuals either read various drafts of the manuscript and made helpful suggestions, or did the same thing in response to a verbal unfolding of these ideas. My thanks go to Professor Beulah Rothman for this kind of help, and to Professor Felice Perlmutter, whose detailed comments were as helpful as her unfailing encouragement. Only Dean Joseph L. Vigilante and I know how helpful he was in carrying this project to completion, and I want to record my deep appreciation.

The basic ideas contained in this book were developed in classes and seminars at the Paul Baerwald School, the Bar-Ilan University School of Social Work, Adelphi University, and the University of Melbourne. As always, I learned much from my teachers but more from my students.

My wife, Frieda, and our children—and their husbands and wives—were unfailingly helpful and supportive, especially during

9

the last, mad race against the deadline, although they expressed difficulty in understanding why one who is basically opposed to work should work so hard at it. Thus, thanks to Varda and Chanan, Yehudit and Itzik, Raanan and Shoshanna, and Annette. The time taken away from writing to be with my grandchildren—Yaron, Michal, and Maayan—was my pleasure.

I have outlined some of the problems inherent in writing about such an emotion-laden subject as work in the final chapter, and I am grateful to the colleagues, students, and family members who suspended their own value judgments in order to give me opportunities for reasoned exposition of these ideas. Nevertheless, for whatever weaknesses and errors the book may contain, I alone am responsible.

—D.M.

Chapter 1

INTRODUCTION

"There is nothing more difficult to take in hand, more perilous
to conduct, or more uncertain in its success, than to take the
lead in the introduction of a new order of things."
—Machiavelli, *The Prince*

The connection between work and welfare has existed so long
and is so deeply rooted in attitudes and structures that it is
usually thought of as part of the natural order and is rarely
examined, let alone questioned. However, an analysis of the
underlying causes for the existence and continuation of poverty
in the Western industrialized world indicates that the link
between work and welfare is a major contributing factor.
Millions of people are poor, and tens of millions more spend
their lives hovering just above the poverty line and in constant
fear of becoming poor, in large part because the very institution
established to prevent poverty and to relieve it when it does
occur the social welfare system restricts its coverage on the
basis of work records and limits its payments to a portion of
others' or previous salaries.

Social workers and social welfare planners not only accept
the existing connection between work and welfare as necessary,
desirable, or both; they reinforce it through their own activities
without questioning the theories and values upon which it is

based and without examining the results. In thus accepting and stressing the overwhelming importance of work, social workers are in the mainstream of societal attitudes and behaviors. However, as the profession most deeply committed to fighting poverty and the social ills which flow from it; as advocates for their clients; and as experts on the nexus between societal structures and individual situations, social workers might be expected to be in the forefront of those questioning the necessity and desirability of the limitations caused by the work-welfare link, and at the cutting edge of planning more humane and equitable systems of social welfare.

Further, work itself is obviously not a source of enjoyment or fulfillment for the great bulk of workers, who constantly struggle for and achieve fewer hours, days, weeks, and years of work. Indeed, for many of them it is a source of alienation, frustration, and mental illness in varying degrees or, at best, a necessary burden for acquiring the pleasures of leisure time. This is particularly true of the majority of people with whom social workers deal, as what active pleasure there is in work is almost exclusively confined to those on the upper levels of hierarchical organizations, or in the free professions. Nevertheless, a very significant part of social workers activities consists of trying to place in or to return people to the labor force—motivating, inducing, training, making household and child care arrangements, seeking jobs, talking to potential employers, using sanctions or the threat of sanctions to get people to take jobs, and evaluating results in terms of the number of people moved off the welfare rolls and onto payrolls, regardless of other considerations.

Analysis of the causes of social workers' uncritical acceptance of work as a basic consideration in welfare arrangements indicates at least four interconnected reasons:

(1) The belief (not confined to social workers) that the economy and the society need as much work as members of the population can produce—i.e., that maximum production of goods and services is desirable.

(2) Since modern society provides no socially acceptable method of acquiring a share of the economy's resources other than through salaries, it is necessary that people hold jobs. In this view, it is the jobholding which is important, not the work done.

(3) Working is normative, causing not working to be labeled as deviant. Work thus becomes a therapeutic device to attain, or to reattain, normalcy. Neither the kind nor the amount of work, nor the level of salary, is paramount in this view—the act of working is the goal to be sought.

(4) Working is regarded as a moral act, and thus not working is seen as ranging from disreputable to sinning. Flowing from this is the concept that welfare payments larger than salaries are themselves immoral, since they reward immorality. In this view, neither production, salaries, nor normalcy is an important consideration— work is a moral imperative requiring no rationale.

It is the thesis of this book that most of these considerations are not valid, and the extent to which they are valid does not justify the human suffering they cause. The present link between work and welfare is not necessary, nor is it defensible. Moreover, it will become increasingly difficult to defend and maintain. The relationship between work and welfare which exists in the modern state was never historically inevitable; it is not the only conceivable arrangement; nor—despite the enormous effort that will be required to break the existing link—is it necessarily immutable.

On the other hand, insistence on maintaining the link will lead to or encourage intellectual and moral corruption, as pseudo-work is engaged in and rationalized. The gap between societal norms—which hold that work is desirable—and individual behavior—which indicates that work is to be reduced as much as possible—will continue to grow, leading to guilt, repression, projection, and scapegoating. Thus, the gap between socioeconomic strata will not only widen, but will result in bitterness and mutual recriminations. Finally, when the number of nonworkers held in poverty reaches critical mass as compared to the nonpoor workers—whatever the tipping point may be—a violent reaction may occur. A society in which, for example, 20 percent of the members do the bulk of the work necessary, and another 10 percent do a little work will not be able to continue terming the other 70 percent "nondeserving," or "lazy bums," or "social cases." Attempts to do so will lead to wrenches in societal structure whose implications are difficult to predict.

If, however, the inevitable results of a continuation of the work-welfare link are foreseen and understood, it should be possible to begin laying the groundwork for a society committed to reducing human labor as much as possible through labor-saving devices; automation; cybernetics; elimination of unnecessary products; production of repair-free, long-lasting items; and creation of an atmosphere in which conspicuous consumption, waste, and dispensable work are frowned upon. Such a society might find a value-base in noneconomic activities—education, music, human relations, sports, or leisure pursuits in general, for example.

Thus, the purpose of this book is to point out that there is, at the very least, a strong possibility that the amount of human labor necessary to maintain a decent standard of living will diminish considerably in the future; that to the extent to which this happens a new value or set of values will be necessary to replace today's dominant work ethic; and that the current linkage between welfare and work, in particular, will be impossible to maintain. We can, on the one hand, simply wait for these changes to take place and attempt to deal with them post hoc, or we can ease the inevitable shocks and wrenches by prior planning. We can even view these developments as healthy and desirable, and through conscious efforts attempt to bring them about sooner or more massively. It is the stance of this book that life with a minimum of required human labor is a consummation devoutly to be wished, and that people can be socialized to regard other aspects of life as just as rewarding and desirable as they have been induced to view work in modern society.

The chapter following this introduction traces the concepts "work" and "welfare" throughout history, pointing out how the present relationship came into being. From this history have come both attitudes toward the deserving and undeserving (or working and nonworking) poor, and the concept of less eligibility (the "wage stop") for nonworkers; as well as structural artifacts like work tests, work relief, and welfare programs rooted in prior and current work records.

The third chapter points out how these historic concepts affect the operation of social welfare today. Insurance-type programs cover only workers and often leave out large groups of them. Vestedness requirements, which demand specified prior periods of work or payments and which limit payments to certain lengths of time, operate to deny benefits to others. Administrative regulations designed to test the desire to work, such as waiting time requirements, carry these limitations further. Finally, the wage-stop (the modern equivalent of less eligibility) makes certain that no one gets from welfare what he or she could get from working, or what others get from working, or what the lowest paid worker gets from working.

The fourth chapter examines the results of this operation in terms of its impact on needy people. How many people are beneath the poverty line, how that line is drawn, and how much (or how little) help they receive are discussed. The role of the work-welfare link in thus creating and perpetuating poverty is explicated, together with some of its side effects on the aged and the disabled, on children, on single heads of families, and on proposals for a guaranteed minimum income.

The fifth chapter dissects one of the four basic reasons why the work-welfare link continues to operate the belief that society needs all the production that people are capable of creating, or needs the work of everyone, or needs everyone's maximum work effort, and that welfare offers an alternative to such productive effort. This assumption is examined in light of past, current, and future unemployment figures, which indicate that more and more people cannot find work. The question of how much current work is actually necessary is also discussed. There is, in fact, little evidence that society or the economy needs everyone's work to maintain present production or even to increase it substantially.

The sixth chapter calls attention to the confusion between the need for work and the attempt to spread and create jobs. Since our society has no widely sanctioned means of distributing resources other than through salaries, it is necessary that work be redefined and redivided to encompass as many people as necessary. The result is make-work, featherbedding, resistance to labor-saving devices, and pseudo-jobs. Not only is this an inefficient and unfair way to provide for the citizenry, but it also gives rise to a socially sanctioned delusional system which is corrupt and corrupting, and whose ramifications can be felt in many other areas.

The seventh chapter analyzes the "normalcy" of working, finding that there is a gap between people's expressed norms and values regarding work, and their feelings and behaviors concerning their own work. The dissatisfactions, mental illnesses, and physical consequences of this situation are examined. The relative nature of current norms indicates that present feelings about work are not the last word, and there are evidences that the norm is changing.

The eighth chapter examines the widespread belief that work is a moral imperative—freestanding and not (or no longer) connected to utilitarian or societal goals. This chapter points out that since morals are basically the result of a socialization process, changes in societal ideology and structure can lead to diminution of this attribute, or even its projection onto some other area of life.

Chapter 9 ventures some projections into the future, based upon current trends. The number of nonworkers will grow, absolutely and proportionately, as the population increases, as labor-saving methods and devices proliferate, as the aged live longer and retire sooner, as the young spend more time preparing for their working careers, as more women enter the labor market, causing greater unemployment, and as relative prosperity makes leisure pursuits more enjoyable. Competition for existing jobs will sharpen, leading to interpersonal and intergroup animosities. The proportionate amounts taken from earnings to support the nonworking will grow, leading to reaction, protests, and resentment. When nonworkers outnumber workers sufficiently, they will reject their second-class status, while the workers will resent their need to work. The flash point will lead to societal changes of incalculable depth, extent, cost, and results.

The tenth chapter proposes some scenarios by which a society dedicated to reducing human labor and placing values on some other societal aspects might be attempted; and how that society might operate and look. Education, creativity, and pleasure are seen as some of the results of such a society.

The eleventh and final chapter is a summation of the main themes of this book, with a call to action.

The data from which this book is drawn are based on the experiences of and published material from the Western industrialized countries, with the exception of Israel and Japan. The former is unique in a number of ways, including the enormous defense budget, the mass of new immigrants who continue to enter the state, and the funds received from other governmental and from voluntary sources. Japan's societal structure, network of interpersonal relationships, and history of emphasis on duties rather than on rights, as well as her emergence as an industrial state relatively recently, also make for uniqueness. Examples from these countries, the communist world, and developing countries are used mostly for contrast. However, it should be noted that most developing countries, with few exceptions (e.g., Burma) are attempting to become industrialized as quickly as possible. To the extent that they succeed and follow the same lines of development outlined here, they may eventually face the same problems.

It should be clear that this book, although based on data, is not value free. The writer is convinced that the connection between work and welfare which exists throughout the Western world is inimical, in that it tends to make many people poor, and to lock many others into the same condition. Further, the economic reasons once advanced for such a relationship are no longer valid, since full production in many countries is not only unnecessary, but harmful. Work itself, despite public protestations to the contrary, is increasingly unsatisfying as compared to leisure activities, and it is simply societal inability or unwillingness to envision or adopt an alternative method of distributing resources which results in efforts to emphasize the importance of work, rather than in efforts to reduce the amount of human labor needed.

For poverty to be vanquished, or even substantially alleviated, the link between work and welfare must be broken. For that to be accomplished, work must be understood for what it is: A historic necessity which has since been sanctified into a positive value, but which has begun to outlive its usefulness, and which, given desire, conscious effort, and skillful planning, can be reduced to a minimum, releasing people for more healthy and enjoyable activities, and freeing their creativity for more meaningful endeavors.

Chapter 2

HOW THE LINK WAS FORGED

"What's past is prologue."

—Shakespeare, *The Tempest*

"I 'spect I growed. Don't think nobody never made me."
(Topsy)

—Harriet Beecher Stowe,
Uncle Tom's Cabin

As is true of many other important concepts, it is difficult to arrive at a generally accepted, exclusive, inclusive definition of work.[1] Attempts range from those as simple as "any physical activity" or any useful activity,[2] to elaborate formulas—e.g., an obligatory economic action involving physical energy with the intention of perfecting or bettering something, which is useful and respectable.[3] Further distinctions are made between labor, which is said to be related to the cyclical and biological nature of human beings and which produces articles immediately consumed, and work, whose products are lasting and a source of satisfaction in themselves.[4] Some other definitions are more hyperbolic: "To labor is to be stamped by the activity; to work is to put one's stamp on the activity."[5] While Neulinger makes a distinction between work, jobs and leisure,[6] others find it difficult to arrive at clear distinctions,[7] and still others term work too complex to make possible isolation of criteria for such a distinction.[8]

At both ends of the complexity range the definitions can be assailed, either concerning their contents, or concerning their usefulness, or both. For example, if only the exertion of physical energy is work, a theoretical mathematician might be surprised to learn that writing down the solution to a knotty problem is work, but the intellectual effort involved in arriving at the solution is not. Similarly, is the planting of a fruit tree, whose produce will be immediately consumed, labor, whereas the planting of an ornamental tree is work? Indeed, there is hardly a sophisticated definition of work to which a commonsense objection cannot be made, and hardly a commonsense definition which stands up to rigorous criticism.

Consequently, it seems more useful to define work on a pragmatic basis, taking into consideration the use to which the definition will be put. For example, those groups which take the Biblical prohibition against Sabbath work literally—e.g., Seventh Day Adventists, the Amish, and the like—have defined that which is allowed and that which is forbidden to their own satisfaction. Perhaps the most detailed definitions of work exist in Orthodox Jewish life, where by the extension of certain basic principles every activity of human life has, for over a thousand years, been examined and categorized as permitted or forbidden on the Sabbath and certain holidays. Riding in a vehicle (except a shi, under way at sea), switching electricity on or off, walking more than a certain distance are all proscribed, and at present discussions are taking place as to whether using diapers which have adhesive tabs is work in this sense—with one view holding that pressing the tabs together is not work, but pulling them apart is.

For purposes of this book, work is operationally defined as *those activities in which people engage in order to acquire material necessities and luxuries.* The emphasis here is specifically on the material aspect, rather than on spiritual, psychological, or social rewards, and, as such, this definition includes all such material-acquisitive activities, whether or not they are thought to be respectable, useful, or productive.

The History of Work

In the early history of the human race, no distinction seems to have been made between work and nonwork activities. McLuhan even holds that work did not exist in the nonliterate world.[9] Certainly, in the language of some of the primitive societies which continue to exist today, there is no word to designate work. The activity of acquiring material goods is so all-important and so time-consuming that no distinction is made between work and other aspects of life. Work *is* life—and life is work—and there are no linguistic distinctions between work and nonwork. Australian aborigines on a "walkabout," constantly moving in search of food, do not designate this as work in contradistinction to some other activity.[10] On the other hand, there may be a rich language concerning aspects of work itself. Eskimos, for example, have many words to describe bears— walking bear, sleeping bear, dangerous bear—since hunting bear is vitally important.[11]

As society continued, however, individuals and groups became more productive through the use of tools, innovations like irrigation, the division of labor, and other discoveries.[12] The amount of work required to support oneself and one's family diminished, making possible a distinction between work and nonwork activities. At no time during this period, though, does work seem to have been viewed as pleasant, ennobling, or moral. On the contrary, in those societies in which slaves were captured by conquest, subjugation, or kidnapping, the role of the slave was to do the most mundane work. Other occupations were considered more prestigious than material-acquisitive activities—that of the warrior, for instance. The ancient Hebrews viewed work as a painful necessity, punishment for the sin of Adam and Eve. Paradise lost was lost indeed, as the necessity to work attested, and it had been paradise because it contained no work. In preindustrial society, no pretense was made that work was anything but a necessity, to be avoided insofar as the consequences were not too unpleasant.[13]

Had this not been so, the many admonitions to work and to work hard which are found throughout the Bible and its commentaries, in royal proclamations, sermons, fables, folk tales, and folk sayings would not have been necessary. As Freud pointed out, much later, there does seem to be a natural human aversion to work.[14] This natural inclination was reinforced by the economic structure of those days. Although some work was required in order to acquire life's necessities, there was no profit or merit in preindustrial society in acquiring a surplus. When arrangements for storage, transportation, and commerce were almost nonexistent, producing more than one's family could consume was simply wasteful—the surplus would rot.[15] Hence, in such societies, religion or custom might dictate more than a hundred holidays a year, and properly celebrating these was more important than working.[16]

In some times and places work was actually frowned upon and denigrated. To the ancient Greeks, work was a curse and nothing else. The Greeks regarded as drudgery physical work of every sort. Work was seen as brutalizing the mind, making man unfit for thinking about truth or for practicing virtue.[17] Socrates said: "Workers at these [mechanical] trades simply have not got the time to perform the offices of friendship and citizenship. Consequently they are looked upon as bad friends and bad patriots, and in some cities . . . it is not legal for a citizen to ply a mechanical trade."[18] To Plato, work, the production of goods and services, was not thought to be of any great importance.[19] As Aristotle saw it, work got in the way of the more proper pursuits of a citizen, corrupting him and making his pursuit of virtue more difficult.[20]

Primitive Christianity is said to have seen work as punishment, but added a positive function: work as necessary in order to share what one produces with one's needy brothers. However, no intrinsic value was recognized in labor—it was still only a means to a worthy end. Even when early Catholicism dignified labor, it was mainly of the religious and intellectual kind. Some cults preached work, not as a good, but, on the contrary, because it was painful and humiliating.[21]

At a much later date, it was widely assumed and accepted that no Victorian gentlemen would sully his hands with work or

even enter "trade." Similarly, in the pre-Civil War South, gentlemen were expected to be concerned primarily with horses and
women—in that order. In many places in the world today,
work—particularly physical work—is seen as demeaning and
degrading. Thus, some Asian and African participants in training
courses abroad ask that all mention of physical work be elimi-
nated from documents concerning them.[22] Indeed, throughout
most of the preindustrial world, and the preindustrial areas of
the modern world, the goal and the hope of most people was
and is to be able to stop working, or to be able to do less work
for the same recompense.

A number of convergent factors led to changes in the role of
work in the world. Improved roads and vehicles made it possible
to transport surpluses from point to point without ruining
them, and the emergence of a money economy to replace barter
made trading in surplus products much easier. Feudal society—
in which the lord exacted work from his serfs or peons, took a
share of their produce, or taxed them arbitrary amounts
through entrepreneur tax collectors—also put a new light on
work. Changes in inheritance laws played their part: Whereas at
one time the eldest son inherited the property, while the others
joined the clergy or the military, laws which gave all the
children equal shares and/or allowed daughters to inherit often
caused property to be divided until only intensive work could
support the owner and his or her family, and sometimes not
even then. The move from agriculture to industry transformed
labor into a commodity to be bought, sold, bargained for, and
exploited. The advent of factories which needed working hands
not only provided a solution for the latter, but led the mass
media of the day—clergymen, newspapers, government pro-
nouncements, public speakers, and the like—to emphasize the
purported positive values of work, creating a favorable valence
in the public mind.

Added to these structural changes were new attitudes and
ideologies. The laissez-faire conception of the economy, explicated by Adam Smith, held that if everyone would seek to
maximize his or her own economic condition, everyone would

benefit. If each were to compete with all others, the most efficient enterprise would survive, and society would profit by a supply of the best merchandise at the cheapest prices. This competitive network becomes the "invisible hand" regulating the market for everyone's benefit. The sine qua non for such a happy state is that everyone seek to maximize his or her own position to the utmost—or, in the case of laborers, that they work as hard as they can. Anything which interferes with the operation of self-interest and competition weakens the invisible hand, and everyone suffers. Work thus became a duty owed by everyone to a healthy economy. Those who do not work—or do not work hard—not only injure themselves, but keep the total economy from attaining its highest potential. The motivation to work hard thus took on tinges of human relations, neighborliness, and interpersonal responsibility.

Flowing from this conception was a second ideological component, mercantilism. The thrust of mercantilism was that the goal of a healthy economy was the wealth of the nation, rather than the welfare of the individuals. Measures which increased the value of the total economy were sought, without regard for, and sometimes in opposition to, the welfare of citizens,[23] with the intent of making the country rich in comparison to other countries. There is little question but that echoes of this philosophy continue to resound as concern for the growth of the gross national product takes precedence in many countries over welfare or other social considerations. The welfare aspects of such policies are sometimes termed the "trickle-down" theory, saying, in effect, that increased benefits depend upon increased prosperity.[24] Unfortunately, experience indicates that even if prosperity is a "necessary" condition (to use research terms), it is not a "sufficient" condition to bring about such trickling down.[25] Rather, increased prosperity strengthens the attitude that if people are poor, it must be their own fault in view of the many opportunities for acquiring wealth which seem to exist. This might be termed the Second Law of Social Welfare: When more welfare is possible, it does not seem needed, and when more welfare is needed, it does not seem possible.[26] In any case, the philosophy of mercantilism, or increasing national wealth through production, made work a patriotic duty, in addition to being a responsibility owed one's fellows.

Undoubtedly the most important attitudinal change regarding work, however, was the beginning and spread of the Protestant Ethic. When Martin Luther nailed his 95 theses to the church door in Wittenberg in 1517, he set in motion two influences regarding attitudes toward work. In denying the efficacy of good works in one's lifetime to earn grace or to guarantee salvation, since these things were predestined, he weakened the previously mentioned rationalization that one worked hard in order to help one's fellows. On the other hand, Luther viewed work of any kind as service to God. He endowed work with religious dignity by defining it as a vocation, or a calling, commanded by God. In his view, one serves God best by doing most perfectly the work of one's own vocation. Conversely, one who does not work, or who will not work to the full extent of ability, is a sinner. John Calvin went a step further: Not only is work a religious duty, but people are called upon to work without desire for the fruits of their labor, simply because to work is to carry out the will of God. Such work will establish God's kingdom on earth, and this is its value and its end. Thus, it does not matter whether people receive less than their subsistence needs for their work or become rich, whether the work is satisfying or stultifying, socially useful or harmful, degrading or elevating: God-fearing people work.[27]

In this manner, Catholicism's emphasis on good works was supplanted by Protestantism's requirement of good work. Work, as such, added a religious motivation to its human relations motivation and its patriotic motivation.[28]

The Protestant Ethic both helped bring about and was strengthened by the industrial revolution. It was the need of middle-class factory owners for labor which created the regularity of work that we know today.[29] Many factory owners (at least, as portrayed in fiction and fictionalized biography) felt themselves to be public benefactors in providing workplaces, and thus helping people avoid becoming sinful vagrants.

Workers were expected to be grateful to their employers, not just for the economic opportunities granted them, but for the opportunity to do God's will.

These changes in structures and attitudes converged to project onto work values, meanings, and goals far beyond those of making a living for oneself and one's family. Further, deployment of manpower, employment policies, wage levels, and minimum wage legislation, laws protecting and limiting working people and labor unions all became important elements in government policies. Determining the proper mix between policies leading to unemployment and those leading to inflation, for example, is seen as a problem to be grappled with on the highest levels of national policy making.[30] Thus, work has become a central element in both the structure and the ideology of most modern societies, and attitudes toward work are a major element in shaping social, economic, and fiscal policies.

The History of Welfare

Alongside this history and these developments as regards work as such, there has been another, parallel, aspect. Even in primitive societies there are individuals who do not directly engage in the acquisition of material items, or who do not do so full time, and they are therefore supported by those who are. This usually includes the young, who are still learning to work or whose work does not produce enough; the mothers of young children, and the aged (although there are societies in which the aged engage in a form of suicide when no longer productive, and others where mothers continue to participate in activities almost without a break). In addition to these categories, there may also be individuals or groups supported by the community despite or because of their non-material-gathering activities. Medicine men, priests, and artists contribute only indirectly to the work as defined, although they may be seen as vital to the success of others or to the community as a whole. Kranzberg and Gies point out that even in its early stages agricultural production seems to have provided surplus enough to support specialists—makers of metal tools and weapons.[31] At first, these were probably part-time specialists, and the priests and medicine men may also have participated part-time in the hunt or in agricultural pursuits. Even so, it is reasonable to assume that they did not do so at their own expense—the group compensated them for their "nonwork" activities. When they became full-time, they were certainly not left to starve or to forage for themselves. Nor did they "sell" their goods or services to individuals—the tribe, herd, or group made arrangements for such specialists.

It could be argued that such "welfare clients" who were supported by society because their roles were socially sanctioned, as exemplified above, were different from the modern poor, whose role is censured rather than sanctioned. However, it has been pointed out that the poor play important roles in modern society. Those who work perform the "dirty, dead-end jobs";[32] those who do not work are, in large part, those whom society has legally prohibited from working—i.e., the young and the old—or those whose roles are sanctioned by specific programs to keep them in those roles—i.e., programs to keep mothers at home with their young children—or societally supported invalids. In addition, the whole category of "the poor" plays an important informal role, as scapegoats, horrible examples, subjects of exploitation, and much more.[33] In short, the categorization of welfare recipients as those who do not engage in material-acquisitive activities but who are supported because their roles are socially sanctioned is equally applicable to modern social welfare, especially—as will be pointed out in detail later—since the proportion of the poor who can and should work and are therefore socially censured, is extremely small.

How much of the material goods nonworkers are entitled to, however, how the contributions are to be made, and how they are to be consumed or used is usually subject to codified or understood regulations. In some societies the warriors ate their fill first, nonwarriors next, then the women, followed by the children, and the aged scrambled for scraps, often taken away to be eaten. The priests in ancient Israel, for example, were to have "that which is left of the meal offering. ... It shall be eaten without leaven ... in the court of the tent of the meeting."[3][4] With the increasing complexity of society, regulations concerning precisely how much help is to be given to whom and under what circumstances constitute in many places numerous volumes of laws, regulations, and administrative procedures.

The mutual aid practiced within tribes devolved upon families when these became the basic unit of society, and upon neighbors when families were nonexistent or unable to help. The term "family" until comparatively recently referred to the traditional or extended family, usually living under one roof. Neighbors were those who lived contiguously. From these developments stem relatives' responsibility laws in many countries, by which certain relatives are legally responsible for the well-being of others, and residency requirements, which limit responsibility to those who have lived in the vicinity for a specified period. Both these have been ruled unconstitutional in the United States,[3][5] but continue to exist in other places. Responsible relatives in Israel, for example, include spouse's parents, adult children and spouses, grandchildren, grandparents and spouse's grandparents, brothers and sisters, and spouse's brothers and sisters.[3][6] Residency requirements in New Zealand range from twelve months for unemployment benefits, sickness insurance, and family allowances, to twenty years for old-age pensions. Both Canada and Australia require ten years' residence for old-age pensions.[3][7]

With the codification of religious beliefs—commandments and instructions—the role of organized religion as a dispenser of social welfare came to the fore. In almost every monotheistic religion, and some that are polytheistic, the commandment to take care of "social cases"—the widow, the orphan, the disabled, and the poor, among others—is important. The Old Testament explicates the responsibility of persons to others. The corners of grain fields are to be left uncut for the needy; that which the gleaners leave behind is not to be picked up. Gautama Buddha established the foundations of Buddhism, with its interpretation of poverty and the relief of the poor, about 500 B.C. Prince Asoka of India, a Hindu, endowed hospitals and shelters for both people and animals 300 years before the beginnings of Christianity. Both the Eastern and the Roman branches of Christianity engaged in charity. In Arab countries, hospitals were built and equipped as early as the twelfth century.

In Christianity, charity was one of the three cardinal virtues, along with faith and hope. The medieval Jewish philosopher Maimonides outlined eight degrees of charity, the lowest being giving with reluctance and regret, and the highest consisting of preventing poverty by helping people earn a living. In the Middle Ages, much charity was dispensed by and through the church, with tithing—contributing part of one's income—the basic source of funds. Eventually, religious motivations became the primary sources for the two main streams from which modern social welfare flows. The clergy, civic leaders, and public-spirited citizens formed loose associations to help the needy on an ad hoc basis. Informed of someone in need, one of them would assemble the pertinent information and appeal to the others for a one-time grant to relieve the problem. The initiative, the appeal, and the response were usually undertaken as part of one's "Christian duty," and to prevent the sufferer from resorting to a life of sin. By 1869 there were 640 such informal associations in London alone, and they federated themselves into the Charity Organization Society, which was the forerunner of most of today's family-service and casework agencies.[3][8]

Similarly, the roots of group work and community organization are in the settlement house movement, usually dated from the establishment of Toynbee Hall in London in 1884. Here, too, religiously inspired men and women acted out their religious beliefs on the one hand, and guarded the religious morals of their charges on the other. Such activities actually came to be identified with various branches of organized religion—the Young Men's Hebrew Association (founded in Baltimore in 1854, or thirty years before Toynbee Hall) being one example, and the Young Men's Christian Association or YMCA, associated with Protestantism, another.

The separation of church and state led both to laws regarding social welfare and to activities of the state as such. The division of responsibility between the church, the state, families, voluntary associations, and the market, insofar as human welfare was concerned, resulted in differing patterns in various countries. In some places, for example, education became the responsibility of the family (through home instruction or private schools); health, the responsibility of the market, whereby one purchased services from doctors, nurses, pharmacists, and so on; housing, the responsibility of the state (through housing authorities and schemes); and welfare that of the church. In other places, education became a state responsibility; health that of the church (through free hospitals and lay nursing orders); housing that of the market; and welfare that of family and friends or of voluntary associations. Other patterns also arose, including those of shared responsibility, wherein both the church and the state engaged in welfare activities.

The activities of the state regarding social welfare have been categorized as those which are residual, designed to help only after church, family, marketplace, and all other systems have failed, and those which are structural or institutional, in which social welfare activities are front-line governmental responsibilities, along with defense, highways, education, and so on.[39]

In 1531, during the reign of Henry VIII, the government of England first took responsibility for the relief of economic distress. Although this merely consisted of granting a license to beg, it was the first time that a type of social welfare right was conferred by an act of Parliament. During the reign of Elizabeth I, a series of laws was passed, culminating in 1603, known until today as the Elizabethan Poor Laws. The Poor Laws were based upon three principles: the responsibility of the state; limitation of this responsibility to those unable to take care of themselves; and administration of social welfare through local units.

These were essentially residual functions, and the first structural step was taken by Bismarck in 1882, when he introduced in Germany comprehensive plans for social insurance, including compulsory insurance against illness and accident and for old age.[40] Bismarck was not moved by religious conviction, nor was he a humanitarian. Rather, he sought to undermine the opposition political party which was advocating such measures. Another large stride forward in government responsibility for social welfare was taken in 1936, when the United States adopted the Social Security Act to counteract the Great Depression. The so-called welfare state as such was launched in England by the Beveridge Plan during World War II, with the intention of creating a country "fit for heroes."[41]

Such steps to include social welfare in the structure of governmental activities usually (although not always) involve insurance-type programs, and there seems to be a growing trend toward such universal programs, rather than those devised for specific categories of people.[42] Hence, an explanation is in order as to why these are referred to herein as "insurance-type" programs, rather than the more commonly used term, insurance programs.

Most such programs do not contain an actual written policy between the insured and the insurer. The insured often has no choice as to whether he or she is to be covered. Both the premiums and the benefits are changed without consultation or agreement of the insured. Premiums do not buy equal amounts of benefits: The well-paid may not be charged beyond a certain amount, and the not-well-paid may get benefits somewhat larger than those to which their premiums entitle them—or none at all, in some cases.[43] Were a private insurance agent to offer policies under such conditions, it is doubtful whether anyone would buy a policy.

In addition, there often is no organic connection between the premiums and the benefits. The Social Security Act of the United States was passed in 1935 in two separate Acts: One was a payroll tax, and the other was a pension plan. Although a trust fund was established to receive monies from the former, and pay them out for the latter, the fund does not sequester or invest the actual cash received—it is basically a bookkeeping operation. Consequently, it seems more correct to call these insurance-type programs.

With the entrance of the government on the welfare scene, the economics of social welfare came to the fore. Governmental programs involved vast and usually growing sums of money. The existence of massive trust funds for insurance-type programs, cost-benefit analyses which contrasted the expenses of programs with the savings of alleviating or eradicating social problems, and the share of taxes which went to social welfare all became crucial elements in predicting and planning. Social welfare expenditures make up over 40 percent of all government expenditures in the United States, and well over half the total expenditures of many states.[44] There are almost half a million social workers in the United States. And, as will be discussed in detail later, the social welfare institution will almost inevitably continue to grow, absolutely and proportionately.

From an instrumental activity designed to provide the needs, and sometimes the wants, of non-material-acquiring persons, social welfare began to take on an ideological hue. Attitudes toward equality, equity, dependence-independence, the standard of living, and the quality of life are often expressed through, and toward, the social welfare system. Humanitarianism and altruism find their expression, in great part, within the system, both as attitudes and as activities like volunteering.

The development of social welfare to the point that it contains elements of mutual aid, religion, politics, economics, and ideology, did not mean that it was free of other influences. In its time, the influence of Malthus's views on population led to current involvement with population and family planning. Darwin's doctrine of the survival of the biologically fittest species was vulgarized, as Social Darwinism, to mean that unsuccessful individuals (or social institutions) should not be helped, since such help interfered with the working out of natural law. Luther's influence, mentioned in connection with work, not only saw those who did not work as sinners, but similarly tarred those who helped them. Adam Smith's laissez-faire philosophy cast social welfare into the role of upsetting the economic system. Sigmund Freud caused many social workers to impute the cause of problems to the person, rather than to the environment. Further, Freud's famous recipe for happiness—"to love and to work"—pushed nonwork in the direction of a neurosis, or at least a personal problem, despite his oft-ignored comment, quoted previously, that there seems to be a natural human aversion to work. Karl Marx, on the other hand, emphasized economic determinism, but had little impact on social welfare thinking outside the communist world.[45]

In the history of the development of social welfare, the question of what is acceptable non-material-producing behavior varies with circumstances. There have been times, and there are still places, where warriors had their needs met by the rest of the community, or the king's relatives were not expected to work, or an entire stratum of religious functionaries—priests, nuns, monks—was supported by others. In many Jewish communities in Europe during the nineteenth century those who studied the Torah were supported by families, each of whom fed a student on a given day of each week, a custom known as being on "kest" with the family. In some current cultures, a father who stops working when his son reaches eighteen and begins a job, expecting to be supported by the son, would be denounced as a monster, while in others, a father who continues working after his son's eighteenth birthday is seen as shaming his son by indicating that the son cannot or will not support him.[46]

Consequently, in most modern states the regulations concerning who is entitled to welfare help, to what extent, under what circumstances, and how the help is to given as well as used (for example: food, yes; toothpaste, no; home rental, yes; home purchase, no) takes up volumes of legal jargon. These define and apply relatives' responsibility, residency requirements, income from various sources, assets of different kinds, work ability and disability, and much more.

The Work-Welfare Link

Welfare can be said to date back to the beginnings of mankind, as non-material-producing or non-material-acquiring persons were permitted to share in the community's resources. In some cases the link was punitive, as in the New Testament admonition that "If any would not work, neither should he eat."[47] This provision, incidentally, is repeated almost verbatim in the constitution of the supposedly anti-religious Soviet Union.[48] In other instances, e.g., ancient Athens, as noted previously, those who worked received only slaves' rations, while those who shunned work—i.e., full citizens—were in receipt of a sufficient amount of food and money to secure their livelihood.[49]

The historical connection between work and welfare insofar as modern legislation is concerned, however, might be said to date back to the Statute of Laborers of 1349. As de Schweinitz explains:

> The King and his lords saw begging, movement and vagrancy, and the labor shortage as essentially the same problem, to be dealt with in one law. They proposed to solve this problem by fixing a maximum wage, by compelling the unattached man to work for whoever wanted him, by forbidding the laborer to travel, and by stopping alms to the man who if he could beg would presumably refuse to work. The beggar, in the Concern of the Statute of Laborers, was not a problem in destitution but a seepage from the supply of labor.[50]

As often happens to this day with laws concerning welfare, the unanticipated effects of the Statute of Laborers on work patterns led to a speedy revision. The agricultural economy of the day required a supply of migrant workers, particularly during harvest time, but the law prohibited such movement. Consequently, the law was amended two years later to allow for travel during the month of August.[51]

There were numerous other attempts to restrict welfare for the benefit of work during the subsequent 200 years, but the legislative and attitudinal bases of modern social welfare can be traced back primarily to the Elizabethan Poor Laws, culminating in 1603. These laws were intended to repress begging, use work as the major vehicle for overcoming need, help children and the handicapped, and punish the idle poor. They assigned responsibility for social welfare to local authorities, thus strengthening the move from exclusive familial or religious concern to that of government. These laws also contained provision for taxes in support of the poor.

The connection between work and welfare which is contained in the Poor Laws is evident, if confused:

> The Elizabethan lawmaker proposes work as training for the youth, as prevention of roguery, as a test of good intent, and as a means of providing employment for the needy. In the background is the House of Correction with its threat of punishment.[52]

More specifically, the Poor Laws contained two concepts which influence social welfare laws and attitudes today: the distinction between the deserving and the undeserving poor, and the concept of less eligibility. In general, the deserving poor were those whose circumstances plainly made it impossible for them to work. These were usually defined in the public mind as children (meaning very young children, for in Elizabethan and later days child labor was not frowned upon), the very aged, those so severely handicapped that they could do no work at all, and widows with several small children. All other poor people were ipso facto undeserving. Those who could not find work, those who were denied work because of prejudice or discrimination, those whose salaries left them starving, and those who could not tolerate the conditions of work (some of which were described by Dickens) were lumped together with those who were capable of working but did not. The distinction thus established made possible an inclination to see poor people as undeserving, and the tendency to blame poverty and other problems on those suffering from them has continued unabated to this day, as will become evident in the fourth chapter.

Determining who was deserving and who was not pivoted on the applicant's ability and willingness to work, and since this was not always evident on the surface, work tests were devised. A work test often consisted of a pile of logs to be cut, in the

case of men, and flax or wool to be spun or pieces of cloth to
be sewn together, in the case of women. Although in some cases
the cut logs were subsequently used, or the garments given to
orphans, in most cases the test consisted of make-work—stones
to be shifted from one place to another and back, or garments
taken apart for resewing. The essential element was that the
burden of proof was on the applicant to show that he or she
really wanted to work. Even so, the underlying assumption
remained that the able-bodied could find work if they wanted
to, and consequently the help given the deserving poor was
always more generous (or, rather, less skimpy) than that given
the undeserving.

Even with the use of work tests, it was not seen as proper
that one who could work should be supported while not working, and, as a consequence, workhouses were established. These
were institutions into which the poor were required to move,
and in which work was provided—household work, farming, or
work contracted for. Workhouses were seen as important addi-
tions to the mercantilist state—in Britain, they were intended to
give a substantial boost to the woolen trade by having wool
carded and spun in workhouses by pauper inmates. Children in
workhouses were also expected to work, of course. Conditions
in workhouses were deliberately made harsh, in order that those
who could avoid them (people capable of working elsewhere)
would choose to do so. In this way, the principle that those
who cannot work or find work should be made to suffer, to
deter those who can work, was established.

Workhouses were considered "indoor relief," because recipients were required to live inside public institutions. However, as
the houses proved uneconomic, not only in terms of how little
work actually got done, but in terms of the high cost of upkeep,
even under Dickensian conditions, there was a swing to "out-
door relief" which allowed people to stay in their own homes.
Much of this help was tied to work through "work relief," in
which people were required to work for their needs. At one
time paupers were farmed out to farmers or entrepreneurs who
bid for their services, but the vicious exploitation to which this

led resulted in a trend toward governmental-sponsored relief work projects.

Work relief (or relief work) is seductive. Inasmuch as people are receiving money anyway, it seems that anything they produce by their labor is gratis. Experience in many places and at various times, however, has proved that relief work is expensive—the cost of tools, records, supervision, transportation, insurance, and the like are sometimes more than the actual work or product is worth. In most cases, normal labor drawing going wages could do the job cheaper (and often faster and better). In addition, the anticipated side effects, like maintaining work habits and skills, improving the recipient's morale, and meeting public criticism of welfare through requiring work do not eventuate.[53] Nevertheless, work tests, workhouses, and work relief continue to be utilized in various ways to distinguish between the deserving and the undeserving poor.

The second seminal concept of early social welfare was that principle known historically as "less eligibility," nowadays referred to as the "wage stop." This declares it illegal, immoral, or both, and makes it impossible, for anyone to acquire from welfare payments as much as or more than he or she could presumably acquire from working. In earlier days (1796) this was judged on an individual basis: "Measures were taken to prevent any man from securing a shilling which he was able to earn himself."[54] By 1834 the principle had become attached to wages in general, rather than to the individual's earning capacity: "The first and most essential of all conditions . . . is that his situation on the whole shall not be made really or apparently so eligible as the situation of the independent laborer of the lowest class."[55]

The inclusion of the word "apparently" is indicative of the force, or the fear, of public opinion, which might misjudge the situation of the pauper as being the equivalent of that of nonpaupers and react accordingly. This fear that the situation of the poor might approximate that of others now marks most social welfare programs, and its apparent violation is sometimes the object of the deepest and most emotional anti-welfare expressions. That nobody should get from welfare that which he or she could get from working (if they could work), or that which others get from working, is such a deeply felt principle on the part of some people that it defies rational discussion or analysis.

The manner in which the earning capacity of the individual is determined varies with program and place. One method is to base payments on the last salary, paying a proportion. Another, used by American Social Security, is to average out the individual's lifetime earnings, based on representative periods, and to pay a proportion of that. Or it is possible to determine the average wage for a country or a region, for an occupation or a group of occupations, and to base payments on that.

The payments which are made in almost every country and program are limited to a portion of this predetermined wage— hence, the term "wage stop." The wage stop not only operates to limit payments in direct and indirect grant programs, but similarly restricts the amount of payments from insurance-type programs, regardless of the fact that recipients may have paid premiums during a lifetime of work. Further, and perhaps even more important: The wage stop limits the amount paid to those who cannot work in any case, like the aged, to those who have never been able to work, like the young, as well as to those whom social policy has decreed should not work, like single parents of small children.

The work-welfare link was also evident in the beginnings of public (or private) social welfare. Of the Charity Organization Society, the prototype of many present-day voluntary organizations in the field of social welfare, it has been said:

> It epitomized that part of England which opposed any extension of governmental activity in this area and which believed that poverty was essentially the responsibility of the individual and that a request for assistance indicated a need for personal reform. It was in those years a strong advocate of the doctrine of less eligibility and played a strategic supporting part to the central body of the Poor Law in a campaign that, lasting through the nineteenth century, endeavored to reduce to a minimum, if not actually to eliminate, public outdoor relief. [56]

Although work tests[57] and relief work continue to be used, they have in large measure been supplanted by insurance-type programs. These, too, are linked to previous and current work records, and subjected to the wage stop, in almost every place and in every form in which they have arisen. The first such government-sponsored insurance program was, as mentioned, adopted by Bismarck's Germany between 1883 and 1889. This included sickness, work-injury, invalidity, and old-age pensions. The beneficiaries of this program were "those who are disabled from work by age or invalidity"—a forerunner of other work-linked programs.

In 1977, of 114 countries reporting insurance-type old-age pensions, 101 specified that benefits were only for employees (and in some cases for the self-employed). Of the remaining 13 countries, 6 paid additional benefits to workers, and 2 required payments to have been made into the scheme, thereby linking benefits to former incomes which in most cases means to former work. Two of the remaining five countries seem to assume that one will have worked and saved money or joined a private pension plan, since payments are limited to those in need. Only Iceland, Australia, and New Zealand report universal, noncontributory, non-means-tested old-age pensions, but one must be 67 years old and resident 40 years in Iceland, and 70 years old for a non-means-tested pension in Australia.[58] Thus, 97 percent of old-age and survivors' insurance plans throughout the world are linked to previous work records.

The same situation holds for sickness and maternity benefits. Of 72 countries reporting such programs in 1977, only 8 are not work related, either for cash grants, maternity benefits, or medical care—a rate of 89 percent work-relatedness.[59] Concerning medical care as such, 74 percent of the programs are for employees only. In the United States, the hospitalization provisions of Medicare are available only to Social Security beneficiaries, which means to those with a sufficient work record.

Even in the case of family allowances, often thought of as the prototype of universal, unrestricted programs, 47 of the 65 programs reported in 1977 are for employees, with an additional 2 being dual programs including work linkages, and one requiring prior payments, thus arriving at 72 percent work-linked family allowances. The importance of work shows through such programs in other ways, too: In East Germany, for example, employees are paid from the first child, but the self-employed are paid beginning only with the fourth child.[60]

Since work disability and unemployment programs are based squarely on work records, the result is that on a worldwide basis national social welfare programs of the insurance type are linked to work records in 72 percent to 100 percent of the instances (see Figure 2.1).

The connection between work and welfare is further illustrated by the sequence in which programs are adopted and by their spread. Workmen's compensation, for example, is intended to assure and reassure labor by promising that work-connected injuries will be compensated for and if possible that the injured will be rehabilitated. So important is this in labor-centered societies that some form of workmen's compensation law has been the first social security measure to be adopted in most countries, and in a few it is still the only branch of social security.[61] In 1977 more countries had work-injury programs than any other social security program, and this was equally true at the times of previous surveys—in 1940, 1949, 1958, 1967, and 1975.[62] Further, work-injury payments are often

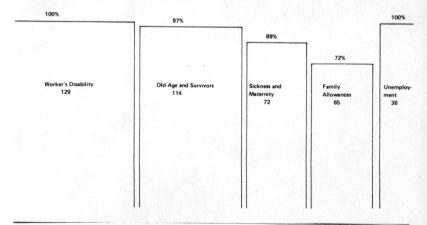

FIGURE 2.1   Linkage Between Work and Insurance-Type Social
Welfare Programs Throughout the World (1977)

significantly higher than those applying in case of ordinary sickness,[63] and are generally somewhat higher than for ordinary invalidity pensions.[64]

Contrariwise, unemployment insurance is usually one of the last social welfare programs to be instituted. Just as the justification for early, wide, and substantial insurance against work injuries arises from the desire to keep people at work, so the lag in initiation, coverage, and amounts of unemployment insurance reflects widespread suspicion or fear that payments in lieu of work will induce people to stop working or to stop looking for work. Consequently, there were only 38 unemployment compensation programs in 1977, as compared to 129 workmen's disability programs.[65] It might be argued, of course, that the lag in adoption of unemployment programs resulted from lack of widespread unemployment, and it is true that in the United States, for example, as well as in some other countries, unemployment insurance was an offspring of the Great Depression. However, in 1911, the year when unemployment insurance was adopted in Britain, the rate of unemployment (as measured then) was 3.0, the lowest it had been since 1900.[66] Similarly, the Unemployment Insurance Law in Switzerland went into effect in 1924, a year in which the number of unemployed was lower than it has ever been since. Four years later it was still lower than at any time until 1957.[67] In New Zealand, the Unemployment Fund was established in 1930, but the effects of the depression were not felt until "the early 1930s."[68] Consequently, the amount of unemployment is not the sole or general consideration for the laggard adoption of unemployment compensation plans (see Table 2.1).

It has also been argued that unemployment insurance is dependent upon industrialization, where the "labor market is sufficiently organized to afford a workable basis for this form of social security."[69] However, it is hard to think of Albania, Algeria, Cyprus, Ghana, Greece, Iceland, and Malta, among others, as industrialized countries, and yet they all have unemployment compensation programs. Further, most of the existing programs were established before World War II. If since that

TABLE 2.1   Number of Insurance-Type Social Welfare
Programs Throughout the World, 1940–1977

	1940	1949	1958	1967	1975	1977
Any Type of Program	57	58	80	120	128	129
Old age, invalidity, survivors	33	44	58	92	108	114
Sickness and maternity	24	36	59	65	71	72
Work Injury	57	57	77	117	128	129
Family allowances	7	27	38	62	66	65
Unemployment	21	22	26	34	37	38

SOURCE: *Social Security Programs Throughout the World 1977*(Washington DC:
Department of Health, Education and Welfare, 1977).

time there has been increasing industrialization throughout the
world, as there has been, it has certainly accelerated.

Consequently, there is good reason to believe, with Adams,
that: "Unemployment compensation . . . has been less popular
and has evoked more disagreement than have other programs to
aid the needy." [70] In a nationwide poll, support for unemployment compensation ranked seventh on a list of nine domestic
programs. While 70 percent of the population favored more
expenditures for help for older people and 60 percent supported more help for needy people, only 29 percent favored
higher unemployment benefits. [71] Further, whatever support
there may have been for this program at its inception appears to
have gradually decreased. [72]

Not only were these programs late, but many were highly
restrictive. Some programs were for building workers only;
some were not for, or only for, government employees; there
were programs for members of trade unions only, for employees
of firms of a certain minimum size, not for domestic workers,
and so on. In fact, about half the programs cover only workers
in industry and commerce. Further, introduction of unemployment compensation plans has slowed almost to a stop: Most of
the programs now in force were established before World War
II, and not only have relatively few new programs been introduced in recent years, but both Algeria and Iraq have discon-
tinued their previous programs since that time. [73]

Insurance-type programs are not alone in being tied to work records and efforts. Those programs which simply give out money to the needy are also conditional, in many cases, on the recipients seeking work. The Work Incentive Program (WIN) added to the Aid to Families of Dependent Children Program (AFDC) conditions the aid given parents of small children on their willingness to undergo job training, and subsequently to accept almost any job offered.

Even in-kind programs, which provide items and services other than money, are tied into the work syndrome. The largest in-kind program in the United States, the food-stamp program, makes such stamps legally available only to people who register for work. [74] Similarly, the spreading network of child-care facilities is available in many cases only to working mothers; this is also true in countries where there are camps, sightseeing trips, and other benefits available to working mothers, but not to mothers who stay home with their children.

Finally, the "personal" social services—in contradistinction to payments and other material items—are geared in large measure to using work for socialization and resocialization, for therapy, and for rehabilitation. [75] In rehabilitation, for example, the measure of success is rarely surcease from pain, or happiness, or family functioning, or improved self-image, but rather the rate of return to the world of work. Even this is sometimes justified, not in terms of the normalcy involved for the person, but as an increase in productivity. In this way, upgrading of poor schools or day care programs for small children are proposed as instruments to improve the future work abilities of those involved. [76] This is sometimes even costed out, in order to prove that rehabilitation repays society ten times over in income taxes received. [77] Indeed, in Iran one of the aims of social welfare is given as "improving the quality of the work force." [78]

As noted in the introduction, social workers "on the line," face-to-face with clients, spend enormous portions of their time trying to induce clients to go to work, helping them find work, directing them to courses to prepare them to work, helping solve problems which deter them from going to work, and in growing measure in solving problems arising from work. In the latter connection the newest burgeoning field of industrial social work, although specifically eschewing productivity goals, is constantly in danger of being manipulated into the position of helping working people with problems, not for their own sakes, but in order that they will be better, more dependable workers, not distracted on the job by outside problems. Indeed, current writings in the field emphasize solving personal problems so that people can go to or stay at work, to an almost total exclusion of changing work conditions or content to avoid or alleviate personal problems.[79]

Despite the closeness of the link between work and welfare, the relationship is never symmetrical. When welfare policies are proposed, discussed, or evaluated, the presumed effect of welfare on the employment patterns of recipients is a major factor considered. Sometimes this springs from a desire to remove certain categories of people from the labor force by offering a welfare alternative, as was true in the original conception of Old Age and Survivors' Disability Insurance ("Social Security") in the United States, which sought—among other things—to make jobs available for younger people; and in the Aid to Dependent Children program, originally intended to make it unnecessary for mothers of young children to go to work. More often, however, the primary considerations in fashioning welfare programs are the desire that people should go to work and the fear that too generous benefits will result in disincentives to work.

Contrariwise, when employment measures are under discussion, the impact of the proposed policies on welfare recipients, or on the poor in general, is rarely decisive.[80] Thus, full employment may be pursued because it is presumed to result in greater productivity and consumption, or resisted because it will lead to inflation. Unemployment may be feared as costing votes or leading to social unrest. However, only for publicity purposes is the claimed impact of full employment on welfare recipients discussed, since in reality the number of people in poverty who can work, or who would be helped by improved work opportunities, is invariably extremely small. In the same way, minimum wage rates in most countries are set by calculating their effect on the total economy or on production efficiency; the desire to raise the working poor out of poverty is not important enough a consideration to result in rates that would accomplish that goal. Similarly, labor mobility is encouraged or discouraged through policies more due to the needs of industry and agriculture than to the needs of workers. Even in programs ostensibly designed to allow people to retire from work with dignity, payments are kept low enough so that many people will want and need to continue working, a right which is being increasingly legalized.[81]

The strength of the work-welfare link is highlighted when viewed against other possible links. Despite the societal value placed upon education, for example, there are no formal educational "vestedness" requirements in social welfare—one does not have to have gone to school for a stated period to be eligible for welfare, nor are payments based upon the amount of prior education.[82] Efforts to turn or to return one to educational settings are almost always instrumental steps in getting into the workforce, and consequently usually related only to vocational education. There is, incidentally, a good deal of question as to how effective even these efforts are, since only very few of those so trained get jobs in the areas for which they have been trained, get any jobs at all, are removed from welfare rolls, or are lifted out of poverty.[83] In fact, as has been succinctly remarked regarding unemployment and as is equally relevant to other social problems: "Education alone as an answer to unemployment will only guarantee better educated unemployed persons."[84] In any case, education is not considered a prerequisite for welfare help, nor are payments limited on the basis that they will thus encourage or discourage people from studying.

One could make the same case regarding all other societal values. Welfare is not linked in any way to prior health records, personal honesty, effective parenting, good relations with others, nor with any other attribute that is considered desirable in individuals or necessary for society. Only work records and work motivations shape the extent and amount of most welfare payments and services. How this link operates is the subject of the next chapter.

NOTES

1. For a thoughtful analysis of the problems of arriving at a definition of work, see S. Parker, *The Future of Work and Leisure* (New York: Praeger, 1974).

2. E. B. Palmore, "Physical, Mental and Social Factors in Predicting Longevity." *The Gerontologist* 9 (1969): 103-108.

3. P. Schrecker, *Work and History: An Essay on the Structure of Civilization* (Gloucester, MA: Peter Smith, 1967).

4. H. Arendt, *The Human Condition* (Chicago: University of Chicago Press, 1958).

5. S. B. Sarason, *Work, Aging, and Social Change* (New York: Free Press, 1977), p. 30.

6. J. Neulinger, "The Need for and the Implications of a Psychological Conception of Leisure." *Ontario Psychologist* 8 (June 1976): 13-20.

7. S. Shimmin, "Concepts of Work." *Occupational Psychology* 40 (1966): 195-201.

8. P. D. Anthony, *The Ideology of Work* (London: Tavistock, 1977).

9. M. McLuhan, *Understanding Media* (London: Routledge & Kegan Paul, 1964), p. 149.

10. C. T. Shipman, *Stone-Age Cultures of the Australian Aboriginals* (Melbourne: Privately printed for the Israel Museum, Jerusalem, 1977).

11. M. Kranzberg and J. Gies, *By the Sweat of Thy Brow* (New York: Putnam, 1975).

12. Ibid.

13. For a thorough debunking of the idealized past in which people presumably enjoyed working, see A. Clayre, *Work and Play: Ideas and Experience of Work and Leisure* (New York: Harper & Row, 1974), pp. 85 ff.

14. S. Freud, *Civilization and Its Discontents* (New York: Paperback, 1958), pp. 20-21.

15. M. Weber, *The Protestant Ethic and the Spirit of Capitalism* (New York: Scribners, 1952), translated by T. Parsons.

16. W. Buckingham, *Automation* (New York: Mentor, 1961).

17. Parker, op. cit., p. 34.

18. Kranzberg and Gies, op. cit., p. 27.

19. Anthony, op. cit., p. 16.

20. Ibid, p. 17. There is even a point of view that today: "The traditional 'Protestant' ethic of work for work's sake has no place in Greek culture. A person works only to the degree that *philotimo* demands and when it is to the advantage of the family group. If the work becomes more important than responsibilities to the family or in-group the priorities are thought to be wrong." J. Walters, K. B. Mellor, D. R. Cox, J. M. Taylor, and L. J. Tierney, *Cultures in Context* (Melbourne: Victorian Council of Social Service, n.d.), p. 102.

21. Parker, op. cit., p. 35.

22. D. Macarov and G. Fradkin, *The Short Course in Development Training* (Ramat-Gan, Israel: Massada, 1973).

23. D. Macarov, "Social Welfare as a By-Product: The Effect of Neo-Mercantilism." *Journal of Sociology and Social Welfare* 4 (1977): 1135-1144.

24. Although Cutright found national affluence to be the strongest predictor of a nation's social insurance program experience, Wilensky reinterpreted the same data and found the age of the program more decisive. P. Cutright, "Political Structure, Economic Development, and National Security Programs." *American Journal of Sociology* 70 (March, 1965): 537; and H. L. Wilensky, *The Welfare State and Equality: Structural and Ideological Roots of Public Expenditures* (Berkeley: University of California Press, 1975).

25. Bequele and Freedman found that "there is no strong or obvious relationship between the rate of economic growth and improvements in the living standards of the poor, whether measured in terms of their share of the total income, their absolute level of income or a defined set of basic needs. . . . These studies suggest a trickle-up in favor of the . . . middle class and the very rich rather than a trickle-down to the poor." A. Bequele and D. H. Freedman, "Employment and Basic Needs: An Overview." *International Labour Review* 118 (May/June 1979): 315-329.

26. The First (or Iron) Law of Social Welfare has been enunciated as: "Those who need the most get the least."

27. Henry Ward Beecher expressed this clearly: "The general truth will stand that no man in this land suffers from poverty unless it be more than his fault—unless it be his sin." Quoted by H. G. Gutman, *Work, Culture, and Society in Industrializing America* (New York: Knopf, 1976).

28. This is not to indicate that the Protestant Ethic is confined to practicing or religious Protestants. As Rotenberg points out, the ethic has become diffused within other religions and among non-Protestant countries. M. Rotenberg, *Damnation and Deviance* (New York: Free Press, 1978).

29. J. W. Osborne, *The Silent Revolution: The Industrial Revolution in England as a Source of Cultural Change* (New York: Scribners, 1970), p. 38.

30. "The issue of full employment is, clearly, the central social policy concern." H. J. Weiner, S. H. Akabas, E. Kremen, and J. J. Sommer, *The World of Work and Social Welfare* (New York: Columbia University School of Social Work, Industrial Social Welfare Center, 1971), ???

31. Kranzberg and Gies, op. cit., p. 15.

32. A. Walinsky, "Keeping the Poor in Their Place: Notes on the Importance of Being One-Up," in A. B. Shostak and W. Gomberg, *New Perspectives on Poverty* (Englewood Cliffs: Prentice-Hall, 1965).

33. H. Gans, "Income Grants and 'Dirty Work'." *Public Interest* 6 (1967): 110; and *More Equality* (New York: Vintage, 1968); and D. Macarov, *Incentives to Work* (San Francisco: Jossey-Bass, 1970), pp. 30-33.

34. Leviticus II : 10, VI : 9.

35. See E. Eagle, "Charges for Care and Maintenance in State Institutions for the Mentally Retarded." *American Journal of Mental Deficiency* 65 (September 1960): 199; and *Shapiro v. Thompson,* 394 U.S. 618 (1969).

36. *Amendment to Family Law (Support), 1959* (Jerusalem: Government of Israel, 1959). (In Hebrew.)

37. *Social Security Programs Throughout the World, 1977* (Washington: Department of Health, Education and Welfare, 1977).

38. K. Woodrofe, *From Charity to Social Work in England and the United States* (Toronto: University of Toronto Press, 1962), p. 23.

39. H. L. Wilensky and C. N. Lebeaux, *Industrial Society and Social Welfare* (New York: Free Press, 1958).

40. C. I. Schottland, "The Changing Roles of Government and Family," in P. E. Weinberger, *Perspectives on Social Welfare: An Introductory Anthology* (New York: Macmillan, 1974), p. 129.

41. W. H. Beveridge, *Social Insurance and Allied Services* (New York: Macmillan, 1942).

42. *Social Security Programs Throughout the World,* 1977, op. cit. p. x.

43. P. A. Brinker, *Economic Insecurity and Social Security* (New York: Appleton-Century-Crofts, 1968), p. 85.

44. M. S. March and E. Newman, "Financing Social Welfare: Governmental Allocation Procedures," in *Encyclopedia of Social Work* (New York: National Association of Social Workers, 1971), p. 426.

45. For a more detailed account of these various motivations and influences, see D. Macarov, *The Design of Social Welfare* (New York: Holt, Rinehart & Winston, 1978).

46. In Scandinavia the bestowing of *Odels,* in which a father and his older son agree as to when the father should give up certain work roles and cease to supervise land use, still exists.

47. Thessalonians III : 10.

48. *Constitution of the Union of Soviet Socialist Republics (1936),* Article 12.

49. J. Hasebroek, *Trade and Politics in Ancient Greece* (London: Bell, 1933), p. 35; quoted in A. W. Gouldner, *The Hellenic World: A Sociological Analysis* (New York: Harper & Row, 1969), p. 137.

50. K. de Schweinitz, *England's Road to Social Security* (Philadelphia: University of Pennsylvania Press, 1943), p. 6.

51. Ibid., p. 9. The current European habit of taking vacations during the month of August probably stems from this amendment.

52. Ibid., p. 27.

53. J. Charnow, *Work Relief Experience in the United States* (Washington, DC: Social Science Research Council, 1943), pp. 114-115.

54. Schweinitz, op. cit., p. 92.

55. Ibid., p. 123. It should be noted that this did not refer to the *average* wage of common laborers, but to the lowest wage that any laborer was known to accept. Similarly, in comparatively modern times, Governor Huey Long of Louisiana defined

the federal requirement for paying the prevailing wage as the lowest wage he could prevail upon a person to accept.

56. Ibid., pp. 152-153.

57. Modern work tests require, among other things, that the unemployed prove their desire to work by going for interviews, following up newspaper advertisements, writing letters of application, and so on.

58. *Social Security Programs Throughout the World,* 1977, op. cit.

59. Ibid.

60. Ibid., p. 84.

61. Ibid., p. xviii.

62. Ibid., p. x.

63. Ibid., p. xix.

64. Ibid., p. xix.

65. Ibid., p. x.

66. *Encyclopedia Britannica,* Volume 22 (Chicago: Benton, 1965), p. 684.

67. A. Saxer, *Social Security in Switzerland* (Berne: Paul Haupt, 1965), p. 92.

68. *New Zealand Official Yearbook 1972* (Wellington: Government Printer, 1973).

69. *Social Security Programs Throughout the World, 1977,* op. cit., p. xxiii.

70. L. P. Adams, *Public Attitudes Toward Unemployment Insurance: A Historical Account with Reference to Alleged Abuse* (Kalamazoo: Upjohn, 1971), p. 21.

71. Adams, op. cit., pp. 20-21.

72. M. E. Schiltz, *Public Attitudes Toward Social Security 1935-1965* (Washington: Department of Health, Education, and Welfare, 1970), p. 93.

73. *Social Security Programs Throughout the World, 1977,* op. cit., pp. 65,112.

74. "It does feature a work test, as well as an assets test." R. L. Lampman, "Employment versus Income Maintenance," in E. Ginzberg, *Jobs for Americans* (Englewood Cliffs: Prentice-Hall, 1976), pp. 163-183.

75. Sommer, for one, holds that work as a "clinical" goal can be a valid focus for treatment. J. J. Sommer, "Work as a Therapeutic Goal: Union-Management Clinical Contribution to a Mental Health Program," *Mental Hygiene* 53 (1969): 263-268.

76. J. A. Kershaw, "The Attack on Poverty," in M. S. Gordon (ed.) *Poverty in America* (San Francisco: Chandler, 1965), p. 56.

77. B. J. Black, "Vocational Rehabilitation," in *Encyclopedia of Social Work* (New York: National Association of Social Workers, 1965), pp. 819-820.

78. C. J. Prigmore, *Social Work in Iran Since the White Revolution* (University: University of Alabama Press, 1976), p. 33. Interestingly, despite the ubiquity of such efforts, "There is no evidence that the provision of social services for welfare recipients has induced labor force participation." S. A. Levitan, M. Rein, and D. Marwick, *Work and Welfare Go Together* (Baltimore: Johns Hopkins University Press, 1972), p. 46.

79. See, for example, Weiner et al., op. cit.

80. In fact, as Weiner points out, the reciprocal relationship between work and welfare is "one vast uncharted iceberg. Little systematic attention has been devoted to the phenomenon." Weiner et al., op. cit., p. 5. Dubin also calls for "more detailed attention than has hitherto been devoted to an analysis of the functions of work institutions as contributing to welfare." R. Dubin, *Handbook of Work, Organization, and Society* (Chicago: Rand McNally, 1976), p. 23.

81. At the time of writing, the United States has raised the limit that a retired person may earn without loss of pension.

82. Even in terms of nonwelfare income, education explains only between 25 percent and 36 percent of variance in incomes. J. E. Tropman, "The Image of Public Welfare: Reality or Projection?" *Public Welfare* 35 (1977): 17-23.

83. "Gains in earnings have been large relative to costs, [but] they have not been large by conventional, social standards. . . . Even those studies with the most optimistic results estimate average posttraining annual earnings level well below the poverty line." J. H. Goldstein, *The Effectiveness of Manpower Training Programs: A Review of Research on the Impact on the Poor* (Washington, DC: Government Printing Office, 1972), p. 14.

84. M. G. Arnold and G. Rosenbaum, *The Crime of Poverty* (Skokie, IL: National Textbook, 1973), p. 191.

Chapter 3

FOUR CHAINS IN THE LINK: Coverage, Vestedness, Administration, and the Wage-Stop

"According to the law of the Medes and the Persians, which altereth not."

—*The Bible*, Daniel VI:12

As the relationship between work and welfare evolved through history, it created a social welfare system whose basic thrust is to induce people to go to work and to punish those who do not work, for whatever reason. The punishment consists of leaving them out of programs entirely, limiting their benefits, restricting the time during which they can draw benefits, making it difficult for them to collect benefits, and stigmatizing them to the point of creating emotional, social, and physical problems. Several mechanisms contribute to this situation: lack of coverage, vestedness requirements, administrative regulations, and—perhaps the most important—the wage-stop, which is extended to nonworkers as well as workers insofar as benefits are concerned. Thus, the historic concept of deserving and undeserving people continues to influence policy.

Limited Coverage

As pointed out in the previous chapter, insurance-type programs are linked to work in proportions ranging from 72 percent to 100 percent. In an overwhelming number of cases (over 90 percent of all programs in all countries), coverage specifies "employed persons," "employees," or "wage earners." This designation excludes from benefits, a priori, two large groups: (1) the self-employed, which includes not only employers of others, but owners of small businesses, freelance technicians like plumbers, electricians, painters, and so on, members of the free professions, artists, and others; and (2) housewives or, more correctly, nonworking wives and single parents. (Some programs, however, allow for voluntary participation by such people on payment of premiums.)

Nor does simple designation as a worker or employee guarantee coverage—58 of the existing 114 old-age programs, for example, specify certain groups of workers as excluded from possible coverage. These are usually agricultural workers, domestic workers, casual workers, or those in firms below a certain minimum size.[1] Some countries do not include school leavers as unemployed or entitled to sickness benefits until they have first held a job. Although there is some evidence that coverage is being gradually extended to different groups, it will be a very long time at the present rate, if ever, that people who are neither working nor making payments will be as fully covered as those who either work or pay, or both.

In grant programs, too, the designation as unwilling, rather than unable, to work is often reason enough to deny help. The Work Incentive Program provisions (WIN) of the Aid to Families of Dependent Children Program (AFDC)[2] are an obvious example of this, as parents in this program—which was devised to allow parents of small children to stay home and devote themselves to child care—are required to undergo job training and accept any available job, while out-of-home arrangements are devised for the children. In other programs and in other places, people who do not accept jobs found for them, or even those for whom it is difficult to find jobs, are often labeled "uncooperative," "unable to use help," or some similar pejorative designation and dropped from the rolls of service.

Lack of coverage even affects the personal social services. When day care facilities are designated for working mothers only, or when these are given preference or subsidies, the lot of other mothers who may have a strong need for such services—those with medical or psychological problems, with many children, with a problem child or children, or in housing unsuitable for children—may be made more difficult by such provisions.

Vestedness

Being eligible for coverage in a work-linked program does not necessarily designate coverage. Many insurance-type programs require a certain amount of prior work time as a condition for enjoying benefits, and benefit amounts and duration are often proportional to time worked. Qualifying periods may entail real hardship: Workers who are injured on the job may not be eligible for help if the injury occurs too early; those becoming ill or pregnant before the end of the required work period are in the same position, despite having paid in the required "premiums."

Further, there are always people who have paid into such programs while working, but have not worked enough to be eligible for benefits. On reaching the condition required for benefit-payment, they not only do not receive the benefits for which they have paid, even proportionally—they also do not receive their premiums back.[3] Sums involved may appear trivial in the total context of a social insurance program, but to the person who paid the premium the amount may seem considerable. In addition, such amounts judiciously invested tens or scores of years previously might have achieved a considerable current payoff.

The amount of time one must have worked to acquire vestedness varies from program to program and from country to country. Insofar as old-age programs are concerned, "The minimum qualifying period for a full pension under some social insurance systems is often 15 years, but variations may be found which range from 5 years up to 45 years."[4] Regarding sickness benefits, "Generally ... a recipient must be gainfully employed when he becomes ill,"[5] in addition to having a past record of sufficiently long employment. The most common qualifying condition for unemployment compensation is that the person have worked at least six months during the preceding year.[6] Even family allowances may be affected by vestedness—in the Federal Republic of Germany, for example, such allowances may continue to be paid for nine years past the statutory limit of 18 if the person is an apprentice or in a vocational school, among other things.[7]

At the other end of the vestedness scale, payments may be limited by statute to a certain period of time, or they may be proportional to the amount of time worked.[8] In this manner, sickness, which is generally considered involuntary, entitles one to financial help only in relation to the amount of time that one has worked, presumably voluntarily. In any case, a proportion of the people in need are in that condition because they have exhausted their social welfare benefits after having filled all the qualifying conditions concerning work.

Administrative Regulations

Although it is fashionable in some circles to think of administration as a value-free technology, not only are there ideologies of administration,[9] but the ideology of the institution must—if administration is to be effective—be reflected in the regulations and practices of the institution. Thus, the influence of the link between work and welfare is not only seen in the policies which govern coverage and vestedness, among other things, but in the minutiae of technical arrangements.

Take the differences between work-disability programs and unemployment compensation on an administrative level. No minimum qualifying period of employment or insurance is ordinarily required for entitlement to work-injury benefits. Temporary benefits are usually payable from the start of an incapacity, and this is replaced by permanent benefits if the incapacity lasts. For unemployment insurance, the worker is ordinarily required to have completed a specified minimum qualifying period—usually six months. A waiting period, often between three and seven days, is required. Some countries require such a waiting period before each period of unemployment, while others limit applications for unemployment compensation to once a year—a limitation that does not seem to apply to work injuries.[10] The administrative inconvenience of handling very short unemployment periods is operative in the case of unemployment,[11] and results in waiting periods, while such inconvenience is overcome for work-disability.[12] Similarly, waiting periods are used to prevent abuses of the system in the case of the unemployed, but not of the injured.[13] In these ways, administrative procedures carry out the ideology.

Waiting periods are also used to make sure one is "really" unemployed, ill, or retired before payment begins.[14] These waiting periods are more serious for the recipient than the administrators or policy makers seem willing to admit. In Australia, for example:

> The seven day waiting period is a myth. In practice, 17 days usually elapse after the claim is lodged. This is because firstly, upon registering the claimant has to wait an initial seven days before becoming eligible for benefit and secondly, because payments are retrospective, the claimant has to wait an additional seven days. This makes a total of 14 waiting days. To this we add three days to cover processing requirements and the fact that benefits are payable by cheque posted to the beneficiary's address.[15]

The Trade Expansion Act in the United States, which was not a welfare program but intended to aid workers displaced by foreign imports, operated so that there was a time lag that averaged 55 weeks between a worker being so displaced and receipt of benefits.[16] Injured workers have their benefits based on their salaries at the time of injury; other programs pay in proportion to salaries earned long ago, at rates which inflation has often made unrealistic. When adjustments are made to compensate for inflation, these are often made only once a year, with some countries moving to make adjustments twice a year. Such adjustments are usually not retroactive. Thus, in a country undergoing, say, 30 percent inflation a year, benefits fall—at the real level—to approximately 75 percent of what they were at the beginning of the year before an annual adjustment is made, or to about 85 percent in the case of semiannual adjustments. What has been lost in the meantime is irretrievable.

Administrative arrangements continue to reflect the historical distinction between the deserving and the undeserving poor. Many insurance-type programs require registration for benefits only once—when one becomes aged, sick, injured, or has a child—after which payments are made automatically until the condition changes. In almost all countries the unemployed worker must register for work at an employment office before benefits will be paid and must report regularly to that office as long as these payments continue.[17] There is, of course, no obvious administrative difficulty in having the unemployed person register, and then continuing the payments until he or she is notified of a job opening. However, the historical concept of work tests surfaces in this manner.

The insurance-type programs, with their work linkages, arose from two goals, neither of which necessarily required such provisions. One goal was to make the taxes required to institute and maintain these programs more palatable, and hence the payroll tax levied was disguised as an insurance payment. The second goal was to give people the feeling that, having paid for their benefits, the benefits were theirs as a right—in short, to remove the stigma from these welfare payments. The former goal is often attained during the early days of programs, but as the proportion grows, there is more widespread designation of the payment as a tax. The latter goal seems to have been achieved to the extent that even insurance-type programs which do not require premium-payment by the designated beneficiaries—e.g., workmen's compensation and unemployment compensation—are usually seen in some countries as paying insurance claims more than as welfare grants.

It is, however, precisely the pseudo-insurance features which make benefits seem to be rights that militate against payments to those who have, for any reason, not paid premiums or not paid enough of them, and against payments disproportionately high relative to premiums paid. Attempts to overcome these limitations include flat-rate payments to everyone in some countries, flat-rate payments based on marital status and dependents, flat-rate payments supplemented by payments proportional to premiums (the "two-tiered" system), flat-rate payments supplemented by means-tested assistance grants, and in the case of Australia means-tested payments only. Lately, however, there seems to be a move toward premium-linked payments in one form or another (the system which has always been operative in the United States).[18] Of this trend, it is said: "The concept of social insurance has almost disappeared in a system which, in effect, levies earnings-related taxes . . . in order to guarantee earnings-related income."[19]

The underlying rationale (or perhaps rationalization) for payments based on the amount of premiums paid in, using old-age pensions as an example, has been stated by the person who was the U.S. Commissioner of Social Security from 1962 to 1973: "Economic security for one no longer earning an income requires that a level of living be maintained that is not too far below what the family was been used to while living on earned income."[20]

This statement contains two clear value judgments. On the one hand, it could as easily be argued that during their old age those who have never had the opportunity to live well during their lifetimes to date—i.e., those who have never had good jobs or good salaries—should be compensated by society, as it were, by being given the chance to enjoy life during their remaining years, while those who were financially well off all their lives should have provided for their own futures or should be prepared to live on a lower standard than heretofore. In short, the ideology of premium-linked programs is that individuals are responsible for their own conditions, including their work-lives, while the ideology of compensation would argue that in most cases these conditions are societally induced.

The second value judgment in the rationale for linked benefits quoted above is contained in the words, "not too far below." The assumption that persons reaching pensionable age should be able to continue living at the same level that they did previously is not even considered. In short, when people stop working—even if they are required to stop working—they should expect, or be made, to suffer.

These value judgments, which are widely shared and are legally embodied in the provisions of the law, represent historical continuities of the distinction between the deserving and the undeserving poor dating, as mentioned before, from the Elizabethan Poor Laws and thus representing the attitudes of the sixteenth and seventeenth centuries: The aged who did not work hard enough, continuously enough, or successfully enough to have paid full and high premiums into social insurance programs should suffer the consequences of such undeservedness; and *all* the aged, since they no longer work, should reduce their levels of living.

These ideological considerations have practical consequences. Not only do they keep many of the aged in poverty, but they also damage the financial soundness of the programs. There is often a top limit to the amount of salary on which premiums are levied. Were there no such limit, and were payments to remain at current levels, considerably more payroll taxes would be collected, thus strengthening the financial structure of the program. However, this suggestion is rejected out of hand on the basis that it would not be fair to collect more taxes from high-income people than their benefits would amount to.

Nevertheless, concern for fairness does not seem to limit or restrict programs which are not related to work behavior. Many people pay for services which they do not use. Childless couples pay taxes which support schools; nonowners of automobiles support highway building through taxes; people who are actively opposed to certain programs or projects are still compelled to participate in their costs.

To summarize: The connection between work and welfare may have commendable goals—to establish benefits as of right, paid for by premiums or by work, and thus nonstigmatizing.

The result, however, is to base benefits on contributions rather than on need. Despite some slanting of benefits toward low wage earners in some programs, those who have been able to work and to provide for themselves at an adequate level usually receive the highest benefits. Those who have worked, but never made much money, receive less. And those who have not been able to work, and are therefore in greatest need, receive least.[21] In fact, the least well off have benefited the least from this system; the position of the poor relative to the rest of the population has hardly altered.[22]

It is difficult to determine how many people are excluded from welfare programs or benefits through limitations of coverage, vestedness, and administration. Most discussions refer to the number of jobs or industries brought into the program, rather than the people.[23] Consequently, such evidence as exists is tangential. One possible index is the difference between the number of people found to be unemployed through surveys, compared to the number officially listed as unemployed, and further compared to the number drawing benefits.

In Australia, in March 1977, surveys indicated 334,800 were unemployed. At the same time, there were only 326,500 registered unemployed, and only 236,400 drawing unemployment benefits.[24] The surveyed unemployed were 14 percent more numerous than the registered unemployed in Japan in 1975; 38 percent greater in Ireland; and 83 percent greater in Sweden.[25] In Britain in 1971 the registered unemployed accounted for only 77 percent of all unemployed persons, and in 1972 over 26 percent of the unemployed failed to register for benefits.[26] Although the results of coverage, vestedness, and administrative limitations differ from program to program, insofar as unemployment is concerned it is generally felt that the real figures are from 50 percent to 100 percent above the reported ones.

Similarly, if still tangentially, regarding old-age programs: In 1935 when American Social Security was passed, it was felt that the direct assistance program to the aged would be phased out as the former extended coverage to the recipients of the latter. But forty years later almost two million people were still in need of the assistance program.[27]

In any case, denial of coverage to nonworkers, linking payments to vestedness, and administrative procedures designed to reward workers and punish nonworkers all combine with the effects of the wage-stop to produce and maintain poverty, as will be demonstrated.

The Wage-Stop

The idea that anyone should get more from welfare than someone else gets from working seems so morally repugnant[28] that provisions against such a contingency have been written into almost every social welfare program in the world, even in the most inappropriate instances. As noted in the previous chapter, this attitude was expressed in the earliest social welfare legislation and was meant to prevent *anyone* on welfare from getting as much as *any* worker. Although this has been amended somewhat to deal with more general definitions—average wages, minimum wages, and the like—the general philosophy remains the same: It is almost universally axiomatic in social welfare policies that benefits are pegged, explicitly or implicitly, at a level so far below income from work that no one would, or could afford to, elect welfare payments over earned income. Throughout the world most systems have developed some mechanism for limiting the size of the pension. Many do this by fixing a ceiling on the amount of earnings taken into account for computing pension amounts. Others establish a maximum case amount or a maximum percentage of average earnings. Almost invariably, however, these maximums are based on the actual or presumed wage levels and are a proportion—often a small proportion—of them.[29]

Methods of determining the wage level to be used in fixing proportions vary, not only from place to place but from program to program within the same locality.[30] For example, work injury compensation may be based on earnings at the time of the accident, unemployment insurance may be paid at a flat rate, and old-age pensions may depend on total work career earnings.[31] These differences reflect value preferences regarding different conditions. As noted, work-injury programs are most prestigious, almost invariably instituted sooner, and (even more so in the case of temporary disabilities) make payments significantly higher than those applying in the case of ordinary sickness,[32] or of non-work-related disability, like automobile accident. Nevertheless, even the compensation paid for work injuries is expressed under nearly all programs as a *percentage* of the injured worker's average earnings during a period immediately before the injury, and a ceiling is often placed on the earnings considered in computing the benefit.[33] The double protection of a ceiling on the earnings taken into account and then payment of only a proportion of that, is obviously intended to place the injured worker in a weaker economic situation than he or she was in while working, thus discouraging malingering, deterring injured workers from applying, or even in some cases encouraging return to work before complete recovery. There is no pretense involved in the explanations of such provisions that the worker's expenses are reduced during the illness, thus justifying the decrease in income. It is clearly the desire to keep people at work that requires them to live on a lower standard while disabled.

Other programs use other methods for determining the size of payments. American Social Security uses a formula involving a number of quarter-years' income. Others use the average or the median wage in the country, in some specific area of work, like manufacturing, or in a geographical area. The basic rate of unemployment benefits is most often based upon a percentage of average wages. However, a ceiling is usually put on the wages to be taken into account for computation purposes. In other words, the payments are based on the average wage, but on condition that the average wage is not high. This might be termed being fair, as long as fairness serves other important considerations.

Many reasons are given as to why the retiree, invalid, or unemployed person must lower his or her standard of living (live on less money). One such rationalization often heard concerning retirees is that the social welfare payment is intended to supplement, not replace, other income. Yet only 20 percent of people over 65 in the United States had any type of supplementary benefits, such as private insurance or private pension plans in 1973;[34] and only about 30 percent in 1975.[35] Two-thirds of public housing families in New York in 1960 had no liquid assets at all, and only 9 percent of 1200 below-poverty-level California families had any savings.[36]

Another rationalization for limiting payments is that the recipient is in a position where less income is needed. It is hard to justify this plea as applied to the unemployed, the injured,[37] or the ill. Their expenses might be much higher during that period, not only for medical and nursing care and special home arrangements in the case of the injured and ill, but due to job-seeking costs on the part of the unemployed.

Insofar as the retired are concerned, Ball argues that they no longer have the expenses of working, they are able to partly substitute their own labor for purchased goods and services, and there is a decreased need for major household goods and clothes.[38] No evidence is cited for any of these statements, and consequently it would be just as reasonable to argue that they now have the expenses connected with leisure activities, many of them need services they did not need when they were younger, such as household help, and their need for clothes has certainly not diminished. It is even hard to imagine any purchased goods that the elderly can produce with their own labor.

Some argue that the retired no longer need to save money, and therefore need less income.[39] If the aged really save less, the cause and effect have probably been reversed—it is because they have less to save. The self-fulfilling prophecy inherent in this situation is obvious: Believing that the aged do not save, we give them less money. When they then reduce savings, it proves that they do not save. However, many aged persons living on pensions are anxious about a future which may last more than another generation, i.e., more than twenty years. Nearly 40 percent of those over 65 in the United States are over 75.[40] Many are concerned with possible failing physical abilities and the costly arrangements this will necessitate, the need for different (and often expensive) living arrangements, medical costs over and above any insurance they may have, and—most of all—inflation. Attempts to save for this uncertain future may be intensified with retirement, rather than abandoned. As a matter of fact, 20 percent of the retired auto workers studied, although admittedly an elite group, *increased* their savings after retirement.[41]

There are, it is true, normal ebbs and flows in the need for income during the average life.[42] The cessation of children's allowances at age 18, when children are presumed to become self-supporting, is recognition of such differences in need. However, the assumption that the day upon which one becomes injured, ill, unemployed, or 65, his or her needs are thereby substantially reduced has no basis in either logic or experience. Again, it is only fear of work disincentives which results in these payment limitations.

The actual effect of the wage-stop on welfare payments can be found by comparing such payments to wages. As mentioned previously, wages are computed differently in various places, nor is there a detailed summary of such comparisons available. Nevertheless, some representative samples culled from various sources will suffice to document the limitations caused by the wage-stop (figures marked with an asterisk should be viewed in light of Ball's estimate that the needs of the single retired drop by 13.6 percent):[43]

Retirement or old-age pensions:

United States (1978):

single persons	52%	of minimum wage
couples	78%	of minimum wage
single persons	41%	of average wage
couples	62%	of average wage
single persons	31%	of maximum covered amount
couples	47%	of maximum covered amount[44]
single persons (1973)	30%	of recent earnings*
couples (1973)	45%	of recent earnings[45]

France (1972):

single persons	25%	of annual wage on
(limited to):		retirement at age 60
	50%	of annual wage on
		retirement at age 65[46]

England (1976):

single persons	23%	of average manual
		worker's salary
couples	36%	of average manual
		worker's salary[47]

Canada (1976):

basic pension	28%	of per capita personal income
with guaranteed income sup.	44%	of per capita personal income [48]

Unemployment compensation:

world (1977):	40%-75%	of average earnings[49]
France (1972) (limited to)	70%	of annual wage[50]
England (1978) (unemployment compensation plus supplementary benefits—		
limited to:)	85%	of earnings per year[51]
United States	34%	of average wage
	25%	of wages lost[52]

Benefits (otherwise unspecified):

England (1976):

single persons	31%	of average male manual
		worker's earnings
couples	60%	of average male manual
		worker's earnings[53]

Canada (1973):

family, one child	82%	of minimum wage
family, two children	93%	of minimum wage[54]

New Zealand (1973):

single persons	32%	of average weekly earnings
married persons	54%	of average weekly earnings[55]

Children's allowances are usually infinitesmal as compared to wages, with the possible exception of France—in England, the benefits for a two-child family were only 3.5 percent of average earnings in 1977.[56]

Noninsurance payments are also limited, implicitly or explicitly, by the wage-stop. In the AFDC program in the United States in more than half the states grants are less than 50 percent of the level established by the states themselves.[57] Throughout the world the ratio of payments to earnings, incomes, average salaries, or minimum salaries seems to be getting smaller.[58]

The underlying (often verbalized) reason for payments smaller than salaries is the fear that people will not work if they can get money in any other way; or, specifically regarding welfare payments, that amounts equal to or near salaries will have a work disincentive effect. The actual effect of unearned income on incentives to work has been discussed in detail elsewhere, [59] and there is an enormous literature concerning efforts to identify work incentives,[60] most of which is based upon the assumption that money is not the only, the most important, or in some cases even a necessary condition.

This question is almost irrelevant insofar as welfare cases or poor people are concerned. As will be seen in the next chapter, the number of poor people or welfare recipients who can work, should work, can find work, and are not working is extremely small. The limitations of the wage-stop, outlined above, which range from 23 percent to 85 percent of wages for single persons, cause poverty among vast numbers of people who are not in the labor force.

NOTES

1. In the United States, for example, one-third of the labor force is not covered by unemployment insurance. *Monthly Labor Review* 102 (March 1979): 91.

2. The name of this program has changed several times. For the sake of consistency, it will be referred to herein as AFDC.

3. R. M. Ball, *Social Security Today and Tomorrow* (New York: Columbia University Press, 1978), p. 118; and Brinker, op. cit., p. 67.

4. *Social Security Programs Throughout the World 1977,* op. cit., p. xiii.

5. Ibid., p. xvi.

6. Ibid., p. xx. Work disability, on the contrary, sometimes requires no vestedness—e.g., in Austria, Canada, Belgium, and Britain, among others.

7. Ibid., p. xxii.

8. Ibid.

9. See, for example, D. Macarov, "Management in the Social Work Curriculum." *Administration in Social Work* 1 (1977): 135.

10. *Social Security Programs Throughout the World 1977,* op. cit., p. xxi.

11. Ibid.

12. Ibid., p. xviii.

13. Ibid., pp. xxi, xviii.

14. Nonwork disability payments in the United States require a six-month waiting period. Ball, op. cit., p. 476.

15. D. Griffiths, *The Waiting Poor: An Argument for Abolition of the Waiting Period on Unemployment and Sickness Benefits* (Fitzroy, Victoria, Australia: Brotherhood of St. Laurence, 1974), p. 3.

16. M. D. Bale, "Worker Adjustment to Import Competition: The United States Experience." *International Journal of Social Economics* 5 (1978): 71-80.

17. *Social Security Programs Throughout the World 1977,* op. cit., p. xx.

18. Ibid., p. x.

19. M. Bruce, "Thirty Years on the Politics of Welfare." *Social Service Quarterly* 52 (September 1978): 5-8.

20. Ball, op. cit., p. 11.

21. In accordance with the Iron Law of Social Welfare, mentioned previously.

22. Bruce, op. cit., p. 8.

23. *Social Security Throughout the World 1977,* op. cit., p. x. Ball mentions that in 1977 the United States covered 83 million people under social security, that the labor force then numbered 92 million, and that 107 million earners paid social security contributions. Ball, op. cit., pp. 185-187.

24. *Employment and Unemployment, May, 1977* (Canberra: Bureau of Statistics, 1977), pp. 10-13.

25. *Main Economic Indicators: Historical Statistics, 1955-1971* (Paris: Organization of Economic Cooperation and Development, 1973), and its *Supplements 1, 2, & 3* (May, August, November, 1977).

26. F. Field, "Making Sense of the Unemployment Figures," in F. Field, *The Conscript Army* (London: Routledge & Kegan Paul, 1977).

27. Macarov, *The Design of Social Welfare,* op. cit., p. 121.

28. "The person who works harder is entitled to nothing more, while the person who works less hard gains a greater claim over what others have produced. The moral

absurdity of this view is transparent." M. F. Plattner, "The Welfare State *vs.* the Redistributive State." *Public Interest* 55 (Spring 1979): 28-48.

29. Great Britain officially abandoned the wage-stop based upon the individual's previous or potential salary in 1975. However, when Parliament sets the amount of supplementary benefits every year, the wage level is tacitly and implicitly taken into account, as the proportions of benefits to wages, mentioned later, indicates. *Supplementary Benefits Commission Annual Report 1975* (London: Her Majesty's Stationery Office, 1976), p. 19.

30. See conditions in various countries for different programs in *Social Security Programs Throughout the World 1977,* op. cit.

31. West Germany, for example, uses full career earnings as a base, specifically growing out of the stated philosophy that "work makes life sweet." "Social Security Abroad: Earnings Index and Old Age Benefits in West Germany." *Social Security Bulletin* 40 (1977): 34-35.

32. *Social Security Programs Throughout the World,* 1977, op. cit.

33. Ibid., p. xix, italics mine.

34. J. Galper, "Private Pensions and Public Policy," *Social Work* 18 (1973): 5-22. This point is also made by official government sources: "Adequate retirement incomes are heavily dependent on income from employee pension plans. . . . Unfortunately, most retired persons do not have access to such income and must rely on their social security benefits alone." *Social Security Bulletin* 40(1977): 15. Of those who do have pensions: "The lowest paid workers . . . tend to get less than a proportional share of the private pension package." Weiner et al., op. cit., p. 114.

35. Ball, op. cit., p. 390.

36. D. Caplovitz, "Economic Aspects of Poverty," in V. L. Allen, *Psychological Factors in Poverty* (Chicago: Markham, 1970), p. 229.

37. "Average income for the totally disabled is half that of the nondisabled." *Work Disability in the United States: A Chartbook* (Washington, DC: Government Printing Office, 1978).

38. Ball, op. cit., p. 39. Nor does the existence of private pensions help very much: A study of $15,000-a year, 30-year employees found that their pensions average one-fifth of their final year earnings. J. H. Schulz, T. D. Leavitt, and L. Kelly, "Private Pensions Fall Far Short of Preretirement Income Levels." *Monthly Labor Review* 102 (February 1979): 28-32.

39. J. Habib and R. Lerman, *Alternative Benefit Formulas in Support Programs for the Aged* (Jerusalem: Brookdale Institute, 1976), p. 9.

40. Ball, op. cit., p. 78.

41. R. E. Barfield and J. N. Morgan, *Early Retirement: The Decision and the Experience and a Second Look* (Ann Arbor: University of Michigan, 1975), p. 324.

42. D. Jackson, *Poverty* (London: Macmillan, 1972), p. 26; G. R. Ghez and G. S. Becker, *The Allocation of Time and Goods Over the Life Cycle* (New York: Columbia University Press, 1975).

43. Ball, op. cit., pp. 39-40.

44. Ball, op. cit., p. 23.

45. Arnold and Rosenbaum, op. cit., pp. 242-266.

46. "Current Information: France—Recent Developments in Social Security Legislation," *International Labour Review* 106 (1972): 367-372.

47. T. E. Chester, "Social Security, Work and Poverty." *National Westminister Bank Quarterly Review* (November 1977): 38-46.

48. *Social Security: 1976* (Ottawa: Statistics Canada, 1976), p. 542.

49. *Social Security Programs Throughout the World, 1977,* op. cit., p. xx.

50. J. J. Oechslin, "The Role of Employers' Organizations in France." *International Labour Review* 106 (1972): 391-413.

51. *Poverty* 39 (April 1978): 6.

52. Arnold and Rosenbaum, op. cit.

53. *Poverty Fact Sheet* (London: Child Poverty Action Group, n.d.). Distributed with *Poverty* 38 (1977).

54. M. Lalonde, *Working Paper on Social Security in Canada* (Ottawa: Government of Canada, 1973), pp. 54-56.

55. *New Zealand Official Yearbook 1974* (Wellington: Government Printer, 1974), p. 168.

56. F. Field, "The Need for a Family Lobby." *Poverty* 38 (1977): 3-7.

57. N. Gottlieb, *The Welfare Bind* (New York: Columbia, 1974) p. 19.

58. R. N. Titmuss, *Essays on "The Welfare State"* (New Haven: Yale University Press, 1959), p. 24. Also: "The SSA poverty-line income has become a smaller percentage of the median family income over the years. . . . In 1959, the official poverty-line income represented about one-half of the median income of all Americans. But by 1974, the poverty threshold for an urban family of four persons had dropped to over one-third of median family income." M. N. Ozawa, "Issues in Welfare Reform." *Social Service Review* 52 (1978): 37.

59. Macarov, *Incentives to Work,* op. cit.

60. See, for example, the papers presented at the international conference sponsored by the Human Factors Panel of the NATO Scientific Affairs Committee, entitled "Changes in the Nature and Quality of Working Life," Thessaloniki, Greece, August 20-24, 1979; to be published as K. D. Duncan, D. Wallis, and M. M. Gruneberg, *Changes in Working Life* (Chichester: John Wiley, forthcoming).

Chapter 4

ALLIANCE FOR POVERTY: Results of the Link

"I've been rich, and I've been poor, and believe me, rich is better."

—attributed to Sophie Tucker

"Rich or poor, it's good to have money."

—Yiddish proverb

The limitations flowing from requirements of coverage and vestedness, ideologically oriented administration, and the wage-stop would only be of academic interest if the results were benevolent or at least neutral. Unfortunately, they tend toward the malevolent. For many recipients, and invariably for those who have no other income, these limitations create, maintain, and guarantee poverty.

In order to document this situation, an explanation as to what is meant by poverty is required.

Determining the level below which people are considered to be in poverty involves, inevitably, value judgments and arbitrary decisions.[1] This is true whether the definition being used is relative, comparing persons to other persons, times, or situations; normative, equating poverty with other conditions or designations; or absolute, based upon some unchanging standard.[2] Both Israel and Australia use relative definitions, although they are quite different. In Israel, poverty is defined by the governmental National Insurance Institute as 40 percent of the median salary and would seem to be value free, being based upon the statistical distribution of salaries. The factor of judgment enters, however, with the designation of 40 percent rather than some other proportion, with the decision to use the median rather than the average, and with the choice of salaries rather than gross or net income from whatever source. The judgmental content of this definition is pointed up by the fact that the median salary is not computed every year, but only once every five years. In the interim, the average salary is used, with whatever distortion this creates.

In Australia, the poverty line is defined as the basic wage plus child endowment. The basic wage, in turn, is defined as "the lowest wage which can be paid to an unskilled labourer on the basis of . . . 'the normal needs of an average employee regarded as a human being living in a civilized community.' "[3] The echoes of the Elizabethan Poor Laws' "less eligibility" are very clear here, but with the addition of a clause clearly based completely on value judgments. When it is recognized that the wage-stop guarantees that welfare payments will not reach this level, it is obvious that the poor in Australia, as in many other places, live below the acceptable level of a human being in a civilized community. Consequently, in the words of the author of the Australian poverty line: "It cannot be seriously argued that those below this austere line, whom we describe as 'very poor,' are not so."[4]

In both Israel and Australia the relative nature of the definition of poverty means that the poverty line varies from time to time—although, in fact, the number of people in poverty remains remarkably steady. Under the Israeli definition it would be extremely difficult to eradicate poverty, although theoretically possible, and more so than if the average salary were used.

Britain uses a normative definition of poverty: Each year Parliament approves a supplemental benefit scale as the minimum income for those out of work,[5] and this is generally used to measure poverty of all groups.

The United States, on the other hand, uses an absolute measure—the number of calories necessary to sustain life for a temporary emergency period. Noting that the U.S. Department of Agriculture issued a "low-cost" budget, and the Department of Labor issued an "economy" budget, both based on the minimum caloric intake required for sustenance, Orshansky, in 1964, sought to determine how much it would cost to acquire those calories, within a reasonably balanced diet, using foods easily acquired in the market.[6]

Extrapolating these costs to nonfood expenditures, and weighting the results for families of different sizes and compositions living in different regions and circumstances, a comprehensive table of the cost of living at the minimum level ("the poor") resulted, based upon one budget, and another table at a slightly higher level (the "near-poor") based on another. At that time, the minimum ("poor") budget for an urban family of two parents and two children came to $3130. This figure was widely used to define and count the poor in America, although it was generally vulgarized to represent $3000 per person or family, without Orshansky's careful differentions. At the time that Orshansky devised the poverty line, it worked out to $.22 per meal; by 1977, with inflation, it came to $.42 per meal. In other words, any family with $.42 per person per meal, and all other necessities of life at the same relative scale, is not considered to be poor.

It should be clear, therefore, that the poor being discussed are not a statistical but faceless concept. Their poverty is of the belly-gripping, face-grinding variety—lack of a bare subsistence living, with all of the deprivations, anxieties, neuroses, and defensive behavior patterns thus created. One study, for example, found that 31 percent of the lowest socioeconomic group were most impaired in terms of their mental health, while only 6 percent of the top socioeconomic group were.[7] Physical defects due to hunger alone are estimated to affect ten million Americans.[8] Sickness strikes the poor more frequently than it does the well-to-do. Bad housing, improper diet, strenuous labor in adverse surroundings, and inability to acquire regular medical attention make the poorer classes more susceptible to the attacks of disease. Poor scholastic achievements and a high rate of school dropouts, juvenile delinquency, crime, and what Caplovitz terms "hustling" are all highly correlated with poverty.[9] Nor is this only a problem for the individuals concerned. In some cities a quarter of the annual budget is used to provide the special services made necessary by slum areas.[10]

Other aspects of poverty have been factually and graphically depicted, including the feelings of indignity, the results of crowdedness, feelings of fatalism and helplessness, hunger, stigma, alienation, poor services, and higher prices.[11] Together, these add up to a wretched, tormented existence in which getting a little more money becomes the most important thing in life. An English study listing seven hardships to which children might be exposed because of poverty (e.g., missing school for lack of clothes or shoes, going to bed early for lack of fuel, a day without a cooked meal) found that one in six faced all seven, and one-half were deprived in at least four respects.[12]

Approximately 12 percent of Americans (about 26 million people) live in the conditions described.[13] In Australia, 10 percent of the population is very poor, and another 7.7 percent is poor.[14] In England, the number of people living at or below the poverty line has steadily increased since World War II, reaching 12 percent in 1976.[15]

The number of people below the poverty line in England is of particular interest, because it epitomizes a widespread phenomenon: On the one hand, Parliament determines the amount of supplemental benefit to which the unemployed are entitled, and this amount then becomes the poverty line by which the poor in England are identified. Since 12 percent of the population is below this line, they do not receive the amount to which they are officially entitled. Thus, the establishment of a poverty line by the government or a governmental agency does not carry with it any obligation on the part of the same body to raise people to or above that line.[16]

Further, the formulas for determining income for purposes of payroll taxes, for purposes of insurance-type payments, for eligibility for welfare grants, and for determining the poverty line may all differ. For example, a favorite device while comparing welfare income to wages is to add together all the possible benefits a hypothetical multiproblem family could acquire— such as maximum medical expenses, rent subsidies, food stamps, day care services, vocational training, income tax relief on social security payments—and compare them to a specific salary. The fact that, fortunately, very few families are so problem-ridden as to need all these services, and that even families using only a few of them are still below the wage level and/or the poverty level,[17] is rarely taken into account.[18] Further, in making these comparisons, the hidden benefits received by the nonpoor are never counted—state stipends for children at universities, capital-gains taxes, a whole array of legal tax dodges, low-interest loans for veterans, and even in some cases oil-depletion allowances.

Due to such differences in formulas, it is necessary to distinguish between and keep in mind the *poverty line,* below which people are officially designated as poor; the level of *welfare payments* or the number of people receiving welfare, which is not the same as and may have little relation to the poverty line; and the number of *the unemployed,* some of whom may be below and above the poverty line, and some of whom may or may not be receiving welfare help. This last is despite the fact mentioned above that the official poverty line may be established as the amount of welfare payments to which the unemployed are entitled, as in England.

Similarly in the United States: In July 1975, the federal SSI standard for aged individuals with no other income was 73 percent of the official poverty threshold for unrelated persons 65 and over residing in nonfarm areas. The comparable figure for aged couples was 87 percent. Only seven states provided supplements sufficient to abolish poverty for single recipients.[19] When other income is available, it produces no dramatic change: Taking into account all income, about 14 percent of retired social security beneficiaries were living below the official poverty level in 1976.[20] Particularly for single workers, current programs are simply inadequate.[21]

The striking fact concerning the number of people in poverty is that the proportion is relatively the same regardless of differences in program structure. The United States links payments to premiums in its major programs. England uses a two-tiered system, paying flat rates and then supplementing these, in some programs with premium-linked payments and in others with means-tested payments. Australia uses means-tested programs only. Israel pays flat rates. But despite these differences in program structure, and despite differences in determining the poverty line, from 10 percent to 13.5 percent of the populations in these countries are below the poverty line. The pervasive influence of the link between welfare and work seems to overcome both program and definitional differences.

The continuation and, in some cases, the growth of poverty is evident despite tens of years (soon to be half a century in the United States) of social welfare programs that are constantly widened, increased, and improved. Programs always manage to stop short, however, of payments that approach salaries for the dual reasons outlined above: that it does not seem fair otherwise, and that work incentives will be affected.

The fear that people will not work if they can achieve their needs (reach the poverty line) through welfare payments concerns three groups: those who are working for salaries below the poverty line, those whose salaries are slightly above that point but who would elect to lose some income for the privilege of not working, and those who are not working and must be encouraged or coerced to do so.

Slaves to the Work-Welfare Link:
The Working Poor

In every country there are substantial numbers of people below the poverty line despite the fact that they are working. In the United States, of the 26 million people defined as poor, 2.3 million are working, and half of them hold full-time, year-round jobs.[22] In fact, one-third of all families classified as poor are within the working community.[23] Further, earnings constituted

37.1 percent of the total money income of families with incomes of $4000 or less in the United States.[24] In Australia, 27 percent of income units defined as "very poor" have a head in the workforce.[25] In England, this group was described in 1974 as the fastest-growing group of poor people, with 70,000 families earning less than the official poverty line.[26]

These working poor—those who "earn their poverty"[27] —are the very nub and crux of the poverty problem. To make payments to them that will raise them above the poverty line means paying them more than their present salaries which are, by definition, below that line. This would presumably remove their incentive to work, and certainly their economic incentive to continue in their present jobs. Not only is it assumed that they will then suffer the psychological, moral, and social deterioration that not working is believed to entail, but society will be deprived of their work in the dirty, dead-end jobs that nobody else wants.[28] In addition, those who are only slightly above the poverty line might decide to sacrifice some income for more leisure and opt for welfare rather than for work.

In this manner, most income maintenance programs operate to guarantee that some people are required to work for income which the society has officially defined as less than that necessary for even temporary and emergency subsistence, or less than the normal needs of a human being living in a civilized community. A system which requires people to work for starvation wages on pain of even greater deprivation can only be called, in the politest of terms, semi-slavery.

One obvious method of alleviating the plight of the working poor is to raise salaries, rather than limiting welfare. However, proposals to institute a legal minimum wage where one does not exist, or to raise it sufficiently where it does exist, run into a number of objections. One argument is that this would require raising all other salaries proportionately, on the basis that present differentials must be maintained. Another argument is that if all salaries were not raised, the wage earners presently just above the minimum would than be making the minimum wage, which they would resist and resent. Both these arguments rest

on the assumption (which may be true) that society wants and
needs a lowest stratum of wage earners below the poverty
line.[29] The third argument is that either "marginal" workers
would be paid more than their production is worth, thereby
contributing to inflation, or that they would be discharged,
thereby contributing to unemployment,[30] and "the general
employment and inflationary consequences of raising minimum
wage levels to a point where the income from 35 to 40 hours of
work would satisfy budgetary requirements at the lower level of
living . . . would probably make such a measure inadvisable."[31]
Consequently, low-paid workers are exploited to keep higher-
paid workers happy, or to serve long-run economic goals. The
result:

> Most poor two-parent families are large families with one member in
> the labor force working at a low wage rate. Twenty million people
> work in industries that pay less than enough to bring a family of five
> out of poverty. Working full time at the minimum wage in 1978 is
> not even sufficient to bring a three-person family out of poverty . . .
> families supported by low wage earners nevertheless pay directly and
> indirectly over one-third of their income in taxes.[32]

This situation arises because the work ethic prevails over the
humane view. Few people have the temerity to question
whether an industry which cannot pay an adequate wage should
be permitted to survive by maintaining its workers at the
poverty level.[33]

Without a minimum wage law covering even the lowest-paid
workers (whose jobs are often excluded from such legislation),
even wage supplements may prove to be unworkable. This was
the experience in Speenhamland, a classic experiment carried
out in 1795. A wage supplement was given those whose salaries
were too low to allow them to provide for their families, but
the experiment foundered on the fact that employers promptly
lowered the wages they had been paying. With the widening gap
covered by the government subsidy, the major beneficiaries
were the employers, whose profits rose steadily, and the experiment was abandoned as too costly and ineffective.[34]

Even with a minimum wage above the poverty level, problems remain. Such wages affect part-time or seasonal underpaid workers very little, and these positions are often excluded from the legislation. More important, since salaries are not usually linked to family size,[35] while the poverty line is, a minimum wage that might suffice to raise single persons or small families out of poverty would not suffice for large families; and were it fixed at a point where it would solve the income problem of large families, it would "overpay" the others. In fact, there is no way that all families can be raised above the poverty line through social welfare while some who work get inadequate earnings.[36]

In short, one of the guiding principles derived from the work-welfare link is: If welfare payments threaten to approach salary levels, lower the payments rather than increase the salaries.

Hostages to the Work-Welfare Link: The Nonworkers

As noted above, from 10 percent to 25 percent of the poor (or poor family heads) are working, and the wage-stop is designed in great measure to keep them working, but the effect on the great majority of the poor who cannot work, should not work, or cannot find work is equally deleterious. In the United States in 1971 half the poverty population consisted of children under fourteen or the elderly. Of the remainder, 43 percent were women with family responsibilities, 28 percent were students, and 19 percent were either disabled or ill. Only about 10 percent of the working-age poor were unemployed for reasons other than school, illness, or family responsibilities.[37]

In 1975 the poor in the United States consisted of:

children less than 16 years old	40%
persons 65 years old or more	20%
disabled persons	5%
female heads of families	25%

the unemployed looking for work   1%
the employed   9%[38]

Persons drawing supplementary benefits in England at about the same time consisted of:

pensioners   57%
sick/disabled   8%
unemployed   22%
one-parent family   10%
others   2%[39]

In Australia, adult income units below the poverty line ("very poor") consisted of

aged   40%
single-headed families   14%
sick or invalid   4%
unemployed   2%
recent migrants   1%
large families   3%
combination of the above   9%
others   27%[40]

In Canada not more than 10 to 20 percent of the 550,000 family units receiving social assistance are able, or should be expected, to work. Of the caseload, 80 to 90 percent are disabled, old, or single-parent families.[41]

In this way, measures designed to ensure that those who can work do so—even at starvation wages—are applied to those who cannot work, who are not permitted to work, who cannot find work, or whom social policy says should not work.

The disabled and some of the aged cannot work for physical reasons. Consequently, concerns about work disincentives and fixing payments at a point where such disincentives will not be created are clearly not applicable to them. And yet their payments are pegged at the same level as those who can, should, or do work.

Similarly, that the aged do not work may or may not be from choice. However, in the case of those who do choose to work, retirement is often mandatory. That is, the rule which allows someone to retire and draw a pension is applied, officially or unofficially, in such a way that everyone is forced to do so.[42] In these cases, the desire to work is also irrelevant, and the wage-stop designed to avoid work disincentives is meaningless— but applied.

One of the largest groups of the poor, in some countries, are single heads of families, and it is for this group that some of the strongest humanitarian motives are felt. The image of the poor widow, struggling to maintain standards in the face of poverty, has been the impetus for several welfare programs—in the United States, the AFDC program. The expressed goal of these programs is to enable the mother (and, in more recent amendments, the father) to remain at home to take care of the children, rather than having to entrust them to others. That such single family heads should have to leave the children to go to work is what the programs try to avoid—and yet the amount of money paid to such cases is just as limited by the wage-stop as in any other program.

It is somewhat surprising that a former Commissioner of Social Security in the United States should express himself as surprised at the effect of the wage-stop—i.e., the amount of poverty among families headed by widows, particularly where there are several children.[43] In 1971 about 40 percent of the families of widows with children were poor. Of those with one or two children, 32 percent were poor; with three children, 49 percent; and with four or more children, 70 percent were poor.[44] In 1977 there were 3.6 million families on AFDC, which was 12 percent of all families with children. The AFDC families consisted of 7.9 million children and 3.3 million adults. Of these, only 4 percent were receiving social security survivor's (or other) benefits.[45]

Nor is this situation new. In 1963 16 percent of the children in the United States were poor. Of families consisting of seven or more persons, 34 percent were poor. Conversely, 22 percent of all the poor were in large families.[46]

One could argue that the wage-stop keeps parents poor, and through them their children, but that it does not affect children as such. Yet the presence of children in a family multiplies the effect of the wage-stop. Since, as pointed out previously, salaries are not linked to family size, but financial need is, pegging payments below individual salary levels automatically makes them even more insufficient for families with children than for individuals, and the more children, the more insufficient, as the figures quoted above testify. At the same time, child labor is illegal in most of the countries being discussed. Work disincentive factors are thus just as irrelevant concerning youngsters as they are concerning all the others who are outside the labor force.

Finally, there are the unemployed whose incentives to work must be maintained. Since, however, in most places unemployment is officially defined as (and payments are made to) those people who have registered for work, who are actively seeking work, and who cannot find work, it would seem reasonable that they have at least demonstrated, to the law's satisfaction, their desire for work. Nevertheless, in the United States, for the poor worker, the benefit levels are too low. Indeed, in most states the normal benefit *maximums* are below the poverty level for families with children.[47]

The impact of the work-welfare link is not confined to existing programs. Even insofar as proposals are made to change existing programs or create new ones, the same limitations apply.

The deleterious effects of the work-welfare link are nowhere more clearly demonstrated than in the various proposals in many countries for some sort of guaranteed minimum income. The methodology through which this is proposed varies from means-tested grants to a reverse income tax. Typically, such plans contain a ceiling for flat-rate benefits which is linked to, or deliberately pegged beneath, employment income; and a provision for proportionately (but not completely) decreasing the benefits as earned income increases. Thus, recipients receive only the flat-rate grant if they do not work; a smaller grant plus earned income, totaling more than the grant alone or the income alone, if they work; or earned income only, when a certain income level has been reached. These are termed the "incentive provisions" of guaranteed minimum income plans, and are intended to make it worthwhile for recipients to work, since the grants are not reduced by the total amount of earned income until a certain point. Arguments as to where the ceiling for flat rates should be set, the proportion of the benefits to be withdrawn with increased earnings, and the "break-even" point where salaries would equal benefits or vice versa, continue to occupy the planners. However, in no case do the flat-rate payments start at the poverty line, at the average salary, or even at the lowest salary. This level can only be attained by work. Thus, the incentive provisions doom those who cannot work, should not work, or cannot find work to remain in poverty, lest their incentive to work be impaired.[48]

It should be quite clear from these figures that the great bulk of poor people are those who cannot work, should not work, or cannot find work. It is equally clear that the various antidotes for poverty which are regularly advanced, such as full employment and education, are irrelevant in terms of raising these people out of poverty.[49] "It is . . . perfectly clear that [even] economic growth will be useless for those persons without strong attachments to the labor force, for whatever reason."[50]

The only way in which the majority of poor people, who are outside the labor force, can be raised out of poverty is by larger money grants, and these grants are withheld for fear that *other* people will refuse to work for lower sums. Since it is obviously impossible that the aged poor will become young, or that children will cease to exist, or that the disabled will become univerally fit; and it is even highly unlikely, despite welfare mythology, that parents would separate in order to be eligible for higher payments, it is clear that the great bulk of the poor are, in effect, held hostage to assure that other people will continue working.

Get 'em Back to Work:
The Personal Social Services

The impact of the work-welfare link is not confined to income maintenance programs. Social welfare services are geared in large measure to using work for training, therapy, and rehabilitation. The measure of success in most rehabilitation programs is not surcease from pain, increased happiness, or better family functioning, but rather the rate of return to the world of work. Even sheltered workshops, as their name implies, are part of the work-welfare link. For those that have return to the workforce as their goal, the link is obvious, but even in cases of sheltered workshops for those who cannot or will not return to the open labor market, such as the physically or mentally disabled or the aged, the desire to keep such people in the work world results in many ambivalences and difficulties.

One of the paradoxes inherent in sheltered workshops is the belief that people should work, but at the same time be sheltered from the exigencies of the work world. Consequently, the work must be of the kind that disabled people can perform, which usually means simple, repetitive tasks. These are precisely the kinds of tasks which can be performed by relatively uncomplicated machines, reasonably cheaply. This makes it economically unprofitable to pay the sheltered workers more than machine work would cost, and at the same time labels their efforts as make-work, both in their minds and in the minds of others. A second problem encountered by sheltered workshops is the inherent competition with commercial firms engaged in the same work, who might tolerate such competition as a humanitarian gesture, provided it is not serious enough or widespread enough. Therefore the work done in sheltered workshops must be highly specialized, or produced in very small quantities, or not put on the open market, or sold at higher than commercial prices on a sentimental basis.

Again, the sheltered workshop must not compete for jobs that are available to other workers, lest it bring down the wrath of labor unions, the unemployed, or other sectors interested in creating and safeguarding jobs.[51] This constraint results in work so menial or difficult that no one else wants it, or payment so low that no one else would accept it. Finally, despite all these limitations, the work must nevertheless be worth doing and paying for, which tends to put a premium on the most productive workers, even within sheltered workshops, and it is not unknown for certain people to be refused entry to sheltered workshops on the basis that they are not productive enough.

In this way, the emphasis on work leads people to accept ridiculous salaries, doing very marginal tasks or producing subsidized products, just so that they can feel they are working. The existence of such workshops is often defended in nonwork terms—e.g., that the people like or need the relationships involved—but these can as easily be provided through lounges, clubs, and groups which do not engage in work. Similarly, the structuring of time for the participants is often advanced as a justification for sheltered workshops, but this, too, could be achieved by programs of other kinds. Finally, whether the participants want or need the feeling of working is itself questionable. There is some evidence, and much experience, to indicate that the major reason why most people participate in sheltered workshops is for the money involved.[52] However, increasing payments—whether through the work or as a grant— would violate the wage-stop. Hence, the widespread existence of sheltered workshops.

Even the use of sheltered workshops to return people to the labor market is more defensible in theory than in practice. The results of training and retraining programs can be summed up in four sentences:

- Most persons starting such courses do not finish.
- Most persons finishing such courses do not find jobs later.
- Most persons finding jobs later find them in fields other than that for which they were trained.[53]
- Most people finding jobs after such courses remain in poverty.

Insofar as the Work Incentive provisions of AFDC are concerned (WIN), only about 2 percent of the eligible welfare population got jobs through the program.[54] Less than 16 percent of the people registered for WIN were employed or trained. In 1975, 34 percent of the people placed in regular jobs stayed in their jobs for less than 90 days, and 53 percent of those who stayed did not make enough to leave welfare. In fact, WIN cost more than it achieved in reduction in AFDC payments.[55] Similarly the WET (Work Experience Through Training) Program had only modest success in reducing dependency through rehabilitation. There is little evidence that the employability of participants improved, and it is probable that those who found jobs would have done so even without the program.[56]

Consequently, it is possible that the money and effort expended on rehabilitation through work, or with work as a goal, might be better used on other methods, or in achieving other ends.

The impact of the work-welfare link on the income of the aged has been pointed out previously: In the countries cited, the aged constitute from 20 to 57 percent of the poor. The dynamics of social welfare insofar as the aged are concerned are an object lesson in the pervasiveness of the work-welfare link. In order to allow people who have worked all their lives to enjoy their old age free of the necessity to work, social security plans are established. Almost invariably, the opportunity to retire is transmuted into a requirement, and at a given age retirement becomes mandatory. The aged person is then paid a small proportion of his or her last salary (although the basis of computation may be various) and finds he or she cannot live on it. Having thus thrust the aged into poverty, society establishes sheltered workshops where, by engaging in demeaning jobs subject to all the constraints noted above, the aged can eke out a small addition to their incomes. And the sheltered workshops are then pointed out as the epitome of social welfare's concern for aged people.

Aside from the financial considerations, the impact of the work ethic on retirement is found in efforts to prepare people for "constructive" leisure-time activities, or even "productive" retirement, including second careers.[57] This approach was carried to its logical extreme by a U.S. Secretary of Health, Education and Welfare who told a congressional committee, "It is important that the retirement test not interfere with incentives to work."[58]

To summarize this chapter: Requirements of coverage, vestedness, administration, and the wage-stop epitomize the work-welfare link in almost every program, resulting in poverty and its attendant ills.[59] Work incentive provisions are applied to those who are already working, those who are looking for work, those who cannot work, and those who should not work. In regard to the results, Dasgupta points out that "much privation, oppression and misery have piled up . . . for the last two decades. . . . What is as shocking, however, is that such results are due not to the failure of methods but to the methods themselves."[60]

In view of the obvious failure of an array of social welfare programs based on the primacy of work to eradicate poverty, even when normatively or absolutely defined, why do social workers and social welfare planners continue to view work as the linchpin, keystone, foundation, and lodestar of social welfare? The following chapters examine four attitudes toward work which bear on this question.

NOTES

1. For some representative discussions, see *The Measurement of Poverty* (Ottawa: Research and Statistics Directorate, Government of Canada, 1970): T. Goedhart, V. Halberstadt, A. Kapteya, and B. van Praag, "The Poverty Line: Concept and Measurement," *Journal of Human Resources* 12 (1977): 503-520; C. Vickery, "The Time-Poor: A New Look at Poverty." *Journal of Human Resources* 12 (1977): 27-48.

2. Macarov, *Incentives to Work,* op. cit.

3. R. I. Downing, "Economic and Social Background to Poverty in Melbourne," in R. F. Henderson, A. Harcourt, and R.J.A. Harper, *People in Poverty: A Melbourne Survey* (Melbourne: University of Melbourne, 1970), p. 1.

4. R. F. Henderson, *Poverty in Australia,* Volume 1 (Canberra: Australian Government Printing Service, 1975), p. 13.

5. *Poverty,* op. cit., p. 7.

6. M. Orshansky, "Who's Who Among the Poor." *Social Security Bulletin* 28 (1965): 3.

7. V. L. Allen, "Personality Correlates of Poverty," in V. L. Allen, *Psychological Factors in Poverty* (Chicago: Markham, 1970), pp. 242-266. While cautioning against imputation of causation, others have found that "on the whole lowered economic status is associated with more psychoses." B. Pasamanick, D. W. Roberts, P. W. Lemkau, and D. B. Krueger, "A Survey of Mental Disease in an Urban Population: Prevalence by Race and Income," in F. Reissman, J. Cohen, and A. Pearl, *Mental Health of the Poor: New Treatment Approaches for Low-Income People* (New York: Free Press, 1964), pp. 39-48. Even determining mental health involves problems. As one of Terkel's respondents says: "Poor people's mental health is different than the rich white. Mine could come from a job or not havin' enough money for my kids. Mine is from me being poor. . . . His sickness is from money, graftin' where he want more." S. Terkel, *Working* (New York: Random House, 1972), p. 114.

8. C. Hampden-Turner, *From Poverty to Dignity* (Garden City, NY: Doubleday Anchor, 1975), p. 91.

9. Caplovitz, op. cit., pp. 229-241.

10. M. Harrington, *The Other America* (New York: Macmillan, 1963), p. 133.

11. Among others, see L. Hamalian and F. R. Karl, *The Fourth World: The Imprisoned, The Poor, The Sick, The Elderly and Underaged in America* (New York: Dell, 1976); *Welfare Mothers Speak Out* (Milwaukee: Milwaukee County Welfare Rights Organization, 1972); R. M. Elman, *The Poorhouse State* (New York: Random House, 1966); O. Lewis, *The Children of Sanchez* (Harmondsworth: Penguin, 1961).

12. Brown, M., *Poor Families and Inflation* (London: Her Majesty's Stationery Office, 1967), quoted in Winyard, S., *No Fault of Their Own: Poverty in Britain* (Liverpool: Liverpool Institute of Socio-Religious Studies, 1977).

13. *Social Security Bulletin, Annual Statistical Supplement, 1975* (Washington, DC: Department of Health, Education and Welfare, 1975).

14. Henderson, op. cit.

15. *Poverty Fact Sheet,* op. cit.

16. In fact, "certain groups of Supplemental Benefit recipients have their income deliberately kept below the official poverty line." Winyard, op. cit., p. 14.

17. Although some sources estimate that somewhere between 10 and 25 percent of recipient families benefit from five or more programs, and that it is "economically disadvantageous for them to work," the extent to which they are still below the poverty line is not examined. Nor is it assumed that salaries are too low in such a case, rather than payments being too high. M. N. Ozawa, "Anatomy of President Carter's Welfare Reform Proposal." *Social Casework* 58 (December 1977): 615-620.

18. This is the logic used by state Senator W. T. Smith II, *Public Welfare: The "Impossible" Dream*. Paper presented at the County Officers Association of the State of New York, Rochester, New York, 1975. (mimeographed)

19. D. L. Grimaldi, "Distributive and Fiscal Impacts of the Supplemental Security Income Program." *Review of Social Economy* 26 (October 1978): 175-196.

20. Ball, op. cit., p. 27.

21. Ball, op. cit., p. 40.

22. S. R. Wright and J. D. Wright, "Income Maintenance and Work Behavior." *Social Policy* 6 (1975): 24.

23. B. Bluestone, "Low Wage Industries and the Working Poor." *Poverty and Human Resources Abstracts* 3 (1968): 1-14.

24. M. N. Ozawa, "Issues in Welfare Reform," op. cit., pp. 37-55.

25. Henderson, op. cit.

26. *Poverty Fact Sheet,* op. cit. "As regards the low paid worker, the Family Incomes Supplement meets only part of the difference between the individual's wage and his assumed needs. A safe gap has to be left to act as an incentive." G. Vic and P. Wilding, *Ideology and Social Welfare* (London: Routledge & Kegan Paul, 1976), p. 113.

27. Henderson, op. cit.

28. Walinsky, op. cit.

29. Gans, op. cit.; Macarov, *Incentives to Work,* op. cit., pp. 31-33.

30. Jackson, op. cit., p. 56. Ragan holds that minimum wages increase youth unemployment particularly. J. F. Ragan, "Minimum Wages and the Youth Labor Market." *Review of Economics and Statistics* 59 (1977): 129-136.

31. M. Ostow and A. B. Dutka, *Work and Welfare in New York City* (Baltimore: Johns Hopkins University Press, 1975), p. 78.

32. J. Bishop, "The Welfare Brief." *Public Interest* 53 (Fall 1978): 169-175.

33. Bluestone, op. cit.

34. Macarov, *Inventives to Work,* op. cit., pp. 10-12.

35. Although Israel pays additional salaries to married workers and those with dependents, the grants—which at one time were substantial—have dwindled with inflation until they are now virtually symbolic.

36. Levitan et al., op. cit., p. 74.

37. Arnold and Rosenbaum, op. cit., p. 31, quoting *Current Population Reports,* P-60, No. 86, p. 5.

38. Wright and Wright, op. cit., p. 24.

39. *Poverty Fact Sheet,* op. cit.

40. Henderson, op. cit.

41. Lalonde, op. cit., p. 16.

42. At the time of writing, the United States has made it possible to retire at 70 instead of 65. Few results have yet been published, but the general consensus is that those who get decent retirement pay retire at 65, while those who need more money keep working. *World of Work Report* 4 (September 1979): 72.

43. Ball, op. cit., p. 140.

44. Ibid.

45. Ibid., pp. 360-361.

46. Brinker, op. cit.

47. Arnold and Rosenbaum, op. cit., p. 45, italics mine.

48. There are many explanations and discussions of various guaranteed income proposals. A good summary and discussion is in J. B. Williamson et al., *Strategies Against Poverty in America* (New York: John Wiley, 1975); and *Negative Income Tax* (Paris: Organization for Economic Co-Operation and Development, 1974).

49. Not only has full employment proved an elusive goal, as pointed out by Weiner and associates in their analysis of 1946 and 1962 efforts in this direction, but Ritti and Hyman found that the AFDC caseload reached record highs while unemployment was achieving unprecedented lows. Insofar as education is concerned, Levitan and associates found that "added educational attainment of welfare recipients does not necessarily result in rising returns." Weiner et al., op. cit., p. 81; R. R. Ritti and D. W. Hyman, "The Administration of Poverty: Lessons from the 'Welfare Explosion' 1967-1973." *Social Problems* 25 (1977): 157-175; Levitan et al., op. cit., pp. 59-60.

50. Arnold and Rosenbaum, op. cit., p. 194.

51. Weiner and associates hold that "concern about competition from cheap labor has periodically led business and trade unions into an alliance against such rehabilitation efforts as sheltered workshops and prison production schemes." Weiner et al., op. cit., p. 114.

52. J. Reingold, R. L. Wolk, and S. Schwartz, "Attitudes of Adult Children Whose Aging Parents Are Members of a Sheltered Workshop." *Aging and Human Development* 3 (1972): 331-337.

53. See Goldstein, op. cit., p. 14.

54. L. Goodwin, *Do the Poor Want to Work? A Social-Psychological Study of Work Orientations* (Washington, DC: Brookings Institution, 1972), p. 113.

55. Lurie, I., "Work Requirements in Income-Conditioned Transfer Programs." *Social Security Review* 52 (December 1978): 551-566.

56. Levitan et al., op. cit., p. 74.

57. Barfield and Morgan, incidentally, found no correlation between enjoyment in "productive" postretirement activities and satisfaction. Barfield and Morgan, op. cit.

58. *Social Security Hearings before the Committee on Finance,* United States Senate, Eighty-ninth Congress, First Session, on H. R. 6675 (Washington, DC: Government Printing Office, 1965).

59. This, despite the fact noted by Lewis that as an a priori principle evidence has been neither asked for nor offered that only destitution will drive the poor to work. V. S. Lewis, "Historical Studies and Social Policy Analysis." *Contemporary Social Work Education* 1 (1977): 36-42.

60. S. Dasgupta, "Facing the New Era: A Plea for a New Approach to Human Well-Being," in *Human Well-Being: The Challenge of Continuity and Change* (New York: International Council on Social Welfare, 1978), p. 52.

Chapter 5

THE MYTH OF NEEDED WORK

"Oh, why don't you work/Like other men do?/How the hell
can I work?/When there's no work to do?"

—Anonymous, *Hallelujah, I'm
a Bum*

Millions of people, making up significant portions of the population in each of the Western industrialized countries, are
beneath the poverty line established by their own governments
as the minimum necessary for decent living. The programs
established to avoid or eradicate this situation, some of which
date back fifty (and in some cases almost a hundred) years are
not only obviously incapable of dealing with this condition, but
contribute to it by their operation and, indeed, by their very
existence. Social workers, welfare planners, and social administrators perpetuate existing conditions by subscribing to the
myths and attitudes upon which they are based, and accepting
without question the structures and processes through which
these operate. These myths and artifacts both derive from and
strengthen the link between work and welfare.

How Much Work Is Needed?

The takeoff point for most assumptions about society and
about social welfare is that work is needed. How much work, by

whom, and what constitutes needed work are rarely examined. From the basic belief that work is needed flow further, if unarticulated, assumptions: that society needs the work of everyone or of everyone capable of working; that more work, more workers, and more productivity are positive contributions to the economy, the society, and human progress; that everyone should work as hard as he or she can. When these subassumptions are examined critically, caveats may develop, but rarely to the point of assaulting the basic assumption about needed work. Hence, the basic sourcebook of American social workers can say, without equivocation, without qualification, and without producing a shred of evidence: "Society needs the productive effort of every person."[1]

Leaving aside the question of whether more is necessarily better, and equally ignoring the fact that the economic problems of industrial nations, including recessions and depressions, usually arise from inability to dispose of products at a profit, rather than from lack of production, there remains the question of whether needed and important work is being left undone through lack of workers.

Three factors point toward a clearly negative answer: the number of people who cannot find work, the constantly diminishing hours on the job put in by those who do work, and the growing rate of technological development.

Unemployment

Unemployment has become a permanent feature in most industrialized countries. Despite variations in methods of measuring and defining those who are employed and those who are unemployed, there remains a steady—and in many cases, growing—number of people whose productive capacity seems to be unneeded or, as will be pointed out in more detail later, not needed to the point that society is willing to pay for it.

Permanent unemployment is not just so-called "frictional" unemployment—a statistical artifact arising from those who are shifting from one job to another or are very temporarily unemployed. It is "structural" unemployment—the inability or unwillingness of the economy to absorb more workers. As a result of constant economic and technological changes, structural employment is increasing in many industrial countries and is the subject of much study, discussion, and research.[2] Many experts hold that this is now a permanent feature of industrialized societies.[3]

As Table 5.1 indicates, there has been an almost steady growth in the number of persons unemployed in the OECD (Organization for Economic Cooperation and Development) countries—the major industrial countries outside the Soviet bloc—since 1955. The exception is those countries whose economies were destroyed in World War II and whose return to "normal" unemployment was delayed. In total, as shown in

TABLE 5.1 Unemployment in ODEC Countries
(in thousands)

Country	1955	1960	1971	1975
Canada	245	446	552	707
United States	2,852	3,851	4,993	7,830
Japan (insured beneficiaries)		469	547	1,000
Australia (registered)	18.5	48.6	73.6	268.9
Austria (registered)	119	83	53	55
Belgium (ins. unemp.)	118	114	71	177
Denmark (ins. unemp.)	62.8	31.5	29.9	103.1
Finland (1958)	64	31	49	51
France	159	130	337	840
Germany (registered)	1,080	271	189	1,074
Greece (registered)		87	30	35
Ireland (ins. unemp.)	32	52.7	42	75.4
Italy	1,479	835	613	654
Netherlands (registered)	33	30	62	195
Norway (registered)	12.5	17.1	12.2	19.3
Spain (registered)	112	114	190	257
Sweden (insured) (1957)	23.5	18.9	45.3	36.7
Turkey (registered)	39	12.9	48	116.8
Gt. Britain (registered)	239	368	776	929
Yugoslavia (unfill. app.)	100	159	291	540
Switzerland (registered)		1.2		10.2

SOURCE: *Main Economic Indicators: Historical Statistics 1955–1971* (Paris: Organisation for Economic Cooperation and Development, 1973); and *Supplements 1, 2, & 3* (May, August, November, 1977).

Figure 5.1, the increase in unemployment in OECD countries
was from 6.5 million in 1955 to almost 14 million in 1975.[4]

These figures cover fifteen to twenty years, or almost a
statistical generation. Children born in 1955 have lived all of
their remembered lives in economies of gradually increasing
unemployment. Those who were twenty in 1955 will have spent
most of their working lives to date in a similar economy. And
these figures are not simply proportions of populations or labor
forces—after all, it makes no difference to the unemployed

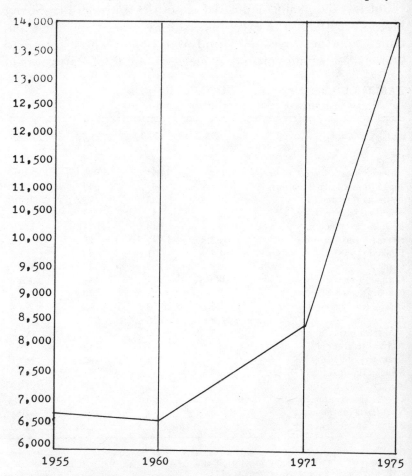

FIGURE 5.1 Number of Unemployed in OECD Countries
           (in thousands)

person whether he or she is part of 1 percent, 5 percent, or 20 percent in a similar category. These are the absolute numbers of individuals who are ready, willing, and able to work, but who cannot find jobs. Even were proportions of the unemployed in the total population to remain the same, continuing increases in populations—true of all the countries under discussion—would result in more individuals being unemployed. However, proportions have not remained constant. Figure 5.2 shows the differences in percentages of unemployed from 1948 to 1975 in the eleven countries reporting such figures to the OECD. In seven of these countries the proportions have increased—decreases are registered only in those countries whose economies reflected defeat in 1948 (Germany, Austria, and Italy), and in Sweden.

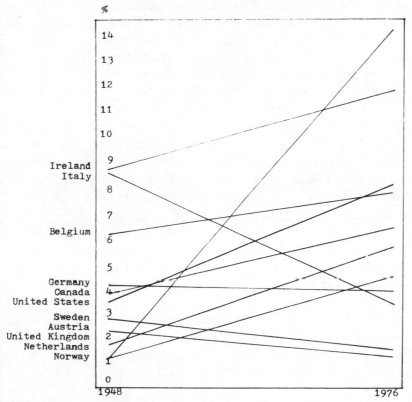

FIGURE 5.2 Unemployment in OECD Countries
(percentage of civilian labor force)

Although there are fluctuations in annual figures, and differences between countries, the long-term trend seems constantly upward. In fact, the major deterrent to anti-inflation measures in countries suffering the phenomenon is fear of increasing unemployment still further.

And these unemployment figures are severely underestimated,[5] being, in 16 of the 21 countries listed in Table 5.1, only those who are registered as unemployed, are insured, or are drawing benefits.[6] They do not include the unemployed who have used up their benefits but remain without work, those who are not covered by unemployment insurance (domestic employees and agricultural workers are almost always excluded),[7] those who find physical access to employment offices too difficult due to illness or other reasons, those who are fed up with the waiting in lines that is required or with the cumbersome procedures, those who are ignorant of their rights, those who choose not to register because they feel it stigmatizing or for other reasons, and those who are not yet eligible either due to insufficient previous work experience or because of "waiting time" requirements. In addition, even the official figures are often underestimated by the very government agencies that supply them. Government employment services have a natural tendency to report success (reduction of unemployment) rather than failure, and, therefore, as Burghes cautions: "It is unfortunate . . . that in looking at who the unemployed are, we must . . . be almost wholly dependent on the official figures."[8] Such official figures usually omit "disguised unemployment"—e.g., unemployed people required to undergo training programs, whose payments are then called "educational subsidies" instead of unemployment compensation.[9] Then there are farmers, who are consistently underestimated or ignored as unemployed, which tends to radically underestimate the actual unemployment.[10] Even mandatory retirement has been labeled an attempt to solve part of the unemployment problem by calling those affected "retired" rather than unemployed.[11]

Official figures are also subject to definitional parameters, and it is possible to change unemployment figures substantially by excluding categories. Field lists five categories often used in England to drop certain groups from discussions of unemployment:

(1) School leavers. Between the time they finish school and the time they get jobs, they can be classified as not unemployed, since they are not eligible for unemployment pay, not having achieved "vestedness" through previous employment. In 1974-1975, however, over 5 percent of school leavers in England were still unemployed nine months after leaving school, and the rest were certainly unemployed in the usual sense until they found jobs.

(2) Unsuitable for regular full-time work. These are, in essence, the people difficult to place—they take longer to obtain jobs and find it more difficult to hold them. It is simply easier to exclude them from unemployment figures as "poor prospects and unenthusiastic," which is done, although experience has proved that this does not mean they would refuse a job if one were offered to them.

(3) The short-term unemployed. These are the people termed "frictionally" unemployed, or temporarily out of work, often due to changing jobs. In England, this category is defined as being out of a job for four weeks or less. Until the end of that period, one is not officially listed as unemployed. By simply lengthening this period to, say, six or eight weeks or more, a much larger group can be termed "temporarily" unemployed, and thus defined out of the unemployment figures. Regardless of the terminology used or the length of the period involved, however, the loss of income for the individuals so defined is no less real.

(4) The voluntarily unemployed. This is the opposite of the above. People who cannot find work within an arbitrarily defined time period can be dismissed as not "really" seeking work. In other words, those who are out of work for an extended period can be declared unemployable, and therefore no longer unemployed—a neat and handy tautology. By making this period short enough, one could substantially reduce unemployment figures.

(5) Fraudulent claimants. Most of these turn out to be people who do not report part-time jobs in hopes of better ones or of benefits. They are actually the underemployed, whose plight is completely ignored by most unemployment statistics.[12]

Thus, by considering anyone out of work for, say, eight weeks or less as only "frictionally" unemployed—that is, between jobs—and therefore not "really" unemployed, and considering anyone out of work for eight weeks or more as not really seeking work, and therefore not unemployed, the unemployment problem can be defined out of existence. This is what two researchers did in England in 1972, when there were approximately one million registered unemployed persons there. By juggling definitions, they were able to prove that the "real" unemployment figure was *minus* 141,000.[13]

As noted in Chapter 3, these definitional solutions result in unemployment figures that may be from 50 to 100 percent below the number of people wanting work. In other words, an official unemployment rate of, say, 6% actually means that between nine and twelve people out of every hundred who want to work cannot find jobs. Nor can the officially reported or real unemployment be attributed solely to unwillingness to work. As Table 5.2 shows, the number of officially reported vacant jobs do not come close to the number of the unemployed in any country except Sweden. In all the rest of the OECD countries reporting, jobs vacant ranged from 11 to 56 percent of the registered unemployed. Overall, there were 22 jobs for every 100 unemployed. In other words, if all the registered vacant jobs were to be filled, there would still remain from 44 to 89 percent of the unemployed in the various countries, or 78 percent total.[14]

Finally, the trends pointed out above are not simply results of the recession which affected some countries in 1975. In December 1977, the OECD *Economic Outlook* said: "Total unemployment in the area is now . . . some half million higher than at the trough of the 1975 recession, and the equivalent of about 5.4% out of the civilian labor force. In Europe . . . unem-

TABLE 5.2   Registered Unemployment and Registered
Vacant Jobs in OECD Countires in 1975 (in thousands)

Country	Unemployment	Vacant Jobs	%
Japan	1,000	338	34
Australia	268.9	30.1	11
Austria	55	31	56
Belgium	177	41	23
Finland	51	18.5	36
France	840	109	13
Germany	1,074	236.2	22
Netherlands	195	47	24
Norway	19.3	6	31
Sweden	36.7	50.3	137
Turkey	116.8	29.7	25
Great Britain	929	150	16
Yugoslavia	540	59	11
Switzerland	10.2	2.8	27
Total	5,312.9	1,148.6	22

ployment has in fact been constantly rising." The same source estimated a rise to 6 percent by the end of 1978.[15] For example:

> Over the last twenty years there has been a steady rise in the level of unemployment in Great Britain ... while unemployment has continued to recover from its peaks as the economy picks up, the noticeable feature of the trend over the last twenty years has been the worsening of the peaks and the lessening of the improvement when it comes. Not only has the total number of unemployed been increasing absolutely, but also as a proportion of the economically active population. In 1956 the unemployed were only 1.1 percent of employees; by 1976 they had jumped to just over 4 percent.[16]

In 1978, the figure was 7 percent.[17] France, too, undertook an all-out drive to check the rise of unemployment in 1978, it being estimated that unemployment in France will top 1.2 million this year.[18]

In the United States, a 5 percent unemployment figure has long been considered not only normative, but desirable. Whereas a higher figure is felt to lead to loss of production and consumption, a lower figure has been feared as inflationary—

i.e., if too many people are working, they will include the marginally productive, which will drive prices up and result in wage demands. Official unemployment at 5 percent meaning from 7 to 10 percent actual unemployment, has been seen as the proper balance for several decades. The only factor reducing unemployment below that figure in the United States during the last quarter century has been war.[19]

In the countries reporting to the OECD in 1955, unemployment remained substantially the same in 1960, rose by 24 percent by 1971, and by another 66 percent by 1975; while, as noted previously, vacant jobs amounted to about one-fifth of the officially listed 14 million unemployed at that time.[20] Thus, a summary of the nineteenth international conference on social welfare concluded that, with the possible exception of Israel and Japan, unemployment is the dominant issue.[21]

Productivity

Increased unemployment, both in proportions and in absolute numbers, is not simply a function of economic bottlenecks or poor planning. The basic reason for increasing unemployment is the continual increase in per unit productivity. From 1956 to 1964 the per person productivity in the major industrial nations increased by 41 percent; from 1966 to 1975, by 37 percent. Using 1970 as the base of 100, there was a 17 percent growth in productivity by 1976.[22] Between 1950 and 1978, the output per hour of all persons in the private business sector almost doubled.[23] The rate of productivity increases in the major Western industrialized countries in 1978 were:

United States	2.5
Canada	4.2
France	4.9
Germany	3.7
Italy	2.9
United Kingdom	1.6[24]

Industrial productivity was matched by agricultural productivity. In 1776, one American farmer provided food for 3 people; in 1976, one farmer provided food for 57 people.[25] In the United States, agricultural output per unit of land increased on the average by 80 percent in 1971-1975, as compared to 1941-1945. Crop yields of wheat have increased by 90 percent, and of corn, 2.8 times within the same time period.[26] In Europe, employment on the farms declined about 40 percent in the last decade,[27] and these ex-farmers and farm workers were not absorbed into industrial employment, since industrial employment between 1959 and 1972 is actually only fractionally higher.[28]

Seen on a longer term, there has been an average of 3 percent annual increase in productivity on the part of all persons in the private sector, from 1947 to 1973.[29] Even those who fear a turn for the worse do not prognosticate a cessation of productivity increases, and certainly not a reduction in productivity as such, but rather a slower *rate* of growth, such as the 2.5 percent predicted for 1979-1985, or the 2.7 percent predicted for 1980-1985.[30] Even if these "pessimistic" predictions come about, it means that in the next ten years per person productivity will increase by 25 percent—in a hundred years, by 250 percent. Were the raw materials and other resources, like energy, to be available, this could mean an increase of 25 percent in goods and services produced. The question with which this chapter is concerned is whether industrialized Western society needs, wants, or can absorb an increase of 25 percent in production. True, there are certain sectors which are undermanned—hospital personnel, for example—but, as unemployment figures testify, this is not due to lack of available people. On the contrary, if increased efficiency and production are not to result in shorter work hours, on the one hand, and unemployment, on the other, the alternative is to seek increases in consumption, through advertising, fiscal policies, and the like. In short, needs and wants must be created in order to absorb productivity increases—a situation which belies the need for maximum productivity on the part of everyone capable of producing.

What is equally obvious is that productivity increases are not achieved through the effort and determination of the workers themselves. As Walbank points out, most people work well within their abilities. Some studies indicate that this is about 44 percent of their capacities.[31] Were the majority of workers to increase their productivity drastically—say, to 75 percent of their capacity—the resultant production would create problems, if not catastrophe, for most industrial countries. They would be (as they have been in the past) forced to literally dump products in the ocean or in pits, to store them for long periods, or to figuratively dump them below cost in foreign markets in order to keep local prices, and thereby salaries and profits, from declining.

Since, despite the rhetoric, increased productivity and certainly not maximum productivity is not really desired, one device for coping with the threat is to limit the hours that people can work. Governments constantly lower maximum permissible hours. Some examples: In Belgium, maximum working hours were reduced in 1965 from 48 to 45; in Switzerland, in 1964, from 48 to 46; in Yugoslavia, in 1965, from 48 to 42,[32] and this trend continues with further limitations being reported to the International Labor Organization every year. In addition to laws, collective work agreements also limit the number of hours that people can work. In Belgium, it runs from 36.25 to 38 hours in different industries; in Germany, 92 percent of the workers have a 40-hour work week; in Luxembourg, permission to work for 43 hours per week, rather than 40, must be obtained from the government; and in France, an hour a week has just been cut from the work time of retail food workers.[33]

Whereas preindustrial society, as noted previously, had so little need for surpluses arising from production that there were often more than 100 holidays a year, modern man has easily surpassed that figure. In areas in which the 5-day week is the norm, there are 52 two-day weekends. In addition, there are holidays (moved from weekends to workdays by law in the United States), and vacations. In 1977, Denmark ruled that there was a general right to at least 24 days' annual vacation (or holiday, in European English).[34] In the Federal Republic of Germany, in 1977, 85 percent of workers had at least 4 weeks' annual holidays, with an average basic minimum entitlement of 22.9 working days; 79 percent of workers had additional holiday pay.[35] In Ireland, an additional annual public holiday was introduced in 1977, as it was in England.[36] In Luxembourg, a uniform annual paid leave of 22 working days was granted for 1977, with the intention of reaching 25 working days in 1979.[37] In short, the modern worker puts in much less time than did his preindustrial predecessor, and many of these limitations are legally enforceable.

Constantly increasing productivity—achieved by people working well within their capacities, to the point that laws and collective agreements are used to limit the hours and days of work—does not add up to a situation in which society needs all the work that everyone is capable of producing.

Technology

It would be fatuous indeed to hold that such constantly increasing productivity is due to the fact that people work harder, better, or longer today than they did in the past. There are, it is true, times or conditions which induce great numbers of people to work harder than they usually do. Wartime is probably the best example of such increased effort. Normally, however, individual work patterns seem to be as ingrained and as constant as are other aspects of the personality—indeed, Neff speaks of a "work personality."[38] To the despair of those who, for over fifty years, have been seeking ways to "motivate" people to work harder, none of the proposed incentives (e.g., job redesign, worker participation, self-actualizing tasks,[39] work groups, and so on) have resulted in permanent, substantial, generalizable changes in human work patterns.[40] Some people work hard at everything they undertake, others at nothing, and still others only at certain things. The reasons for these differential work patterns as stable components of the personality have hardly begun to be investigated.

Further, we are constantly being reminded that modern men and women do not work as hard as their parents and grandparents did. Consequently, the increases in productivity must have occurred despite decreases in human effort or in any case not as a result of people working harder than they used to.

As a matter of fact, productivity increases arise almost exclusively from changes in technology, processes, and products—not in humans. Such technical changes are usually synergistic: Each change feeds into, calls for, and brings about additional changes, joining with them so that the total change is greater than the sum of the individual innovations. It is this factor which leads Davis to state, without equivocation, that advanced technology has already demonstrated that it can produce *more* than society needs and that, moreover, the higher the level of technology, the fewer people are needed.[41]

What Work Is Needed?

It seems clear, from the continued and growing existence of unemployment despite measures to disguise this fact, and from legal restrictions on the amount of work that people are allowed to do, that there is no need for more work in total, more productivity from those working, or more workers. Indeed, it is possible to go a step further and examine how much of the human work now being done is actually needed.

Discussions of need invariably involve value judgments, and the question arises of who is to determine need.[42] Nevertheless, there is the commonly expressed view that we need more people in the human services—more teachers, more social workers, more hospital attendants of various kinds, more people to help with the elderly, and so on. The feeling seems to be that if more people were released from the necessity of participating in goods production, there would be more people available for these positions. It is true that there has been a shift from production to service in most Western countries. In 1929 service employment in the United States was about 40 percent of total employment.[43] In 1950, it had reached 51 percent,[44] and in 1967, 55 percent.[45] By 1980, the service sector should be about double the size of the productive sector.[46] This shift, however, does not seem to be due to unemployment in the productive sector nor does it seem to reduce unemployment as such.

Part of the reason is that automation has made inroads in the amount of human labor needed in the service sector, too. The clerk who answered the telephone has, in many cases, been replaced by an answering service or recorder. Doormen have given way to closed-circuit television; elevator operators, to push-buttons; messengers and even mail personnel to devices which transmit documents through telephones, and so on. Shorthand clerks have been replaced by dictating machines, and bookkeepers by computers.

Even in the more direct human services, there are devices which monitor heartbeat, temperature, respiration, and the like on a continuing basis, alerting a nurse when tolerances are exceeded. In education, audio-visual aids and programmed learning reduce the pressure for more teachers. University satellites teach at a distance through closed-circuit television and intercom systems.

In those cases where the human touch is necessary, there is increasing use of volunteers, rather than employees. Teaching how to work with volunteers and paraprofessionals is becoming increasingly important in social work education, and there are even calls for a curriculum devoted entirely to supervision and administration, with all direct service being carried out by volunteers and paraprofessionals. This list could be extended indefinitely.[47]

However, it is possible to question the whole concept of need as posed above. If one views society as a whole as the arbiter of need, and the willingness to pay for the goods or services as the gauge, then the existence of unemployed people alongside unfilled needs indicates that the purported need is not felt strongly enough by enough people to create the conditions and incentives necessary to provide the service or the product. The need to put a man on the moon before the Russians did so was sufficient to create a whole new industry and many subindustries in the United States; the need for more human service personnel in homes for the aged, for example, is simply not felt to be important enough to pay the salaries, establish the conditions, create the prestige, and undertake the other steps which would induce otherwise unemployed people to undertake such jobs. However, where the pay for garbage and trash collectors approaches a living wage, as in New York City, there is intense competition for the work that is elsewhere shunned and accepted only as a last resort.[48] In short, if supply and demand is used as a criterion for needed work, the demand exhibited for such work is too weak to qualify the work as needed.

There is another way of looking at the question of need, and that is as synonymous with usefulness. Some workers, particularly young workers, make a distinction between "meaningful," "relevant," or "life-enriching" work, and that which they see as detrimental to society—e.g., war-connected work, making products or engaging in processes which cause pollution, or producing items with built-in obsolescence, thus using up natural resources unnecessarily. In this view, building a better mousetrap is not only unnecessary, but counterindicated, if existing mousetraps work well enough.

Take, for example, the backbone of the American economy, the manufacture of automobiles. Over 10 million cars are sold each year through a combination of minor (usually cosmetic) changes and massive advertising. There is little evidence that cars are better, more efficient, safer, longer-lasting, or more comfortable as year follows year. Rather, advertising which makes new cars seem more attractive, combined with engineering which requires various repairs after two years or so, creates the illusion that it is necessary, desirable, or economical to buy a new car about every two years. Consequently, whether there is a "need" for over 10 million new cars every year depends upon whether one judges by supply and demand or by usefulness. In short, need is a value judgment, not a datum.

The same criterion of usefulness applied to the cigarette, alcohol, and pornography industries, among others, would raise similar questions concerning usefulness. Consequently, applying the test of supply and demand, the purported need for more workers or more work in certain areas is not sustained.

Applying the test of usefulness, the same questions are raised in other areas. Unless one tendentiously applies different criteria to different areas, the overall need for more human work in modern society is in serious question.

However, even leaving aside the question of how much work being performed today is necessary, it is obvious that a determined effort to reduce human labor as much as possible (even including "unnecessary" work) would result in dramatic decreases in the number of people in the workforce or in the amount of time those in the workforce spend on their jobs. For example, if per capita gross national product in the United States had remained at the 1965 level, the work week today would be 22 hours, or the work year 27 weeks; or retirement could begin at age 38.[49] The plain fact is that industry is potentially capable of creating wealth with half its current labor force.[50]

To summarize this chapter: Increases in per person productivity arise almost entirely from changes in technology, processes, and products, and not through changes in individual work patterns. These increases have led, are leading, and will probably continue to lead to constant diminution of the amount of human labor needed. This exhibits itself in the continuous reduction in hours, days, weeks, and years of work—legally determined in most cases—to which the last few decades have been witness, and in the high level of unemployment which the last generation, at least, has suffered. In addition, much of the work being performed is not really needed, whether judged by supply and demand or by value judgments. Last, most people work far below their capabilities.

Thus, to say that society needs all the work of which everyone is capable, or even that there is a need for more human labor, is to reiterate a belief, not to state a fact. Such contentions simply perpetuate a myth or repeat a slogan. A world which cannot provide paid work for everyone ready, willing, and able to work, which legally limits the hours that people are permitted to work in a constantly decreasing fashion, which legislates more and more holidays/vacations, and which requires people to retire at a given age cannot be seriously viewed as a world short of workers or one desirous of or needing more work, except through the most self-deluding or cynical contortions of logic and data.

Why, then, the continuing insistence that people must work, not only as a prerequisite for social welfare help, but as a talismanic incantation throughout society? One reason is the confusion between work and jobs. It is the fear of unemployment or, conversely, the need for jobs that maintains the present system of distinguishing between the deserving employed and the undeserving unemployed. And it is the existence of jobs as the only socially sanctioned method of sharing in the resources of society which results in the work-welfare link, with all the ramifications outlined previously in terms of the suffering entailed for the old, the young, the disabled, and single heads of families. It is with this aspect of the situation that the next chapter deals.

NOTES

1. E. B. Whitten, "Disability and Physical Handicap: Vocational Rehabilitation," in *Encyclopedia of Social Work* (New York: National Association of Social Workers, 1965), p. 236.

2. A. Bernfield, "Structural Improvements with a View to Employment Maintenance." *International Social Service Review* 31 (1978): 123-143; see also C. C. Killingsworth, "The Fall and Rise of the Idea of Structural Unemployment," *Proceedings of the Thirty-First Annual Meeting* (Madison: Industrial Relations Research Association, 1978), pp. 1-13.

3. S. Shimmin, "The Future of Work." Paper delivered at the NATO Conference on Changes in the Nature and Quality of Working Life, Thessaloniki, Greece, August 1979; to be published in K. D. Duncan, D. Wallis, and M. M. Gruneberg, *Changes in Working Life* (Chichester: John Wiley, forthcoming).

4. *Main Economic Indicators,,* op. cit., and *Supplements 1, 2, & 3,* op. cit.

5. L. Burghes, "Who Are the Unemployed?" in F. Field, *The Conscript Army* (London: Routledge & Kegan Paul, 1977). Straussman points out how severely understated unemployment is in the United States. J. D. Straussman, "The 'Reserve Army' of Unemployed Revisited." *Society* 14 (1977): 40-45.

6. "Ever since the regular collection of unemployment statistics by the Federal Government began ... the criterion has been that to be counted as unemployed a person should be an active jobseeker." J. E. Bregger, "Unemployment Statistics and What They Mean," in *Monthly Labor Review Reader* (Washington, DC: Government Printing Office, 1975), pp. 6-13.

7. As noted previously, one-third of the U.S. labor force is not covered by unemployment insurance. *Monthly Labor Review,* op. cit., p. 91.

8. Burghes, op. cit.

9. Although it is sometimes argued that there is equal or more disguised employment, i.e., people holding more than one job, in May 1971 only about 5 percent of all employed workers held more than one job. H. V. Hayghe and K. Michelotti, "Multiple Jobholding in 1970 and 1971," in *Monthly Labor Review Reader* (Washington, DC: Government Printing Office), pp. 161-168.

10. It has been found that "official procedures ... may radically underestimate the actual unemployment." P. F. Korsching and S. G. Sapp, "Unemployment Estimation in Rural Areas: A Critique of Official Procedures and a Comparison with Survey Data." *Rural Sociology* 43 (Spring 1978): 103-112.

11. H. L. Sheppard and S. E. Rix, *The Graying of Working America: The Coming Crisis of Retirement-Age Policy* (New York: Free Press, 1977), p. 140.

12. Yankelovich is actually speaking of the underemployed when he mentions those who would take jobs if they were available. "The official unemployment figure of about seven million ... grossly understates the potential demand for jobs." D. Yankelovich, "The New Psychological Contracts at Work." *Psychology Today* 11 (May 1978): 46-50.

13. J. Boulet and A. Bell, *Unemployment and Inflation* (London: Economic Research Council, 1973).

14. *Main Economic Indicators,* op. cit. Although van Wezel calls registered demand an unreliable datum, it is questionable whether it is any more unreliable than unemployment figures, as pointed out in the text. In any case, the former derive from the same official sources as do the latter. J.A.M. van Wezel, "Re-entry into the Labour Process: A Research Among Unemployed." *Sociologia Neerlandica* 10 (1974): 162.

15. *Economic Outlook,* 22 (1977): 4.

16. Burghes, op. cit.

17. *Poverty,* op. cit., p. 4.

18. *World of Work Report* 3 (November 1978): 96.

19. *Yearbook of Labour Statistics: Sixteenth Edition; Twenty-Sixth Edition; Thirty-Sixth Edition* (Geneva: International Labour Organization, 1956, 1966, 1976).

20. *Main Economic Indicators,* op. cit.

21. D. Scott, "A View of the XIXth International Conference on Social Welfare: The Discussions and the Organization." Paper delivered at the closing session of the conference, Jerusalem, August 27, 1978. (mimeographed)

22. *Yearbook of Labour Statistics,* op. cit.

23. *Monthly Labor Review,* op. cit., p. 107.

24. *World of Work Report* 4 (August 1979): 59.

25. *The Secret of Affluence* (Washington, DC: Department of Agriculture, 1976).

26. W. Leontiff, "The Future of the World Economy." *Socio-Economic Planning Sciences* 2 (1977): 171-182.

27. *Work in a Changing Industrial Society* (Paris: Organisation for Economic Co-operation and Development, 1975), p. 22.

28. Ibid., parenthesis mine.

29. R. E. Kutscher, J. A. Mark, and J. R. Norsworthy, "The Productivity Slowdown and the Outlook to 1985." *Monthly Labor Review* 100 (May 1977): 3-8.

30. Ibid.

31. M. Walbank, "Effort in Motivated Work Behavior," discussion of paper presented at NATO Conference on *Changes in the Nature and Quality of Working Life,* Thessaloniki, Greece, August 1979; to be published in K. D. Duncan, D. Wallis, and M. M. Gruneberg, *Changes in Working Life* (Chichester: John Wiley, forthcoming).

32. *Encyclopedia Britannica Yearbook 1967* (Chicago: Benton, 1967), p. 324.

33. *European Industrial Relations Review* 56 (September 1978): 6.

34. Ibid.

35. Ibid.

36. Ibid.

37. Ibid.

38. W. S. Neff, *Work and Human Behavior* (New York: Atherton, 1968).

39. See, for example, D. Macarov, "Reciprocity between Self-Actualization and Hard Work." *International Journal of Social Economics* 3 (January 1976): 39-44.

40. "There is no simple relationship between satisfaction and productivity. Happy workers do not necessarily work harder, and, in some cases, the most dissatisfied ones are the ones most motivated." G. Strauss, "Job Satisfaction, Motivation, and Job Redesign," in *Organisational Behaviour: Research and Issues* (Madison: Industrial Relations Research Association, 1974). Studies which purport to show increased productivity from changes in the quality of working life are beset by methodological weaknesses, including the short time span of the studies. See *Productivity and the Quality of Working Life* (Scarsdale, NY: Work in America Institute, 1978).

41. L. E. Davis, "Changes in the Working Environments: The Next 20 Years." Paper presented at NATO Conference on *Changes in the Nature and Quality of Working Life,* Thessaloniki, Greece, August 1979; to be published in K. D. Duncan, D. Wallis, and M. M. Gruneberg, *Changes in Working Life* (Chichester: John Wiley, forthcoming).

42. For an interesting discussion of the difference between individuals' needs and wants, see E. Allardt, *Dimensions of Welfare in a Comparative Scandinavian Study* (Helsinki: University of Helsinki, 1975).

43. C. Gersuny and W. R. Rosengren, *The Service Society* (Cambridge, MA: Schenkman, 1973).

44. A. Gartner and F. Riessman, *The Service Society and the Consumer Vanguard* (New York: Harper & Row, 1974).

45. Gersuny and Rosengren, op. cit.

46. Gartner and Riessman, op. cit.

47. Gabor, for example, although enthusiastic about the inherent possibilities of technology, did not see—in 1963—how the milkman could be replaced. There are now large sections of the West where milkmen have not been seen in years. Most people buy milk together with other items in supermarkets and carry it home in their cars or have it delivered with other groceries. Where milk comes in plastic bags, it is often bought in quantity and put in the freezer until needed. Thus technology has its way, even if indirectly. D. Gabor, *Inventing the Future* (New York: Knopf, 1971), p. 130.

48. E. Liebow, "No Man Can Live with the Terrible Knowledge That He Is Not Needed." *New York Times Magazine* (April 5, 1970).

49. J. M. Kreps, "The Allocation of Leisure to Retirement," in M. Kaplan and P. Bosserman, *Technology, Human Values, and Leisure* (Nashville: Abingdon, 1971), pp. 239-244. In 1923 Bertrand and Dora Russell estimated that an average of four hours work per day would suffice to produce the goods then considered necessary for a good life. Gabor, op. cit., p. 143.

50. D. Gerard, "Democracy—a Fiction?" *Social Service Quarterly* 52 (September 1978): 24-27.

Chapter 6

THE JOB SCRAMBLE: Corrupt and Corrupting

"More men are killed by overwork than the importance of the world justifies."

—Rudyard Kipling, *The Phantom Rickshaw*

"From the factory dead matter goes out improved, whereas men there are corrupted and degraded."

—Pope Pius XI

Whereas, as discussed in the last chapter, the need for more human labor—or even for as much as presently exists—is open to serious question, people's need for jobs and consequently the need for society to provide jobs are together one of the most obvious features of modern economics and politics. Many policy discussions are confused, however, by lack of clear distinctions between work and jobs. In common parlance, a person's work and his or her job are considered the same. We speak of a person at work or on the job, working or doing his or her job, synonymously. Even in the cases of scientific or scholarly studies, work is usually identified with employment.[1] Although distinctions are sometimes made between work and nonwork or between work and leisure,[2] differentiation between work as such and jobs is hard to come by. Thus, writing from an economist's point of view, Wanniski says that the chief reason that politicians and economists throughout history have failed to grasp the idea of the Laffer curve is their confusion between work and productivity.[3] Scott, speaking from a social welfare point of view, makes the same point in different terms: "Provision of work [jobs], rather than increase in production, should be [the] primary aim of policy."[4]

The distinction between work and jobs is not merely pedantic—it has enormous practical consequences. When getting the work done is the goal—i.e., producing goods and services—utilization of more or even better human labor is rarely the most efficient method. Increasingly, the move is toward new machines or new methods. Contrariwise, when providing jobs is the major goal, then the efficiency of the worker, his or her productivity, and even the quality and quantity of the product become subordinate considerations.

The inherent conflict between production goals, and thereby profits, and job-creation and -maintenance goals, basic to income maintenance, provides the battlefield on which economic, fiscal, and employment policies are fought out.[5] In seeking compromises between these goals, or in attempting to maximize them, government, labor, and business enter into a complex maze of relationships which result in an intricate web of subsidies, guarantees, restrictions, laws, training programs, and much else. Were either unrestricted production without regard for effects on labor, or full employment regardless of productivity, to be an unrestrained goal, many of these measures would be unnecessary.

However, since currently the only socially sanctioned method by which the majority of people can acquire a share of the production results is by holding a job, it has become a necessary goal of labor, government, and—to some degree—business to make sure that there are enough jobs. Given the conditions outlined above—productivity not primarily dependent on human labor, but people primarily dependent on jobs—the result is inevitable. The goal of manpower, employment, and economic policies is to redefine and redesign work to provide employment for more and more people. Tasks are thus reduced to smaller units; jobs are redivided among more people; unnecessary work is not censured; new jobs are artificially created. This is necessary because, in the final analysis, *there are not enough jobs.*[6] The problem is to spread jobs continually in a situation of static or diminishing need.

Thus, it is not surprising that many new economic proposals do not have increased production as their goals, but more work opportunities. The avowed purpose of many current proposals for reduced work time, flexible hours, and alternative work patterns is not to produce more goods and services or to create them faster or better, but rather to create and spread the work.[7] This is also the underlying purpose of the emerging concept of shared jobs, in which two people undertake the same job, dividing the time, the tasks, and the proceeds among themselves.[8] There are calls for drastic reductions in permitted work hours, or lowering retirement ages—all with the intention of creating more job opportunities. In short, in the absence of full employment, jobs must be and are rationed, one way or another.[9]

To avoid this situation, several methods of creating full employment are used. One of these is the previously discussed work relief (or relief work). Perhaps the most widespread of such programs was that of the WPA in the United States during the Great Depression, when it was considered more desirable to create jobs than simply to pay a dole. Despite many solid achievements in terms of projects completed, the experience did not prove its expectations insofar as most participants are concerned. People did not maintain pride that they were working rather than just receiving payments—make-work was seen for what it is. Nor did people learn work habits and skills nor work hard and well. On the contrary, they were the butt of endless jokes, in many cases suffered deterioration in their self-images, and developed contempt for their work.[10] This experience was not confined to the United States; in New Zealand it is reported that the view that there should be no relief without work persisted until it led to absurd results.[11]

Work relief as a substitute for real work has given way, in many places today, to the demand that the government become the "employer of last resort." In countries where such policies have been put into effect, even for limited groups of people, the results are informative. Egypt, for example, guarantees every university graduate a job, accounting for the crowds of government clerks in every office without work to do. Iran also made payments to workers who did not work, rather than engaging in the more complex methods of getting money into the hands of people, as through social welfare.[12] The United States provides "jobs" on farms by paying millions of people *not* to plant certain crops.

As the employer of last resort, some countries use public works projects, rather than work relief, to provide jobs. These are projects whose work is not generally seen as important enough to be undertaken when labor is in short supply, as during a war, but which are carried out by surplus labor, as it were. This work is important enough to get done only when providing people with jobs is part of the rationale. With the current move from a productive to a service economy, public works proposals are now being supplanted by public service proposals[13] –hospital workers, teachers aides, and indigenous personnel in various capacities with funds provided by government. The rationale remains the same: The need is to provide people with jobs rather than simply to get needed work done. If the latter were truly the goal, such work would not be proposed as relief measures, but on its own merits, paying prevailing wages and offering competitive employment conditions. The need for the work is simply not important enough to result in jobs; the need for jobs is important enough to get the work done.

It is the need for jobs, as an instrumental method of acquiring income, which leads to informal work quotas designed to make sure there is enough work to go around. This is also the source of featherbedding—the creation or maintenance of unnecessary work activities—which arises from fear of job losses with increasing efficiency. Resistance to new machinery and methods—e.g., the use of containers on railroads and ships—arises from justified fear of job losses.[14] Longshoremen have been particularly noted for resisting job losses through introduction of labor-saving systems. Their recent contract, consequently, guarantees wage payment for a minimum number of hours per year whether or not the worker has been called onto the job.[15] Thus, much unproductive and even detrimental work is excused on the basis that it gives people jobs.

At the opposite end of the continuum from the government as employer of last resort, but with the same goal in mind, is the creation of an economy of full employment.[16] In this case, the government encourages or aids private business to increase the number of jobs available. This may be done through tax credits, loans, subsidies, or in a number of other ways. In some cases, this simply results in disguised unemployment: As long as the government pays the salary, or a major part of it, the employee is kept on. When the subsidy ends, the job ends. Thus, unemployment figures are held down by making subsidy payments rather than welfare payments. "Creating" permanent jobs has been found to be very expensive. It has been estimated that it requires $16,000 to create a job in Australia,[17] and we have no data as to how long the job lasts, what it pays, or its conditions.[18] In other settings, creating jobs has been estimated to require an investment of 25 percent to 48.5 percent.[19] In Germany, where a widespread job-training and -creation plan was tried, the results are described as a palliative, rather than an effective remedial program.[20] In short, no country has succeeded in creating enough self-sustaining jobs to effectively counter widespread unemployment. In addition, attempts to provide employment for everyone runs afoul, as noted above, of the criteria of profitability of investment,[21] and the latter almost always wins.

This brings up the question not only of the necessity for newly created jobs, but even for many jobs which now exist. The designation of certain kinds of work as necessary or unnecessary is value laden, as has been pointed out. The same thing can be said about judgments concerning the necessity or usefulness of certain jobs. But take the automobile industry again as an example.

Would it be possible for the engineering which went into the space program to create a popularly priced car which would need only minor upkeep for five or even ten years? The answer is almost certainly yes. Henry Ford created such a vehicle in the Model-T. German engineers built the Volkswagen almost according to such specifications. The U.S. Army produced the wartime jeep along these lines. And all of this was before space-age technology was generally available. Could American advertising convince the public that it is a patriotic duty to hold onto the same car for a decade? They did almost that during World War II regarding many items. The slogan was:

> Use it up,
> Wear it out,
> Make it do,
> Or do without.

Such a slogan would be considered almost treasonable as regards today's economy.

What prevents such a step, which would conserve natural resources, reduce pollution, and relieve financial strain for many people, from being taken? Obviously, the fear of loss of jobs. Changes in American car-buying habits in the direction of holding onto current models for five or ten years would wreck the American economy. Workers in iron mines, steel plants, components factories, auto assembly lines, car sales, advertising, and a myriad of other activities would lose their sources of livelihood, and so would many of those who supply them with goods or services. Consequently, the provision of good, long-lasting (or even just serviceable) cars can be viewed as almost a by-product of the American automobile industry. Its major role is to provide millions of jobs directly and indirectly, and it is the number and quality of jobs provided, not the number or quality of cars produced, which is the real contribution of the automobile industry to American life and its economy.

Similarly, when a shipyard is to be closed down, the cry of the local Member of Congress and his or her constituents is not that national security will suffer, but that jobs will be lost. Localities fight for new industries, even those that offer pollution, danger, and traffic problems, to the extent of offering zoning exceptions and tax exemptions, not because of the product manufactured, but because of the jobs involved. Jurisdictional strikes between unions have nothing to do with whose members are better trained to do the work, but with whose jobs will be threatened.

Social workers, social welfare planners, and policy makers not only accept the myth of needed work, and the artifact of needed jobs—they actually strengthen them with their own activities. Efforts and activities designed to get parents off the welfare rolls by inducing and helping them go to work result in need for day-care centers for small children, after-school activities of various kinds, vacation camps, and a myriad of other programs, including counseling concerning the problems caused. Similarly, adults who are so busy at their jobs that they cannot take care of their aged parents create need for homes for the aged, meals-on-wheels, community-based outreach programs, and similar activities, all of which could be handled by the adult children if they did not have to leave home for work. Thus, getting people to go to work creates jobs which people have to be induced to undertake, thereby strengthening the illusion that society is short of workers.

The net result of the widespread endeavors to redefine, redivide, artificially create, and spread jobs is an understanding on the part of many workers that although holding the job is important to them, the work they do, and the amount of work they do, is not really important.[22] Many of them also realize that the work they do could as easily be done by a machine— better, faster, cheaper, and for 24 hours a day all year. And not only do they realize this, they know that others know it, too.[23] The result of such understanding is the widespread malaise about which so much is written and said, and the previously mentioned fact that most people work far below their innate capacities. This leads to an even more serious and threatening social problem—individual and societal corruption.

The artificial creation of jobs, the insistence that people work when their productivity is not needed, the tacit acceptance of informal work-regulating norms, the condoned resistance to new machinery or methods, and contractual legitimation of various forms of widespread featherbedding all amount to moral corruption on the part of society. Rather than devising, adopting, or sanctioning methods of sharing societal resources other than through job-holding, it avoids the problem through use of the subterfuges discussed above. Thus the majority of mankind can be kept in equilibrium "only by conditioning and by lies."[24]

The corruption inherent in such a system inevitably communicates itself and spreads to the individuals concerned. Workers who sign in and then go out to take care of personal matters, those who have others insert their cards in the time-clock in their own absence, those who deliberately or unconsciously stretch their work to fill the assigned time, in fulfillment of Parkinson's Law, those who dawdle, gossip, and simply idle, those who hold other jobs during their ostensible working hours, those who do not come in or come in late on Mondays —all of these are the products of nonserious work, not its causes.[25] The results of this situation in terms of self-doubt and self-hate, guilt, and negative self-images, together with the defensive reactions thus caused, have never been calculated and are not even taken into account very often. Yet, as Schumacher has pointed out, people are destroyed by the inner conviction of uselessness.[26] One of the basic errors in the well-intentioned Quality of Working Life movement is that it attempts to make life on the job more satisfying by changes in the work. It is the lack of important work which is the problem—simply having to be at the work site to satisfy the demands of society.

The illusions which are necessary to maintain such a system, the cheating—by society and by individuals—which is accepted as normal, and the self- and other-images which are thereby created constitute a socially sanctioned delusional system which is both corrupt and corrupting.[27] Just as laws which are obviously unenforced eventually create contempt for laws in general, so unnecessary work and artificially created and maintained jobs lead to other "cons" on and by society. The result of societal hypocrisy regarding jobs—that they are necessary, important, and fulfilling—counterposed to the feeling of many job-holders that what they do is basically unimportant, unnecessary, and boring is spreading cynicism, dishonesty, immorality, and human relationships based on fraud rather than on friendship.

In summary: The need of individuals for jobs, and the requirement that society provide jobs, is very real and deadly serious. However, once it is understood that the need for jobs is not due to productivity demands, but in order to provide income, then it becomes easier to grapple with the problem of providing income as such. Disentangling the need for production from the need for jobs would enable industry and services to proceed with all deliberate speed toward mechanization and "cybernation," while freeing social planners to create and experiment with variations on the job-leisure-income structure.

One obvious solution to the problem of relentlessly pursuing the creation of jobs at whatever cost to society and to individuals is to create or adopt a system whereby those whose efforts are not needed for the production of goods and services would be compensated without the necessity of putting in time at a workplace. One possibility is expansion of the present social welfare system, removing its stigmatizing features, as through the adoption of a universal reverse-income-tax plan. Another possibility is the substitution for the present work ethic of another ethic which society values—e.g., education. Another is the equal distribution of material items, as is the practice in the Israeli kibbutz. These and other possibilities will be examined in Chapter 10. First, however, it is advisable to see to what extent holding jobs has positive values for people, other than as an economic necessity. The next chapter deals with this question.

NOTES

1. Shimmin, "The Future of Work," op. cit.

2. Neulinger is one of the few who distinguish between work, jobs, and leisure on the basis of coercion versus freedom and implicit motivation versus explicit motivation. J. Neulinger, *The Psychology of Leisure* (Springfield, IL: Charles Thomas, 1974).

3. J. Wanniski, "Taxes, Revenues, and the 'Laffer Curve'." *Public Interest* 50 (Winter 1978): 3.

4. Scott, op. cit.

5. Thus, a social policy in relation to employment for all finds itself in juxtaposition with an "effectiveness measure" based on "criteria of profitability of investment." Weiner et al., op. cit., p. 85.

6. B. Olmsted, "Job Sharing: An Emerging Work Style." *International Labour Review* 118 (May/June 1979): 283-297. Italics in original.

7. S. A. Levitan and R. S. Belous, "Reduced Worktime: Tool to Fight Unemployment." *Worklife* 3 (April 1978): 22-26.

8. Olmsted, op. cit.

9. Straussman, op. cit.

10. Charnow, op. cit.

11. *New Zealand Official Yearbook 1972,* op. cit., pp. 7-8.

12. H. Cleveland, G. J. Mangone, and J. C. Adams, *The Overseas Americans* (New York: McGraw-Hill, 1960).

13. See C. C. Killingsworth, "The Role of Public-Service Employment," in J. L. Stern and B. D. Dennis, *Proceedings of the 1977 Annual Spring Meeting* (Madison, WI: Industrial Relations Research Association, 1977), pp. 489-495.

14. This fear, along with the reactions caused by it, even predates the Luddites, who destroyed machinery in England, beginning in 1811.

15. Weiner et al., op. cit., p. 83.

16. Johnston refers to this as the government as employer of first resort. D. F. Johnston, "The Future of Work: Three Possible Alternatives," in *Monthly Labor Review Reader* (Washington, DC: Government Printing Office), pp. 462-470.

17. Dasgupta, op. cit., pp. 51-69.

18. Attempts to create jobs through subsidies to employers have also been disappointing: "Despite the fairly large sums offered as Job Creation Subsidies [in Holland and in Ireland] the rate of take-ups on the subsidies was disappointing." T. Buck, "Experiments with Job Creation Subsidies." *Industrial Relations* 8 (Winter 1977/78): 12-18.

19. Bernfield, op. cit.

20. U. J. Hanby and M. P. Jackson, "An Evaluation of Job Creation in Germany." *International Journal of Social Economics* 6 (1979): 79-117.

21. Weiner et al., op. cit.

22. In a study of Israeli factory workers, those who indicated they did not work as hard as they could were asked the reason. Almost invariably the answer was that the job did not require any more work. D. Macarov, *The Roots of Hard Work: A Preliminary Study* (Jerusalem: Hebrew University, 1978). (Mimeographed)

23. Gabor says that the leading minority really believe the majority to be objectively useless because they can be replaced by machines. Gabor, op. cit., p. 140.

24. Ibid., p. 134.

25. In this connection, it should be noted that it is customary to blame poor workmanship on disaffected workers, but Waller holds that the reverse is true: "The shoddy nature of products affects the job attitude of the worker which in turn contributes to decreased job satisfaction." R. Waller, "Job Satisfaction: The Throw-Away Society." *Business Horizons* 16 (October 1973): 51-52.

26. My thanks to Dr. Alec Dickson for calling my attention to this comment.

27. For this felicitous phrase I am indebted to a personal communication from Professor Beulah Rothman, School of Social Work, Adelphi University.

Chapter 7

WORK AS NORMALCY: Everybody Does It
So It Must Be the Right Thing To Do

"Life wasn't meant to be easy."

—Malcolm Fraser, Prime
Minister of Australia

Social workers participate in and support the work-welfare structure not only because they believe the work to be needed and the jobs to be required, but because work is a normative activity, and in order to be normal, one must work.

That working is normative in most societies is not open to serious question. Some even define humanity in terms of working animals.[1] Most people do work, and those who do not are either pitied or scorned, depending upon their reason. People define themselves and each other in terms of their work: "What do you do?" Work structures the day, the week, the year, and the career. People who do not or cannot work are viewed as somehow outside the mainstream of life.[2] Thus, the women's movement, among others, wants to have housework defined and viewed as "real" work, through the payment of salaries and through other means.[3] Otherwise, the housewife is seen as inferior.

Although Strauss holds that it is possible that genetic factors affect attitudes toward work,[4] it is more generally assumed that work patterns are the result of socialization, and much of the normal socialization process is devoted to inculcating attitudes toward work. Neff, for example, speaks of the "work personality."[5] Fox details socialization to work:

> Attitudes to work are socially and culturally moulded. Men are taught what to expect and want from work—taught by a variety of socializing agencies. . . . Not only will the state itself implicitly or explicitly encourage certain attitudes to work and discourage others, but so also will social institutions such as industry, business and commerce, religion, and the educational system. Relevant strands in the cultural tradition will exert their influence through education and communication media. The local community, the family and the work group will also contribute their effect.[6]

From such socialization stem the widely accepted attitudes toward work and working which are currently prevalent.

Although it would be naive to believe that public attitudes toward work, toward poverty, and toward welfare impact immediately and directly on the appropriate social policies, it would be equally incorrect to ignore the influence of attitudes on policy determination and application. Although many other variables may intervene, in democratic countries public attitudes do ultimately impact on social policy.[7] For example, alternative conceptions of poverty have implications for income maintenance policies. *Situational* views of poverty involve simple causality and the belief that manipulation of a prior variable, like income, is translated into an improvement in work performance or an increase in scholastic attainment. *Cultural* views of poverty, by contrast, posit the existence of values and aspirations appropriate to poor people, which militate against the type of manipulation prescribed for situations, and which require direct treatment of the value as such[8] through education, guided group experiences, and similar means. In the same way, a social problem seen as deviance is dealt with differently from a problem seen as pathology. Deviants are believed to be in control of their behavior and therefore able to change at will. Such change can presumably be brought about by exhortation, rewards, and punishment. But when the problem is seen as pathology, the victims should not only be supported and helped, but may have to have decisions made for them, may have to be separated from the nonpathological, and may have to be induced to partake of distasteful remedies.[9] Further, the "law of anticipated reaction" operates to create universal programs like children's allowances from which everyone receives some benefit, on the assumption that this will be approved and supported, rather than selective or categorical programs which aid only certain groups, like raising the welfare grants of the poor, which would presumably be resented and fought by the nonpoor. A good example of the impact of attitudes on programs, and their effect, is the approbation offered insurance-type versus grant programs:

> Social Security continues to benefit politically from its characteriza-
> tion as a social insurance program. But the price of such an insurance
> scheme is that the program is not an efficient means of eliminating
> poverty.[10]

Thus, understanding attitudes toward work, welfare, and the connection between them is of importance in analyzing present policies and predicting or informing the future. In fact, much welfare policy is explicitly based upon the purported or antici-pated views of taxpayers concerning use of their money for welfare purposes, or how workers might feel about nonworkers receiving more income than they themselves do.

Attitudes Toward Work

Although there had been broad, speculative discussions of work and its meaning previously, scientific inquiry into work can be said to have begun in the United States with the work of F. W. Taylor in the 1880s, followed by that of Frank Gilbreth. However, their concern was almost exclusively with efficiency, seen in time-and-motion study terms. It was not until after 1910 that pioneers such as Munsterberg and Spearman began empirical studies of work as such. These studies were all part of the "scientific management" school of thought. Attitudes did not really come to the fore until the results of the work begun by Mayo in 1927 and 1930, and continued by others, became known. This was the famous research generally known as the Hawthorne studies. Both industrial psychologists and occupational sociologists then began a veritable flood of studies.[11]

Attitudes toward work have been examined, reexamined, and cross-examined in an enormous number of surveys, interviews, and experiments. Many of these proceed from different assumptions, use different methodologies, and examine different aspects of work. It is becoming increasingly clear that attitudes toward work, as well as its performance, are extremely complex and differ with social class, individual personality patterns, work conditions and content, and many other variables that are not yet fully understood. Hence, as more than one researcher has discovered, one can prove almost anything one wants to from existing research results. Generalizations, therefore, must be surrounded by numerous caveats.

From the various studies available, it is possible to distinguish between responses which deal with a specific job or occupation and its attributes, and those that probe attitudes toward work in general. The former include questions like: "If you had the chance to start your working life over again, would you choose the same kind of work you are doing now?"[12] or "If you have or were to have a son (daughter), how would you feel if someone suggested that he (she) work for the same company that you work for?"[13] or "What things do you particularly like about the job?"[14] Questions about work in general tend to be like: "Suppose you inherited enough money so that you and your family could live comfortably without your ever working; would you go ahead and work anyway?"[15] or "Some people feel work to be a burden; others feel it is a necessity; still others feel it to be a pleasure. How do you feel about work?"[16] Methodologically, one can also distinguish between those studies which simply ask people to talk about their work, in the manner of Terkel,[17] and those which pose specific questions.[18]

Work in general

Mindful of the difficulty of generalizing from such a large and diverse pool of findings, there nevertheless seem to be certain attitudes toward work in general and toward one's own work common to the majority of people in Western industrialized countries. The overwhelming majority of people in these countries not only see work as necessary for individual maintenance and for societal order, but as the source of happiness, health, and morals, and thus desirable. In this view, people both need to and should want to work in order to create and maintain an ordered, secure, moral universe, and to be happy, healthy, and respected individuals. A world without work is inconceivable to most; when it is envisioned, it is seen as a catastrophe.[19] A succinct summary of this attitude has been expressed as: "Employment is an end in itself; it provides an individual with the opportunity to participate in society and enhance his sense of worth and dignity."[20]

The view of work as both necessary and desirable is so widespread and deeply held that few studies even probe it, except in relation to certain groups who are suspected of holding other, heretical, views. Goodwin studied work attitudes of poor people, finding that their views coincided almost entirely with those of the nonpoor.[21] Others have studied the attitudes of young people, as compared to their parents, and have similarly found no great differences.[22] Still others have looked at the attitudes of various minority groups. Van Til, for example, found that contrary to popular belief, it is the black poor who exhibit a stronger attachment to the labor force.[23]

Insofar as young workers are concerned, however, researchers using an open-ended technique have remarked a countertheme.[24] As noted in Chapter 5, it is mainly the young workers who distinguish between socially useful and unnecessary or detrimental work and products. Others question the work ethic as such. The Canadian Minister of National Health and Welfare says:

Canadians are coming to question the social value of certain kinds of work, and to question whether there is an inherent value in work, no

matter how unpleasant or dehumanizing it may be. This, indeed, is a
questioning of the work ethic in its original sense: that work as such,
whatever form it takes, and whatever its objective, is of and by itself
a good thing. Canadians—particularly young Canadians—have come
to question this view.[25]

In the United States, the new generation does not seem to
talk about their work as much; their tavern conversation centers
about their softball team or bowling league.[26] Similarly, a study
of 3000 men in 53 U.S. companies found that young workers
valued hard work and craftmanship less, were less satisfied with
their jobs and the company, and when asked whether it is more
important to get along with your friends or to work hard on a
job, the younger group valued hard work less than did the older
workers.[27] A French study found that young workers were
interested in pleasant working relationships—sometimes even
more than in pay. If a job presents any obstacles to personal
relationships or regular contacts with other people, young
people will find another job.[28] Or, as a poster observed during
the French student riots of 1967: "Work—It Will Make You
Ugly."[29]

With the exception of this young element, the significance of
whose responses will be discussed later, the overwhelming
response to questions about the necessity or the desirability of
work in general is positive. So positive and so overwhelming, in
fact, that one is led to suspect that the lady doth protest too
much.

In any case, were consensual validation to constitute truth,
the value of work would be proven. Since, however, there was
once universal consensus that the world is flat, it is legitimate to
look at how people view their own work, in contradistinction to
how they view work as a principle. Here people sing a somewhat
different tune.

One's own work

Despite their stated belief that work as a concept is necessary, desirable, moral, normative, and good, attitudes toward

people's own work and jobs show up in study after study as, at best, a resigned acceptance. Even when people express themselves as satisfied through survey research, caution is indicated. Gutek, for example, found that people tend to say they are satisfied with everything.[30] Rubin, too, found that her subjects tended to call their situation satisfactory, but after a discussion came around to "confessing" that their situation was actually very unsatisfactory.[31]

It seems that, accepting the fact that they must work, most people resign themselves to it and seek to make the best of it. This exhibits itself in the widespread dissatisfaction and apathy among America's labor force found by a presidential commission,[32] and, on a less conscious level, the untold personal and mental problems which have their roots in the world of work.[33] Widespread studies indicate not job contentment, but, at best, lack of discontent. Even workers reporting themselves as satisfied often mean they have made the best bargain under the circumstances. That is, they are satisfied *in,* but not *with,* their jobs.[34] In short, although not all workers hate their jobs, very few love them. Many philosophically point to other, less desirable, work and console themselves that their jobs are not as bad as some others.[35]

Further, since satisfaction may be defined as fulfillment of expectations, people with low expectations from their work may have these easily met—that is, they are satisfied in the sense of not being disappointed in regard to what little they expected.[36] However, increased educational opportunities and higher standards of living create a growing disparity for many people between their aspirations and their realizations.[37] The Revolution of Rising Expectations brings with it more discontent at work. Thus, there is said to be a "surrender process" taking place, in which workers report themselves as reasonably content in their jobs, but have achieved contentment only by surrendering aspirations.[38]

Such surrender may take a while: Three times more respondents under age 30 express dissatisfaction with work than do those over age 44,[39] but eventually many workers seem to

arrive at what Robinson terms "fatalistic contentment"[40] Such
contentment can also be achieved, not by giving up aspirations,
but by never holding them—if expectations are low, they can be
easily satisfied,[41] and part of the general attitude toward work
which comes through from the bulk of the research is that
people expect little joy from work. Few people in all the studies
reported speak of their work as challenging, exciting, or fulfilling,[42] and those that do are almost always on the upper
rungs of the hierarchy, or in prestigeful free professions.[43] Part
of the reason may be because one component of job satisfaction
has been found to be perceived authority or opportunity.[44] In
general, there is a negative correlation between the skills
required on the job and the number of problems which workers
experience.[45] The management literature is highly consistent in
showing a positive relationship between status (or level) of
occupations and job satisfactions.[46] Gavin found 48 percent of
his sample of workers often trapped in situations of role conflict; 45 percent complained of work overload; and 35 percent
were disturbed by a lack of clarity about the scope and responsibilities of their jobs.[47] In those studies which show work
satisfactions as growing, reanalysis of the data indicates that
there is a significant decrease in job satisfactions among low-
paid workers, which is masked by an increase in satisfaction
among higher-paid workers.[48] Overall, however, the number of
workers who are satisfied with their jobs has declined between
1973 and 1977 by large percentages, ranging from 11.3 to 43
percent, in all occupational groups.[49]

It is the acknowledgment of this widespread unhappiness
among the mass of workers which has led to the Quality-of-
Working-Life (QWL) programs now being instituted in a number
of workplaces. QWL programs, like industrial social work, purport to be concerned with workers' health and happiness as
such, rather than in increasing production and/or reducing
absenteeism, tardiness, and turnover. Practitioners are probably
sincere in seeking the former goal. But when companies or
unions are involved, the ultimate goal is "to raise the productivity rate. This is, essentially, what the quality of working life

is all about."[50] Nevertheless, regardless of divergent goals, the very existence of QWL programs or industrial social work bespeaks the presence of worker dissatisfaction. This dissatisfaction is confirmed by a labor spokesman, who suggests a realistic acceptance of the employee view of work as an unpleasant necessity.[51]

There is also evidence that dissatisfaction is not confined to the lower levels. It has become very frequent among a large variety of highly educated, professional people in business, finance, and industry.[52] Indeed, one study shows:

> Dissatisfaction with lack of fulfillment on the job (and what that implies about achievement of life hopes) may be as high as 80 percent among managerial and technical people. The critical point is that such feelings are part of a new ethos, and *not* the life style of one particular class (or race).[53]

In the same vein, a Cornell University interdisciplinary conference on work and mental health found that, increasingly, workers at all levels are uncomfortable with their milieu.[54]

Although, as one worker put it, looking back ruefully at his youthful illusions, "work was supposed to be fun,"[55] most people report their fun at work comes from daydreaming, the coffee break, or from chatting with others—not from the work itself.[56] Indeed, the central life interests of most workers seem to be outside the workplace,[57] and their enforced participation in work has led to serious questions about the mental health of the American working person. We are becoming concerned with what work does to human beings as well as what it does for them.[58] The evidence in the literature does point to a link between work monotony and poorer psychological and physical health.[59] Others have found that nonphysical aspects of work such as job dissatisfaction, low self-esteem, and rapid and continuous job changes are found to be associated with a high risk of heart disease.[60] The effects of monotonous work are not just confined to the workplace, but may result in people who are less capable of creativity off the job.[61] Nor is monotony the only problem. Lack of fulfillment in work in general is so great that only those who do not depend upon their work to fulfill their lives are able to function as healthy human beings.[62]

The presence and effect of work stress has reached the point that courts in some states of the United States award compensation for stress in the same manner as they do for purely physical injuries.

At the other end of the continuum, too, more interesting jobs have been found to lead to increasing amounts of stress, the pressured ulcer-ridden executive being the stereotype.[63] Indeed, it might be well not to ignore the possible influences of socially acceptable answers in surveys concerning work attitudes of executives and members of the free professions. Novels about the men in grey flannel suits, the tribulations of the organization man, the self-doubts of advertising workers, stockbrokers, and others concerning the usefulness of their endeavors may reflect the actual feelings of such people more than do more conventional probes.

Insofar as there is a satisfaction gap between lower- and higher-paid workers or those high and low in the hierarchy, it has enormous significance for social welfare policy. Those who make policy and plan programs are, almost without exception, high in both hierarchical position and salary and, given the power and prestige that they wield, sincerely enjoy their work. They often do not know and cannot conceive of the fact that most people do not enjoy their work. They perceive people who do not enjoy working in general, and their present work in particular, as aberrant, and almost deviant, and policies are thus devised to reward the majority who presumably enjoy their work and to punish the deviants and bring them into line.

In summarizing people's expressed attitudes toward their own work, one can ask, with Sarason: "When one considers how the work scene has changed in a century, how work and its conditions have changed and presumably 'improved,' why is it that so many people are unhappy about their work experience?"[64]

Objective indices

Since most of the reservations expressed by people concerning their own work have not been elicited within the context, nor placed in apposition with, their views about work in general, it is difficult to know which, if either, represents a deeper or more genuine feeling. However, there are external indices which point to a general disaffection from work. One of these is the general desire of individuals to reduce the amount of work they have to do. Although there are "workaholics" who cannot stand being deprived of work even for short periods, and who might demand or manufacture more work for themselves,[65] such people are exceptions and, to some, psychopathic. For most people the amount of work required of them, or the amount they do, is marked by an inexorable downward trend. As Table 7.1 shows, the average hours of work per week in the major industrial countries has been shrinking steadily for the last quarter-century.[66] From 1957 to 1965 alone, hours of work in manufacturing in developed economies decreased by 2.14 percent, and the trend continues.[67] Basic paid holidays for manual workers increased from 1.75 weeks 25 years ago to 3.50 weeks in 1977.[68] The amount of leisure time available to people today (even omitting from the definition of leisure time spent in housework, child care, household care, personal needs, non-work travel, study, participation, and perusal of mass media) is only 2.75 hours per week less than work, even when second jobs are included,[69] and this gap is rapidly narrowing. Leisure time will outweigh work time very shortly.

It is clear that despite people's protestations concerning the desirability of work in general and their own pleasure in working, they continually work less and less as compared to previous generations and times. The average American has four more hours of leisure a day than his or her grandfather had,[70] and if the ratio of reduction in work hours continues as it has since 1880, before today's children retire the work week will be halved again.[71] As the work week has contracted and life expectancy has been extended, the average American has added about twenty-two more years of leisure to life.[72] In 1875,

TABLE 7.1   Weekly Average Hours of Work

	1948	1951	1954	1957	1960	1963	1966	1969	1972	1975
United States	42	41	40	41	40	40	39	38	37	36
France	45	45	45	47	47	47	47	46	45	43
Germany	45	45	45	46	45	45	44	44	43	41
United Kingdom	45	46	47	48	48	48	46	47	45	44
Japan				46	46	45	45	44	42	40
Israel				44	40	41	40	40	40	37

SOURCE: *Yearbook of Labour Statistics* (Geneva: International Labor Organization), Sixteenth Edition, 1956; Twenty-Sixth Edition, 1966; Thirty-Sixth Edition, 1976.

when the world population was 1 billion, the average work year was 4000 hours. In 1975, with a population of 3 billion, it was 2000 hours.

Nor does all this increase in leisure come from involuntary retirement. Slightly more than half the recent retirees studied by Barfield and Morgan had taken reduced social security benefits in order to retire early; [73] a major rallying cry in a recent auto workers' strike was "thirty and out"; while transport workers in New York City have gained half-pay retirement after twenty years. [74] Ball found that in the first twelve months after the opportunity to retire at any age with thirty years of service became effective, nearly 40 percent of the eligible workers between the ages of 51 and 55 retired, and 30 percent of the eligible under 50 retired. [75] Similarly, Stagner found that only 7 percent of those male workers retired due to company policy described themselves as willing and able to work but incapable of finding jobs. A Michigan survey found even fewer job seekers—only 2 percent. In the Harris study, only 25 percent of those over 65, retired and/or unemployed, said they would like to work. [76] Men 45 and older have been withdrawing from the workforce in large numbers during the last fifteen years, and the trend seems likely to continue into the next decade. [77] Davis holds that by 1990 there will be no male workers in the 55-65 range. [78] The majority of American social security beneficiaries have been retiring before age 65 [79]—that is, *more than half* of new awards are reduced because of early retirement. [80]

There has also been a very sharp increase, since 1960, in the number of private pension plans allowing for early retirement. By 1975 plans allowing retirement at 55 or less outnumbered plans allowing retirement at 60 by roughly 5 to 2.[81] In 1963, 23 percent of persons 45-54 years old indicated that they planned to retire before 65, but by 1976 this proportion had increased to 41 percent. Although some of these change their intention as they approach that age, probably because the reality of their upcoming financial situation as retirees is brought closer to them, 31 percent still maintain their plans.[82] Nor does early retirement occur just among the lower-level, presumably disaffected, workers. A 1974 study found that among the twenty-eight major companies included, about three-fourths of the executives had retired "substantially" early. The president of one large oil company noted that in 1975 about 80 percent of the eligible employees in his firm were selecting early retirement.[83] Throughout the world there is public pressure for earlier retirement ages, and payment of benefits before the normal retirement age:[84] One of the more notable trends in the pensions branch continues to be legislative changes to lower the retirement age.[85] Once more leisure is acquired, people generally do not regret it. When work and leisure were compared in Yankelovich's studies, only one out of five people (21 percent) said that work meant more to them than leisure. The majority (60 percent) say that while they enjoy their work, it is not their major source of satisfaction. (The other 19 percent are so exhausted by the demands work makes of them that they cannot conceive of it as even a minor source of satisfaction).[86] Barfield and Morgan found that an overwhelming majority of all retirees (87 percent) believe their decision to retire when they did was the right decision.[87] When people do work beyond retirement age it is almost invariably because they need the money—not because of any intrinsic quality in the job or in working.[88]

That this is not just an American phenomenon is attested to by the fact that during the last twenty years in Sweden work as the main source of meaning in life was cut in half (33 percent to

17 percent). The position of family eroded slightly (45 percent to 41 percent), but dedication to leisure more than doubled (13 percent to 27 percent).[89] It seems that for many people the satisfactions of life free from the demands of work are both pervasive and abiding.[90]

In summary, people have fought hard to cut and succeeded in cutting the number of hours, days, weeks, and years they have to work, and this is true even when extra work is concerned.[91] The work ethic measured by hours of work indicates that workers are increasingly preferring increments of paid nonwork to paid work.[92] Work is becoming an instrumental means of enjoying longer and more frequent periods of leisure.[93] The evidence thus points to a wide gap between societal norms, which induce people to speak of work as a positive and desirable experience, and actual behavior, which treats work as an economic necessity, to be reduced in every way possible without harming one's income. In short, people can be dissatisfied with the job they are presently holding and yet still believe that working is an important and virtuous activity.[94] This gap between norms and behaviors as regards work has important consequences for social welfare policy, as will be indicated.

Attitudes Toward Welfare

Attitudes toward work affect attitudes toward welfare, and consequently it is important to look at the latter in attempting to understand social welfare policy and its future. Although studies of popular attitudes toward welfare cannot be compared with those toward work insofar as quantity is concerned, there have nevertheless been enough studies of attitudes toward welfare to allow some conclusions to be drawn. However, differences in sampling, methodology, and interpretation make it difficult to compare studies directly. In addition, many such studies are characterized by ambivalences and misconceptions concerning poverty, welfare, and work, making the results difficult to categorize.

Surveys of attitudes toward welfare cover many aspects— sexual behavior, adequacy of benefits, costs of programs, and so on—in addition to those regarding work. Limiting findings to the latter, it is clear that the historical differentiation between the deserving poor, who cannot work; and the undeserving poor, who can but will not or do not, remains operative. However, in many cases there is a tendency to lump the former with the latter, and this is the area in which most misconceptions show up.

Feagin conducted a study in 1969 in which 1017 respondents in 86 widely scattered sample areas gave antiwelfare answers to six of seven questions. Insofar as the work-welfare link is concerned, 84 percent of the respondents felt that there are too many people receiving welfare money who should be working, and 49 percent felt that most people on welfare who can work do not try to find jobs.[95] Kallen and Miller interviewed 300 white women and 300 black women in Baltimore in 1967. Eighty-one percent of the whites felt that too many people receiving welfare should be working and only 31 percent that welfare recipients seek work. Black responses were not significantly different.[96] Asking the same question, Carter and Fifield reported in a seven-state study in 1973 that consistently in all seven states, over 55 percent of the respondents believe welfare payments are being received by able-bodied unemployed adults, who chose leisure over work.[97] When Williamson asked 375 men and women in the Boston area, in 1972, "What percent of welfare recipients are able-bodied unemployed males?" the mean of the total responses was 37 percent.[98]

Although these responses are given as totals, there are obviously differences in the responses given by individuals and by groups. Some researchers have sought for differential determinants of attitudes toward welfare. Alston and Dean, for example, using data from 1964 Gallup poll responses, found attitudes toward poverty to be associated with socioeconomic status. Specifically, those social categories which were especially negative in their definition of the poor were the males, the younger, the well-educated, and those who were employed in managerial, clerical-sales, and farming occupations.[99] Rytina, Form, and Pease also found that the high-income respondents imputed more lack of motivation to the poor.[100] Ogren found that the nonpoor tended to blame poverty on circumstances to a lesser extent than did the poor—those who might be considered poor themselves felt that it was due to circumstances beyond their control.[101] Grimm and Orten looked at social work students' attitudes toward the poor, simply scoring them as positive or negative, and found correlations between such attitudes and the sociodemographic backgrounds of the students and their educational experiences prior to entering graduate school. Interestingly, their findings were that the *higher* the students' socioeconomic background, the more positive the attitude toward the indigent.[102] Williamson is not sanguine about the impact of socioeconomic determinants in any case, since many so-called middle-class attitudes, specifically about work, welfare, and poverty, are held by the poor themselves,[103] a finding that Goodwin's extensive study confirms.[104]

Despite these differences between groups (and different findings regarding the same groups), the overall attitude toward poverty, welfare, and the poor remains generally substantiated. At best, it can be said with Ogren that if the poor and/or welfare recipients are not regarded as inherently less worthy than others, they are viewed as less worthy because they are less strongly motivated than "more successful" members of society.[105] Ginzberg probably speaks to the more pervasive public attitude when he says: "There runs deep in the American experience the belief that people who find themselves on welfare lack some basic personal strengths, above all a desire to work and be independent."[106]

Misconceptions

As mentioned, one feature which seems to run through most polls of attitudes toward welfare is the extent of misconceptions of reality—that is, the myths as opposed to the facts.

At the time that Feagin's respondents characterized welfare recipients as not working (84 percent) and not looking for work (49 percent), welfare recipients in the United States were roughly the following:

AFDC children	49%
Elderly persons	19%
Heads of one-parent families	17%
Permanently disabled	7%
Blind	1%

The remaining 7-8 percent were receiving general relief.[107] Able-bodied men accounted for less than 1 percent of the nation's welfare recipients, and eligibility for payments requires these recipients to be actively seeking work.[108] This situation had been little different at the time of the Kallen and Miller study two years earlier, in which 81 percent and 78 percent of white and black women, respectively, said that too many people were receiving welfare who should be working; only 31 percent and 43 percent felt that welfare recipients do seek work.[109]

When Williamson's respondents estimated 37 percent of welfare recipients as able-bodied unemployed males, the actual figure was something less than 1 percent.[110] While 55 percent of Carter and Fifield's respondents believed welfare payments were going to able-bodied unemployed males, "Survey research results show over and over that welfare recipients prefer work as their source of income."[111] Podell found that seven in ten welfare mothers in New York said they would rather work for pay than stay at home.[112] A California study found that three-quarters of the welfare mothers interviewed were very work oriented.[113] In addition to these reports of what people said, in 1971 75 percent of all poor, male family heads worked during the year and 51 percent of those working worked full-time, year-round.[114]

In view of the prevalence of such factual misconceptions about welfare recipients and the poor, Williamson raises the question as to whether, from a policy viewpoint, the facts are as important as the feelings:

Correcting the factual misconceptions about welfare recipients held by the general public would be a difficult task. However, this task would be quite easy in comparison to the task of changing basic ideology. Unfortunately for those whose goal it is to increase the income of the welfare poor . . . the real payoff is likely to come, not with changes in factual misconceptions, but rather with basic ideological change.[115]

Ambiguities and ambivalences

The strength of the work-welfare ideology exhibits itself regarding the poor not only in facts which are misconceived, but in the confusion which people exhibit when they are asked to discuss the causes of poverty and its possible remedies. It is common for people to agree that the poor are mainly victims of circumstances beyond their own control—but if they tried hard enough they could get out of poverty.[116] Similarly, most people would agree that the aged, children, and the disabled should not be expected to work, but would oppose welfare grants which would give them as much or more income than a working person.

Just as there is a gap between norms and behaviors regarding work, so there is a conflict between that which people believe regarding welfare and that which they know—or in some cases between what they believe intellectually and what they want to believe emotionally. Although there may be some groups which are exceptions, the general, immediate, emotional—almost instinctive—reaction to welfare is that it permits those who should be working to avoid it; or that it permits nonworking people to be better off than working people. Given discussion, explanation, or other kinds of pressure, this may be followed by a more thoughtful or detailed analysis indicating that this is true of only some welfare recipients (whose number is almost invariably exaggerated). Thus, regarding welfare, as regarding many other things, feelings go up in the elevator, while the thoughts trudge up the stairs.

Attitudes Toward the Work-Welfare Link

Putting together the salient facts from the studies quoted, it seems clear that most people believe in work as a principle and feel that everyone should work, both as a societal obligation and as a personal desideratum, although they are not actively happy in their own work, and constantly seek opportunities for more leisure. One way of understanding the continuing existence of this gap between beliefs and actions is in light of the psychological phenomenon known as cognitive dissonance.[117] In part and in brief, this theory holds that when people act in a way that is at variance with their beliefs, a tension is set up. There are a number of ways in which this uncomfortable tension can be reduced, and one of them is to deny to oneself the significance or the importance of the action and to emphasize—and sometimes overemphasize—the importance of the belief; in this case, tension is reduced by lauding work and ignoring or denying the existence of work-avoidance behavior. However, such unconscious moves to relieve the tension of dissonance inevitably leave some elements of ambivalence or self-doubt. Such doubts can be allayed by seeking others who express the same beliefs, thereby reinforcing the hitherto shaky position.

In this way, support for the work ethic in the face of efforts to reduce work can be seen as a mutual support system, in which masses of people declare to each other their allegiance to the importance of work as such, while they seek and enjoy shorter hours, longer vacations, and earlier retirement. Poor people and welfare cases are threats to this internal accommodation and to this mutual support system, since they are seen as participating in the work-avoidance activity rather than in the work ethic belief; the welfare system is viewed malevolently as making possible, if not encouraging, such treachery.

The cognitive dissonance theory gains credibility from the existence of a supplementary way of reducing tension between action and belief, and that is the attempt to acquire information which supports the preferred attitude or action, while ignoring information in the other direction. This is exhibited in the manner in which reports of lack of worker happiness, negotiations for shorter hours and longer vacations, statistics concerning the existence of more leisure time, and other such bits of information are ignored, denied, or seen as aberrations,[118] while statements concerning the importance of work, the value of work, the need for work, and the deleterious effects of not working are accepted and believed.[119]

One example of rejection of information in order to maintain a belief system has to do with attitudes regarding unemployment and the unemployed. The image of the lazy, good-for-nothing exploiting society by drawing unemployment compensation may date back in America to the G.I. Bill of Rights, which paid unemployed veterans $20 for up to 52 weeks, and was therefore jocularly referred to as the "52-20" club. However, only 9.5 million of the 15.1 million World War II veterans eligible filed claims. The average number of weeks of benefits paid to these claimants averaged 29; only 11.1 percent drew their full 52 weeks' benefits.[120] Seventy percent of Korean veterans went to work during the first six months after discharge.[121] Nevertheless, as Miller points out:

> Clearly, information and education seem to make little difference in people's attitudes toward unemployment. . . . It must be, therefore, that this attitude is a manifestation of a more or less deeply held belief that is not susceptible to alteration or modification merely through exposure to the thinking and opinions generally regarded as "expert."[122]

Another example of rejection and distortion of information has to do with the reactions of retirees. As pointed out earlier, many retirees are happy in their retirement, not sorry they retired, and wish they had done so earlier, and, in fact, more and more people are voluntarily retiring earlier. However, the image of the retired person is that of the bored, unhappy person.

It is true that some studies have found retirees to become ill and to die at a greater rate than nonretirees.[123] However, this has also been found true of aged persons moving to new homes—it is the change in the situation, not the lack of work as such, which may be responsible.[124] Similarly, it is also possible that much of the illness affecting retirees is psychosomatic—an assumption of the "sick role" which is socially a more accep-table motive for not working than is retirement.[125] Finally, it is also possible that the sickness/death rate is correlated with the reduction in income which accompanies most retirement. This is a factor not controlled for in most such surveys, and yet there is a drastic drop in income for most retirees. There is also a myth that large numbers of, if not most, retirees return to work. Research indicates that only a small number actually does.[126] Nor—at least insofar as early retirees are concerned—are retirees by and large unhappy: The life experiences of the worker who remains healthy after retirement are quite likely to be generally enjoyable.[127] Even in the case of normal retirees, one must be careful not to attribute the results of age or illness to the fact of retirement.

In short, having chosen to work rather than to suffer the consequences of not working, people unconsciously defend their choice by imputing values to working, associating with others who espouse the same values, seeking information which will support their position, and rejecting evidence to the con-trary. This is the classic pattern arising from cognitive dissonance.

In this connection, it is interesting that some of the younger generation of workers, more exposed to the influence of con-sciousness-raising movements, protest manifestations, the coun-ter-culture, and in general more inclined to "let it all hang out," are less affected by the need to conform to societal mores regarding work. Shimmin holds that this is not so much a change from one generation to the next as a change in social outlook and circumstances which permits the young to express what their elders thought but were not allowed to say because they had been socialized to accept the coercive necessity of employment.[128]

Another way of explaining the connotations for social wel-fare which arise from the gap between work beliefs and behav-iors has been termed scapegoating.[129] In this conception, people are aware of their own feelings about work—that they do not enjoy their work, that they try to avoid work, that they do not believe their work to be essential or even necessary—and since societal norms do not permit expression of these feelings, they feel guilty about them. Such guilt is handled by repressing the feelings, but repression results in tension. The tension is discharged by the classic method of projecting the forbidden feelings onto others (in this case, the poor), blaming them for such antisocial attitudes, and punishing them. The manner in which poor people or welfare cases are punished for their putative guilt in not upholding the work ethic is through welfare programs that demand attachment to the labor force as a prior or current condition of benefits, and through limitations of vestedness, administration, and the wage-stop, all of which serve to keep the masses of the poor in their poverty. This is what Ryan succinctly calls "blaming the victim."[130]

Scapegoating, which includes guilt arising from appealing but forbidden ideas or action, really has little to do with the victim. No matter how he twists, turns, changes, proves facts, and so on, the problem is in the persons doing the scapegoating. As Tropman points out regarding poverty:

> The persistent distortions surrounding characteristics of the poverty population suggest that attitudes may unconsciously serve to buttress important values in American society. Specifically, we believe that more accurate ideas about the poor might threaten societal mores and personal security in a variety of ways ... respondents seemed unable to accept the possibility of public dependency, and to reject it doubly because the idea might be unconsciously appealing.[131]

In buttressing important societal and personal values, such as independence, self-determination, and moral probity, our beliefs function to enhance self-image and reduce guilt.[132]

In other words,

> So long as the organization of our industrial society remains essentially work-centered, the timing of work continues to be central to the organization of all other activities. . . . Preparing people for and maintaining people in work has presented a guiding principle for

most of our social institutions. . . . The individual has been expected
to accommodate to the predetermined structure.[133]

This accommodation requires the strategy of turning inevitable drudgery into a virtue by stressing the inherent nobility of
work and the desirability of the compensation it offers. Freedom from drudgery, impossible in any case, is presented as
decadent and experienced as unnecessary.[134] Further, in such a
situation, to proclaim one's dissatisfactions or doubts is tanta-
mount to questioning the significance of one's life and future,
to appear to others as "deviant," and to raise questions in their
minds about one's personal stability.[135]

In summary, the aspect of normalcy which inheres in work
makes it one of the most difficult barriers to overcome in search
of a new basis for social welfare. Normalcy feeds on itself. That
which is normative demands adherence, and continued or additional adherence strengthens the normative. Thus, the normality
of working has become all-pervasive, despite the fact that it
involves all the unhappiness, mental illness, and ambivalences
described previously, as well as the misery and afflictions of
poverty, which flow from the nonnormative nature of not
working.

And yet norms, being themselves the results of socialization,
are not ultimate truths, nor even necessarily accurate reflections
of reality. Although we are all trapped in our own modalities,
norms have changed and do change over time. Even relatively
recent years have witnessed changes in norms regarding slavery,
racism, marriage and divorce, abortion, women, homosexuality,
premarital chastity and living arrangements, and much more.
Not all of these changes are unanimously accepted, but neither
are they as monolithic as they once were. So, too, the normalcy
attached to working is a reflection of the current resource-distribution base and system. When the present situation changes—
i.e., when nonworkers heavily outnumber workers or when
other methods of distributing income receive societal sanction—
then normalcy will consist of participating in activities other
than work.

Unfortunately for the future, however, the work ethic has become a free-standing value system which will probably outlast its original utilitarian origins. Overcoming the feeling that one should espouse one's belief in work, judge others by how they work and what they do, and structure one's life around work will probably take longer and be more difficult than making changes in the work situation and resource-distribution methods themselves. Part of the reason is the fact that work is not only seen as normalcy, but has taken on moral attributes—which is the subject of the next chapter.

NOTES

1. "Work is the *differentia specifica* of the human species, pivotal to the formation of human character, and the process by which individuation is achieved." J. R. Stanfield, "On Liberalism and Capitalism: A Reply to O'Boyle," *Review of Social Economy* 36 (October 1978): 209-211.

2. "The certification as a 'poverty person' means that the recipient has been certified as outside the economy, not fully participating in society." Ritti and Hyman, op. cit.

3. Weiner and Akabas suggest that only by terming mothers "workers" can programs to reduce family dependency on government be successful. H. J. Weiner and S. H. Akabas, *Work in America: The View from Industrial Social Welfare* (New York: Columbia University School of Social Work, 1974), p. 7. See also D. G. Gil, *Unravelling Social Policy* (Cambridge, MA: Schenkman, 1973).

4. G. Strauss, "Workers: Attitudes and Adjustments," in J. M. Rosow (ed.) *The Worker and the Job: Coping with Change* (Englewood Cliffs: Prentice-Hall, 1974), p. 80.

5. Neff, op. cit.

6. A. Fox, *A Sociology of Work in Industry* (London: Macmillan, 1971), p. 2.

7. See, for example, Schiltz, op. cit.; D. S. Sanders, *The Impact of Reform Movements on Social Policy Change: The Case of Social Insurance* (Fairlawn: burdick, 1973); Macarov, *The Design of Social Welfare*, op. cit.

8. S. Spilerman and D. Elesh, "Alternative Conceptions of Poverty and Their Implications for Income Maintenance." *Social Problems* 18 (1971): 358-373.

9. Macarov, *Incentives to Work,* op. cit.

10. Arnold and Rosenbaum, op. cit., p. 43.

11. P. Kimmel, "Research on Work and the Worker in the United States," in J. P. Robinson, R. Athanasiou, and K. B. Head, *Measures of Occupational Attitudes and Occupational Characteristics* (Ann Arbor: University of Michigan, 1969), pp. 17-24.

12. R. Blauner, "Work Satisfaction and Industrial Trends in Modern Society," in W. Galenson and S. Lipset, *Labor and Trade Unionism* (New York: John Wiley, 1960).

13. M. Patchen, *Some Questionnaire Measures of Employee Motivation and Morale: A Report on Their Reliability and Validity* (Ann Arbor: University of Michigan, 1965).

14. A. Kornhauser, *Mental Health of the Industrial Worker* (New York: John Wiley, 1965).

15. Goodwin, op. cit., p. 30.

16. Macarov, *The Roots of Hard Work,* op. cit.

17. Terkel, op. cit.; see also K. Lasson, *The Workers* (New York: Grossman, 1971).

18. Such questions are characteristic of the 77 scales reviewed by J. P. Robinson, R. Athanasiou, and K. B. Head, *Measures of Occupational Attitudes and Occupational Characteristics* (Ann Arbor: University of Michigan, 1969).

19. When asked their views about a world in which automation would make most present work unnecessary, 50 percent of the members of an Israeli kibbutz under study saw that as undesirable, while another 21 percent termed it catastrophic. D. Macarov, *Work Incentives in an Israeli Kibbutz* (Jerusalem: The Hebrew University, 1971).

20. Bequele and Freedman, op. cit. Similarly, from a psychoanalytic a point of view: "The normal person seeks not only to work, but to work at a level of responsibility that taxes his capacity to the full." E. Jaques, *Work, Creativity, and Social Justice* (London: Heineman, 1970), p. 13.

21. Goodwin, op. cit.

22. See study by Simon and Gagnon quoted in R. J. Krickus, "White Working-Class Youth," in L. Zimpel, *Man Against Work* (Grand Rapids, MI: Eerdsman, 1974), p. 110.

23. S. B. van Til, *Work and the Culture of Poverty: The Labor Force Activity of Poor Men* (San Francisco: R&E Research Associates, 1976).

24. Terkel, op. cit.; Lasson, op. cit.

25. Lalonde, op. cit., p. 6.

26. E. E. LeMasters, *Blue Collar Aristocrats: Life-Styles at a Working-Class Tavern* (Madison: University of Wisconsin, Press, 1975), p. 195.

27. *World of Work Report* 4 (January 1979): 8.

28. Ibid.

29. D. Jenkins, *Job Power: Blue and White Collar Democracy* (Baltimore: Penguin, 1973).

30. B. A. Gutek, "The Relative Importance of Intrapsychic Determinants of Job Satisfaction." Paper delivered at the NATO conference on *Changes in the Nature and*

Quality of Working Life, Thessaloniki, Greece, August 1979; to be published in K. D. Duncan, D. Wallis, and M. M. Gruneberg (eds.) *Changes in Working Life* (Chichester: John Wiley, forthcoming).

31. L. B. Rubin, *Worlds of Pain: Life in the Working Class Family* (New York: Basic Books, 1976).

32. Weiner and Akabas, op. cit., quoting *Work in America,* (Cambridge: MIT, 1973).

33. Ibid.

34. W. W. Daniel, "Industrial Behaviour and Orientation to Work: A Critique." *Journal of Management Studies* 6 (1969): 366-375.

35. M. Fein, "Motivation for Work," in R. Dubin, *Handbook of Work, Organizations, and Society* (Chicago: Rand McNally, 1976), p. 465-530.

36. Gutek found that 25 percent to 28 percent of the variance concerning job satisfaction is related to aspirations. Gutek, op. cit.

37. Shimmin, op. cit.

38. Lasson, op. cit.

39. C. R. Price, *New Directions in the World of Work: A Conference Report* (Kalamazoo: Upjohn, 1971), p. 7.

40. J. P. Robinson, "Occupational Norms and Differences in Job Satisfaction: A Summary of Survey Research Evidence," in *Robinson* et al., op. cit., p. 66.

41. High satisfaction of discharged reservists with centers established to help them after the Yom Kippur War was found to be linked, in part, to low expectations of the centers. D. Macarov and U. Yannai, *A Study of Centers for Discharged Reservists* (Jerusalem: Ministry of Labor, 1974). (In Hebrew)

42. Even when jobs are reported as self-actualizing, there is reason to believe the report arises from the personality of the worker, rather than from the content of the job. See D. Macarov, "Reciprocity Between Self-Actualization and Hard Work," op. cit.

43. C. N. Weaver, "Relationships Among Pay, Race, Sex, Occupational Prestige, Supervision, Work Autonomy, and Job Satisfaction in a National Sample." *Personnel Psychology* 30 (1977): 437-445.

44. A. S. Tannenbaum and W. J. Kuleck, Jr., "The Effect on Organizational Members of Discrepancy Between Perceived and Preferred Rewards Implicit in Work." *Human Relations* 31 (1978): 809-822.

45. A. Hanlon and S. Jacobs, "Social Work and Private Industry." *Social Casework* 50 (1969): 152-156.

46. Weaver, op. cit.

47. J. F. Gavin, "Occupational Mental Health: Forces and Trends." *Personnel Psychology* 56 (1977): 198-201.

48. R. P. Quinn et al., "Evaluating Working Conditions in America." *Monthly Labor Review* 96 (1973): 32-43.

49. B. Walfish, "Job Satisfaction Declines in Major Aspects of Work, Says Michigan Study; All Occupational Groups Included." *World of Work Report* 4 (February 1979): 9.

50. *World of Work Report* 4 (January 1979): 5.

51. L. Woodcock, "Changing World of Work: A Labor Viewpoint." Paper delivered to the American Assembly, November 1, 1973, New York City, quoted in Weiner and Akabas, op. cit.

52. Sarason, op. cit., p. 1.

53. Price, op. cit., p. 6. Italics and parentheses in original.

54. A. McLean, "Work and Mental Health: Summary and Recommendations," in A. McLean, *Mental Health and Work Organizations* (Chicago: Rand McNally, 1970), pp. 5-22. Insofar as attitudes toward work and welfare are concerned, even among researchers, it is revealing how many studies have been done concerning the impact of mental illness on work, and how few are concerned with the impact of work on mental and physical health, except as therapy. See, as examples, B. J. Black, *Industrial Therapy for the Mentally Ill in Western Europe* (New York: Altro Health and Rehabilitative Services, 1965); W. T. Query, *Illness, Work, and Poverty* (San Francisco: Jossey-Bass, 1968); and O. Simmons, *Work and Mental Illness: Eight Case Studies* (New York: John Wiley, 1965).

55. Terkel, op. cit., p. 333.

56. M. Csikszentmihalyi, *Beyond Boredom and Anxiety* (San Francisco: Jossey-Bass, 1975).

57. R. Dubin, "Industrial Workers' Worlds: A Study of the Central Life Interests of Industrial Workers," in A. M. Rose (ed.) *Human Behavior and Social Processes* (London: Routledge & Kegan Paul, 1962): in less than one-third of fourteen studies did informal social relationships constitute a significant source of work attachment. R. Dubin, R. A. Hedley, and T. C. Taveggia, "Attachment to Work," in R. Dubin, *Handbook of Work, Organization, and Society* (Chicago: Rand McNally, 1976), p. 283.

58. D. Coburn, "Job-Worker Incongruence: Consequences for Health." *Journal of Health and Social Behavior* 16 (June 1975): 198-212.

59. D. Coburn, "Job Alienation and Well-Being." *International Journal of Health Services* 9 (1979): 41-59.

60. Weiner and Akabas, op. cit.

61. Coburn, "Job Alienation and Well-Being," op. cit., p. 56.

62. Fein, op. cit., p. 493.

63. Coburn, "Job-Worker Incongruence," op. cit., p. 198.

64. Sarason, op. cit., p. 19.

65. M. M. Machlowitz, *The Workaholic* (New Haven: Yale University, 1976) (mimeographed); "Working the 100-Hour Week—and Loving It," New York *Times,* October 3, 1976; see also the letters to the editor in the New York *Times* of October 24, 1976.

66. *Yearbook of Labour Statistics,* op. cit.

67. Ibid.

68. D. Bell, "The Future That Never Was." *Public Interest* 51 (1978): 35-73.

69. A. Szalai, *The Use of Time* (The Hague: Mouton, 1972).

70. M. Kaplan, *Leisure in America: A Social Inquiry* (New York: John Wiley, 1960).

71. Buckingham, op. cit.

72. R. L. Cunningham, *The Philosophy of Work* (New York: National Association of Manufacturers, 1964).

73. Barfield and Morgan, op. cit.

74. Weiner et al., op. cit., p. 114.

75. Ball, op. cit., p. 504.

76. R. Stagner, "The Affluent Society Versus Early Retirement." *Aging and Work* 1 (Winter 1978): 25-31.

77. S. H. Rhine, quoted in *Newsday* (October 30, 1978), p. 2A.

78. Davis, op. cit.

79. Sheppard and Rix, op. cit., p. 138.

80. B. R. Herzog, *Aging and Income: Programs and Prospects for the Elderly* (New York: Human Sciences Press, 1978), p. 111.

81. Sheppard and Rix, op. cit., p. 111.

82. Ibid., p. 109.

83. Ibid., p. 5.

84. *Social Security Programs Throughout the World, 1975* (Washington: Department of Health, Education, and Welfare, 1975), p. xiv.

85. "Development and Trends in Social Security 1974-1977." *International Social Security Review* 30 (1977): 271-313.

86. Yankelovich, op. cit.

87. Barfield and Morgan, op. cit., p. 320.

88. *World of Work Report* 4 (April 1979): 25.

89. Yankelovich, op. cit., p. 49.

90. Barfield and Morgan, op. cit., p. 334.

91. M. Kaplan, *Leisure: Theory and Policy* (New York: John Wiley, 1975).

92. *Work in a Changing Industrial Society,* op. cit., p. 24.

93. Kaplan, *Leisure: Theory and Policy,* op. cit.

94. R. A. Buchholz, "The Work Ethic Reconsidered." *Industrial and Labor Relations Review* 31 (July 1978): 450-459.

95. J. R. Feagin, "America's Welfare Stereotypes." *Social Service Quarterly* 52 (1972): 921-933.

96. D. J. Kallen and D. Miller, "Public Attitudes Toward Welfare." *Social Work* 16 (1971): 89-95.

97. G. W. Carter and L. H. Fifield, *Welfare Concepts and Welfare Services: Results of an Opinion Poll of Public Attitudes* (Los Angeles: University of Southern California, 1973). This, incidentally, is the only widespread poll which does not report general antiwelfare attitudes.

98. J. B. Williamson, "Beliefs about the Welfare Poor." *Sociology and Social Research* 63 (1974): 163-175.

99. J. P. Alston and K. I. Dean, "Socioeconomic Factors Associated with Attitudes toward Welfare Recipients and the Causes of Poverty." *Social Service Review* 40 (1972): 13-23.

100. J. H. Rytina, W. H. Form, and J. Pease, "Income and Stratification Ideology: Beliefs about the American Opportunity Structure." *American Journal of Sociology* 75 (1970): 703-716.

101. E. H. Ogren, "Public Opinions about Public Welfare." *Social Work* 18 (1973): 101-107.

102. J. W. Grimm and J. D. Orten, "Student Attitudes Toward the Poor." *Social Work* 18 (1973): 94-100.

103. J. B. Williamson, "Beliefs About the Motivation of the Poor and Attitudes Toward Poverty Policy," *Social Problems* 21 (1974): 634-648.

104. Goodwin, op. cit.

105. Ogren, op. cit.

106. Ostow and Dutka, op. cit., p. xv.

107. Feagin, op. cit., pp. 922-923.

108. Ibid., p. 934.

109. Kallen and Miller, op. cit.

110. Williamson, "Beliefs About the Welfare Poor," op. cit., p. 164.

111. Carter and Fifield, op. cit., p. xii.

112. L. Podell, *Families on Welfare in New York City* (New York: Center for the Study of Urban Problems, City University of New York, n.d.).

113. M. Warren and S. Berkowitz, "The Employability of AFDC Mothers and Fathers." *Welfare in Review* 7 (1969): 1-7.

114. M. C. Barth, G. J. Carcagno, and J. L. Palmer, *Towards an Effective Income Support System: Problems, Prospects and Choices* (Madison: University of Wisconsin, 1974), p. 62.

115. Williamson, "Beliefs About the Welfare Poor," op. cit., p. 173.

116. Ogren, op. cit.

117. L. Festinger, *A Theory of Cognitive Dissonance* (Evanston, IL: Row, Peterson, 1957).

118. A revealing piece of denial concerns the use of work as punishment. Although it is widely known that work is often used as punishment in court sentencing, in jails and prisons, and in the army (quite distinctly from work as rehabilitation), expressed attitudes toward work ignore this fact. When confronted with it, a facile rationalization is that work is punishment only to those who do not like to work.

119. Work "succeeds in communicating its imperatives because they are acceptable to the audience it addresses. But ideology would be ineffective if there were not some readiness to be convinced." Anthony, op. cit., p. 312.

120. *Employment Security Review* 22 (1955): 57-58.

121. *House Committee Print Number 291.* Eighty-Ninth Congress, Second Session, Part B, September 12, 1956.

122. G. W. Miller, *Use of and Attitude Toward the Ohio Bureau of Unemployment Compensation: A Research Report* (Columbus: Ohio State University, 1963), quoted by Adams, op. cit., p. 34.

123. E. W. Busse, "Psychoneurotic Reactions and Defense Mechanisms in the Aged," in P. H. Hock and J. Zabin, *Psychopathology of Aging* (New York: Grune & Stratton, 1961).

124. E. J. Markus, *Post-Relocation Mortality Among Institutionalized Aged* (Cleveland: Benjamin Rose Institute, 1970).

125. G. Friedmann, *The Anatomy of Work* (New York: Free Press, 1964).

126. S. Grad, "New Retirees and the Stability of the Retirement Decision." *Social Security Bulletin* 40 (1977): 3-12.

127. Barfield and Morgan, op. cit., p. 152.

128. Shimmin, op. cit., p. 12.

129. For a good explanation of social scapegoating, see K. Heap, "The Scapegoat Role in Youth Groups." *Case Conference* 12 (1966): 215; Macarov, *Incentives to Work,* op. cit., pp. 35-36, 224-225; see also Gans's fifth positive function of poverty, in Gans, *More Equality,* op. cit., p. 108.

130. W. Ryan, "Blaming the Victim: Ideology Serves the Establishment," in P. Roby, *The Poverty Establishment* (Englewood Cliffs: Prentice-Hall, 1974), pp. 171-179.

131. Tropman, op. cit.

132. Ibid., p. 23.

133. A. S. Glickman and Z. H. Brown, *Changing Schedules of Work: Patterns and Implications* (Kalamazoo: Upjohn Institute, 1974), p. 49

134. E. V. Kohak, "Being Young in a Postindustrial Society." *Dissent* (February 1971): 30-40.

135. Sarason, op. cit., p. 103.

Chapter 8

WORK AS MORALITY: The Opium of the Classes

"In toil shall thou eat. . . . In the sweat of thy face shall thou eat bread."

—*The Bible,* Genesis III 17 : 19

There is a further aspect of the work-welfare link to be considered. Social workers, along with others, see work as more than needed, income-producing, and normative. These utilitarian aspects have become clothed with a moral value to the point that the former have been obscured by the latter, and the real reasons why people work have been made to appear somewhat disreputable.

As detailed in Chapter 2, the Industrial Revolution, the free market economy, mercantilism as government policy, and the Protestant Ethic all combined to clothe work, which had previously been viewed as a necessary but not very enjoyable part of life, with moral attributes. Throughout industrial society, and not just in Protestant areas, work has been elevated to a moral necessity.

The fact that one works, what one does, and how one is viewed as a worker have become important criteria for judging one's worth, without relation to the economic aspects involved. "Hard-working," "productive," and "ambitious" have positive connotations wherever they are used; "lazy," "poor worker," and "unmotivated" are damning indictments. Work is placed in the panthenon of moral values which contains truth, friendship, patriotism, and love of mother, and woe betide the iconoclast who questions or derides any of them.

Attempts to question the value of work are either looked upon as amusing or are ignored. Mention Russell's "In Praise of Idleness" and be met with a smile. The fact that Karl Marx's son-in-law, Lafargue, put forward as one of the goals of the Revolution the right of the working class to be lazy[1] is discreetly overlooked, even by historians. Such purported immorality even imparts a bias to scientific endeavors. Despite thousands of articles and studies on work incentives, work satisfactions, the meaning of work to individuals, and the like there are no studies of laziness as such—why some people never work hard, the determinants of such behavior, the characteristics of such people, or the dynamics of laziness. MacGregor[2] is an exception, with his Theory X people, who do not want to work and Theory Y people who do, but the former are given cursory attention and the balance of his presentation deals with people who want to work. Even studies of deviance, which deal with such immoral subjects as prostitution, crime, gambling, and "hustling," do not include people who do not want to—or do not—work.

Imputing immorality to nonworkers has a good deal of social utility. Since poor people in general, and social welfare clients in particular, are normally assumed to be not working, they are therefore ipso facto immoral. They should be grateful for whatever is done for them and are impertinent, if not worse, if from their immoral situation they ask, like Oliver Twist, for more.[3]

From this situation there naturally flows the postulation of two cultures. In this formulation, the majority of Americans share and are guided by the traditional views concerning the meaning of work. They are hard-working, self-reliant, thrifty, productive people who take pleasure in their work and receive their major satisfactions from the work which they do and from the relationships which they have with others at work. Their activities keep the economy sound and the society healthy.

There is, however, another element in society often referred to vaguely as "they." "They" do not really want to work, find all kinds of excuses not to work and methods of living without work, stop working as soon as they have enough for minimal needs (often defined as beer and cigarettes), and are immune to desires for upward mobility, more material satisfiers, and respectable social status. "They," in fact, have their own culture, which puts premiums on different activities and values than does the majority culture, and within their own culture they find social and psychological satisfiers that do not arise from work. In the United States, the vague "they" are a mixture of blacks, new immigrants, Latin Americans, urban slum dwellers, rural (usually Southern) farmers, dwellers in areas like Appalachia, welfare recipients, Medicaid participants, teenage dropouts, drug abusers, alcoholics, derelicts, and the current equivalent of hippies. The one thing they all are said to have in common is their immoral attitude toward work.[4]

The imputation of two cultures,[5] one of which is basically immoral as regards its attitude toward work, offers a rationalization for dealing with the poor and with welfare recipients in a punitive, begrudging, manner: "All modern societies . . . hold that men who possess the capacity and opportunity for productive (or otherwise useful) work yet refuse to perform it have no moral claim upon society's resources."[6] Hence the meagerness of social welfare payments, as explicated in Chapter 4, is not only based upon fear of work disincentives, but has within it a punitive aspect—such people do not deserve more.

Together with the disincentive factor, and the question of deservedness (with its echoes of the Elizabethan deserving and undeserving poor), there arises the attitude toward fairness. It is not considered fair that people who have paid less into various social security programs should receive benefits higher than those who paid more. It also is not considered fair that those with good incomes should have to pay more into such programs than they will get back in benefits—hence income limitations on payroll taxes. But most important: It is considered patently unfair that someone who does not work should have an income greater than one who does (unless, of course, it is inherited wealth, income from investments, wealth married into, or fraud on a gigantic scale).

This "moral" view of fairness is expressed by Plattner in discussing a hypothetical situation in which "the person who works harder is entitled to nothing more, while the person who works less hard gains a greater claim over what others have produced. The moral absurdity of this view is transparent."[7] Equally transparent is the fact that this statement is true only in a situation where work is considered moral, and division of resources is on a quid pro quo basis. In contrast, however, take a situation in which group membership or group loyalty is considered the highest expression of morality, and resources are divided equally, or according to need. A homely example would be a combat unit sharing out packages received. A more elegant example is the Israeli kibbutz, where there are those who work harder and those who work less hard,[8] but in which everyone is provided with his or her needs, without regard to work patterns. Or, on a more limited basis, take a university. To be eligible for stipends students must maintain a certain average, but they are not entitled to larger stipends on the basis of better grades. Thus, the just-passing student and the leader of the class get the same stipend—a situation which, in terms of work as morality, would be considered unfair, if not transparently absurd.

In some respects work has been elevated beyond the realm of mere morality and invested with the attributes of religion. This has its roots in the expressed attitudes toward work of all major religions and was given overwhelming reinforcement by Luther and the subsequent Protestant Ethic, in which working was equated with serving God. The religion of labor may be sincerely believed in, as it is by many people who hold the Puritan distrust of leisure; the lack of occupation or at least preoccupation is thought to be sinful.[9] A. D. Gordon, for example, a pioneer Israeli, traveled the length and breadth of the country in the early years of this century advocating "The Religion of Labor." Gordon sought to inject a religiouslike fervor into the efforts of the early pioneers who were basically secularists, at the same time reacting against what he and they saw as the sterile life of Torah study, on the one hand, and that of commercial middlemen, on the other, in the Diaspora. The religious aspect of work also exhibits itself as the previously quoted basis for social security in Germany: "Work makes life sweet."

On the other hand, the religious aspect of labor might be used exploitatively, as by factory owners during the industrial revolution. The owners expected gratitude for making it possible for people to work and thus avoid being sinners. Or it might be used cynically, as in the enormous sign over the entrance to the Auschwitz death camp: "Work Makes Us Free."

In a number of ways one can identify traces of religious rites and commitments in the workplaces of many people. In a way, the workplace becomes the shrine at which people serve, with its own mysteries and miracles. The executive lunchroom and/ or the lavatory may be barred to the masses or to neophytes. In some places this is also true of certain elevators, parking places, or entire parking lots. The office of the president, guarded by a secretary, is often referred to as the Holy of Holies. What takes place in the Boardroom—or even in some offices—remain mysteries to most workers. The time clock reigns as an implacable deity, to be served, but not to be cajoled. Supervisors, foremen, or "middle-management personnel" perform the functions of priests, keeping workers and the mysterious "management" (usually referred to as "them") apart, carrying communications upward and downward, and mediating between them. One tithes—to Social Security, to pension funds, to group insurance, to United Fund drives, and so on. Proper dress and badges of office exist, and in some cases are enforced: ties, briefcases vis-à-vis lunchboxes, hardhats, and other safety devices. Rites at various levels include coffee breaks, attendance at conventions, office parties, and retirement ceremonies. And above all, to suggest that one does not want to or like to work—or even worse that people should not have to work—is to be accused of blasphemy or heresy.

The religious aspect of work may be even stronger in the

so-called irreligious communist societies than in others, with work seen as the goal, meaning, and justification for life, therapy for all problems, and the major duty of all citizens. The adulation of Stakhanov, who allegedly dug 102 tons of coal in one night, as the role model to be emulated, and the very description of countries as "workers' republics," indicates the morality attached to working in that sector. This emphasis dates back at least to Marx, who declared: "What individuals ... are ... coincides with their productivity, both with *what* they produce and *how* they produce."[10] As concerns Cuba, too, it is held that the major incentive to work there is a sense of morality, reinforced by social pressure.[11]

It is not only that people are socialized to work; they are taught to like, revere, and even worship work, to see in work a value over and above its results. Since, obviously, men have no innate, genetically given orientation toward work,[12] belief in the moral value of work is transmitted to individuals via the same instrumentalities as is the belief that work is necessary and desirable: schools, child-rearing practices, and all the other instruments of socialization, including the mass media. In his well-known discussion of the development of morals, Kohlberg points out that attitudes which were at one time instrumental—i.e., punishment-avoidance—may in time divest themselves of their utilitarian roots and become free-standing value systems, not only operative in the absence of the previous motivations, such as threats of punishment, but believed in, defended, and acted upon as parts of the ideology of the individual.[13]

In this manner the internalized value acts to create a society that invests work with great spiritual and historical necessity, seeing in toil, advancement, tenacity, a virtue beyond material reward—the definition of self.[14] Economic difficulties serve to reinforce, rather than to weaken, the morality of working:

In times of scarcity, unemployment, or when cheap labor is needed ... the poor and their problems become more visible ... a resistance to reforms develops among some who are in power ... these groups communicate their ideas to the public, usually espousing the virtues of hard work, the sanctity of laissez faire economics, the propriety of low wages, and the unworthiness of the poor.[15]

Consequently, welfare enters that which Beck calls a moral category, and not working becomes a public scandal to the structure.[16] In this way, hard work developed a halo, and the rejection of dirty, dead-end, low-paying jobs was associated with laziness and indolence.[17]

It is the moral aspect of work which creates difficulties in thinking about, discussing, planning, projecting, and trying to create a new socioeconomic structure. The facts appear insignificant in face of the moral outrage provoked. Raising a question as to whether work is really necessary or desirable is rather like asking for proof of God's existence from a truly pious person. Nevertheless, unless a distinction is made between work as production, work as job holding, work as an appropriate and normal reaction to the present situation, and work as a moral or even a religious act, the future of society cannot be described, predicted, or prescribed.

Holding these distinctions in mind, we can venture into prediction. Before doing so, however, it might be well to summarize the arguments and data to this point, in order to provide a basis for extrapolation. As seen in the historical section, the growth of social welfare has been created and conditioned by changes in methods and structures of human work. Welfare is not only a side-product of industrialization, but a grudging recognition of some of the inequities of the work world— inequities which are seen as inevitable and a small price to pay for the progress of productivity.

Welfare's role as an unfortunate necessity connected with the world of work is institutionalized through coverage which is extended only to those who are working or who have worked; through vestedness requirements which condition help on length of attachment to the labor force; through administrative regulations which tilt toward programs and benefits which turn and return people to work; and through the wage-stop, which assures that nobody—including those who cannot or should not work—can attain an income equal to those who work.

The result of these ideological and practical limitations is to create poverty among those who cannot work, those who cannot find work, and among a large percentage of those who do work for low wages. The aged, the young, the disabled, single parents of small children, the unemployed, and the underemployed are kept in or near poverty on the assumption that larger benefits would keep them from working, or would induce some of those now working at close to the poverty level to quit.

The institutionalization and enforced continuation of poverty through the idealization and enforced continuation of work rests upon four assumptions. The first of these is that society needs all the work that all its members can produce. That this assumption is faulty is indicated by the level of structural unemployment which has existed for over twenty years in all the industrialized Westernized countries, with the exception of Israel and Japan, and which seems to be growing. Not only is there severely understated permanent unemployment, with hidden unemployment and underemployment rife, but a great deal of work which is now done is redundant, and some of it is harmful. This situation has arisen due to increasing technological advances, resulting in growing per-person productivity. Were technology freed from restraints arising from fears of job losses and unemployment, were the goal to be the greatest possible efficiency in the production of needed goods and services, were the inventive and creative capacity which went into the space program, and from time to time into a war effort, to be unleashed and given the resources to replace human labor whenever possible, the amount of work performed by people would be reduced to a small fraction of the current total.

However, people's need for jobs in order to acquire income, and consequently society's need to provide such jobs, militates against an all-out effort to reduce human labor through technology. This results in available work being redefined and redivided into smaller and smaller jobs—namely, shorter work days, more time off, "shared" jobs, and the like. It also results in a socially sanctioned delusional system whereby people pretend that their jobs are necessary and important, whereas they know and others know that this is not so. The result is individual and societal corruption. The faulty assumption upon which this system is based, and which social workers and welfare planners share with the rest of society, is that the job method is the only conceivable, practical, desirable method of dividing the results of production.

The third assumption is that the work-based system offers satisfactions other than monetary ones to those who hold jobs, that people find companionship, time-structure, and self-actualizing experiences in their jobs, and that working is a measure of normalcy. The data indicate, however, that despite rhetoric to the contrary, large and growing numbers of people do not find satisfaction in their work, prefer leisure, look forward to retirement, and—given sufficient means—are glad they retired. Further, despite assertions concerning the positive virtues of work, people work fewer hours per day, days per week, weeks per year, and years per lifetime than in the past, and increasingly request and demand more leisure time. It is evidently possible to find in nonwork activities as much or more companionship, time-structure, and self-actualizing experiences as at work. In fact, the normalcy which work bestows is an accommodation to existing ideologies and structures. Changes in the latter would result in new definitions of normalcy. Thus the normative aspects of work arise from the current situation. They, like the work structure itself, are not necessarily inevitable or immutable. Certainly the normalcy involved does not arise from the inherent characteristics of work itself.

Finally, there is the assumption on the part of many people that working is a moral act. This view has deep roots in history and particularly in the history of religions. The deinstitutionalization of morals usually follows practice, rather than preceding it—namely, prohibitions against interest, which became prohibitions against usury (high interest rates), which have been legally abandoned in some countries as inflation and other changes in the fiscal system required such changes. Consequently the moral aspects attributed to work can also change with changed circumstances, and there is compelling evidence to indicate that morals are changing in a number of areas—e.g., birth control, abortion, and other areas mentioned previously. Morals can also change in regard to work, with freedom from unnecessary work or meaningless jobs becoming valued as a step toward human happiness, and thereby toward the goal of religion, or God's design for man.

Thus, none of the purported reasons for society's current predominant emphasis on work as essential to human happiness or societal continuance stands up to critical scrutiny. We have been caught in a closed circle of myths, artifacts, and beliefs which is increasingly creating unhappiness ranging from self-doubts to near-starvation. The next chapter looks at what the future may hold if the circle is allowed to continue.

NOTES

1. M. R. Marrus, "Introduction," in M. R. Marrus, *The Emergence of Leisure* (New York: Harper & Row, 1974) p. 2.

2. D. McGregor, *The Human Side of Enterprise* (New York: McGraw-Hill, 1960).

3. "We know that it is unpopular for welfare recipients . . . to bite the hand that feeds them." Milwaukee County Welfare Rights Organization, *Welfare Mothers Speak Out* (New York: Norton, 1972), p. 114.

4. Macarov, *Incentives to Work,* op. cit.

5. Not to be confused with C. P. Snow's two cultures—the sciences and the humanities.

6. Plattner, op. cit.

7. Ibid.

8. Of 218 respondents, 39 were identified as underworkers and 38 as overworkers. See D. Macarov, "Work Without Pay: Work Incentives and Patterns in a

Salaryless Environment." *International Journal of Social Economics* 2 (1975): 106-114.

9. L. Braude, *Work and Workers: A Sociological Analysis* (New York: Praeger, 1975), p. 203.

10. Quoted by C. W. Mills, "The Meaning of Work Throughout History," in F. Best, *The Future of Work* (Englewood Cliffs: Prentice-Hall, 1973), pp. 6-13 (italics in original).

11. R. M. Bernardo, *The Theory of Moral Incentives in Cuba* (University: University of Alabama Press, 1971).

12. Fox, op. cit.

13. L. Kohlberg, "Development of Moral Character and Moral Ideology," in M. L. Hoffman and L. W. Hoffman, *Review of Child Development Research* in Volume One (New York: Russell Sage, 1964), pp. 383-431.

14. E. Hardwick, "Domestic Manners." *Daedalus* 107 (1978): 1-11.

15. K. Heise, "Changing Perceptions of the Poor." *Public Welfare* 35 (1977): 6-10.

16. B. M. Beck, "Welfare as a Moral Category," *Social Problems* 14 (1967): 260-264.

17. J. M. Rosow, "Introduction," in J. M. Rosow, *The Worker and the Job: Coping with Change* (Englewood Cliffs: Prentice-Hall, 1974).

Chapter 9

THE LEISURE MAN COMETH: The Transitional Phase

> "The philosophies of one age have become the absurd-
> ities of the next, and the foolishness of yesterday has
> become the wisdom of tomorrow."
>
> —Sir William Osler, quoted
> in *Montreal Medical Journal* (1902)

Predicting the future is a risky business. Striner says it is wise
never to forecast for any period shorter than the balance of
your own life expectancy plus five years.[1] For example, estimates of forthcoming birth rates, made in 1947, were 20
percent wrong as early as 1950.[2] In 1953 the Census Bureau
projected a 1975 population of persons 65 and older amounting
to 20.7 million, but the actual figure was 8 percent higher. In
1970, 1971, and 1972 the Census Bureau's projections for the
year 2000 called for a 65-plus population of 28.8 million, but in
1975 this estimate was raised by 1.8 million, or more than 6
percent. In 1975 55-64-year-old males in the labor force were
11 percent fewer than projected in 1959—1.1 million more
people of that age were out of the labor force than had been
projected.[3] It would be easy to continue this listing of poor
predictions. On the other hand, good predictions are far more
numerous. Were this not so, the present inconveniences of
living—the law's delay, the insolence of clerks, as well as traffic,

pollution, density, and many others—would be simply unbearable, and society as such would have ceased to exist. As Ferkiss puts it: "Ability to predict technological change is far from absolute, but usually the unanticipated event occurs in addition to the anticipated rather than as a substitute for it, so most of what is predicted probably will occur."[4]

Projections into the future may be straight-line extrapolations of past and present situations with stated margins for error, or high-, medium-, and low-rate alternatives.[5] Or projections can be extrapolations which take into account anticipated, probable, and possible changes in present situations. In addition, there are projections which may include that which has been called "ideals,"[6] or "tacit knowledge,"[7] or ways of thinking that do not exhibit the logical structure of deduction or induction.[8] In this chapter, all three of these will be used.

Since both the history and the structures of work and welfare are inextricably interwoven, it is impossible to project the future of one without keeping in mind what will happen in the other. Welfare, however, as pointed out earlier, assumes its shape and size from work—it is basically an outgrowth of the work situation—whereas policies and arrangements regarding work are rarely based upon or conditioned by the effect they will have on welfare, even though they may impact profoundly and immediately, as in the case of deliberately contrived unemployment to relieve inflation. Consequently, the future of work will be discussed first, followed by the future of welfare.

The Future of Work

Some straight-line extrapolations

Continued reduction of work hours. There seems to be almost unanimous agreement among most sources and experts that the amount of work (or work time) required of individuals will continue to decrease in the near and distant futures.[9] Although here and there in the literature one finds a caveat that work time has not decreased, or that productivity has not really increased, almost no one predicts that people will work more or harder in the future. To both experts and laymen, it is clear that standard hours have decreased considerably, during this century at least. Vacations and statutory holidays have also increased over the years, and pressure for further reductions will continue. [10]

There is less agreement about the extent to which hours, days, weeks, and years of work will be curtailed. In 1875, when the world's population was 1 billion, the annual hours of work amounted to 4000. One hundred years later, when the population of the world had tripled to three billion, the annual hours of work were 2000. Using a straight-line projection, one could predict that in 2075 when, according to the United Nations *minimum* projection the population of the world will have again tripled,[11] the annual hours of work will be 1000. Some see this happening much sooner: 1100 working hours by the year 2000,[12] which is roughly a 30-hour week and thirteen weeks of vacation a year.[13] Others predict that the working week in the West will become a four-day, 35- or 36-hour week, soon changed to a week of four 8-hour days, with both summer and winter vacations.[14]

Continued growth of the aged population. Not only will the hours of work continue to decrease, but so will the number of years of work. The number of people retiring and retiring early will continue to rise both absolutely and proportionately. The simple increase in the number of the elderly which is taking place will account for the absolute numbers, while increasing early retirement, as well as probable lowering of the retirement age in some countries, will increase the proportions, as will the growing proportion of the aged as such.

For example, at the turn of this century, only 4 percent of Americans reached the age of 65. In 1970, almost 10 percent, or 20 million people, reached that age. By 1980 there should be about 25 million. In the year 2000, there should be about 12 percent, or 31 million, aged people. And by 2030 (only 50 years from now) this will probably be 17 percent of all Americans, or 52 million people.[15] When the elderly were 4 percent of the population, they tended to remain in the labor force until completely physically disabled. By 1975, only 14 percent of those 65 and older remained in the labor force. Projections to 2010 indicate that the decline in labor force participation of the elderly will continue. In the 20 years since 1955, the participation rate of 65-69-year olds has declined at a rate of nearly 40 percent (down to 22 percent). Among males, the ratio of years of work to years of retirement has declined from 14 : 1 to about 5 : 1 during this century.[16]

Nor will 65 continue to be the cutting point for aging or retirement. The definitions of aging and retired are becoming more and more synonymous. Because more people are retiring younger, they are being defined as elderly. Consequently, in the literature on aging the term "young old" is being applied to those reaching 55, mostly because so many of them are retiring.[17] Using this definition of aging, 15 percent of the population will be between 55 and 75 before the end of the century,[18] and about another 5 percent will be above 75—that is about one in every five Americans will be "aged" if 55 years old becomes the cutting point.

It should be obvious from the above that retirement from work is not and increasingly will not be due to physical inability to continue working. On the contrary, the 65-year-old of today is probably considerably healthier than his father or grandfather was, due to advances in medicine, nutrition, housing, and such. The 55-year-old retirees are even less likely to be unable to work. It is possible that in the future people in their 60s and 70s will be in a physical state comparable to people now in their 30s and 40s.[19]

These extrapolations of past and present trends, without any quantum breaks to be caused by new inventions or new methods taken into account, indicate that both hours and years of work will continue to decline, absolutely and proportionately. Thus, the need for more work as such, or even as much work as is now being done, seems no more compelling when contemplating the future than it does when viewed objectively today.

Continuation and growth of structural unemployment. The amount of work needed (or, rather, not needed) has obvious implications for the number of jobs needed. The growing number and rate of the unemployed is very likely to continue. This growth has now existed for twenty years in most countries, despite all the correctives administered, ranging from freer enterprise, fiscal manipulations, pump-priming, jawboning, vocational training, job creation schemes, and public service jobs, to "cracking down" on welfare recipients.

Population increases, which are estimated to increase the present 4 billion people in the world to either 9.5 billion (low forecast) or 15.8 billion (high forecast),[20] will not solve the problem of unemployment through creation of additional needs, and thus creation of additional jobs. Since 100 workers support 30 people other than themselves and their families today and since this will probably become 45 other people, if not more, relatively soon,[21] then the available labor force will outstrip additional need at a constantly growing rate, leading to ever-increasing unemployment.

A further factor that will feed into increased unemployment is the growing number of women who are entering the labor force. Whether inspired by the women's movement, freed to work by more and better child care arrangements, or driven by economic necessity, it seems almost certain that this trend will not only continue but grow in volume. Around 1980 large age groups of both men and women born during the years of high natality will enter the labor market. Thus, the curve of unemployment will rise considerably for demographic reasons alone, and in the 1990s this will become even more acute.[22]

Further, if moves toward freer trade become truly worldwide, including the developing countries, the result will be a large-scale displacement of workers in the developed countries, especially those engaged in labor-intensive, low-skill industries[23] (which are precisely the antidote prescribed for high-unemployment regions). Finally, as the developed countries themselves become increasingly high-consumption, leisure-wealthy societies, they simply will not need cohorts of young workers every year. They will not be able to employ more than a fraction of youngsters fresh out of high school.[24]

Not only is there likely to be a decline in employment, but technological changes are beginning to affect occupational groups not affected in the past—namely, the more stable, high-skilled craft groups.[25] Taking all these factors into consideration, it is not surprising that the World Bank predicts mass unemployment for the end of the century.[26]

Shorter and shorter hours, longer and longer retirement periods, continuing and growing unemployment all add up to a ground swell of social problems. These include more and more people unsatisfied by their work, widening collusion between workers and between workers and employers that "putting in time" is all that is required, increased competition for jobs, and more and more dropping out of what is essentially a useless, demeaning, and in some cases, harmful pretense. These results have been deduced from extrapolation of present trends. If more uncertain, yet quite possible, events are taken into consideration, the problems will be intensified enormously.

Riskier, but very possible, predictions

Demographic. Suppose, for example, that recent increases in longevity do not level off, but increase greatly due to scientific breakthroughs. If a method of preventing, inhibiting, controlling, and/or reversing cancer were to be discovered, or if death from heart disease could be drastically reduced—neither of which is very far outside the realm of possibility—the number of aged would increase almost overnight. Or in a slightly more visionary vein, can lifetimes be lengthened far beyond present limits? At least one biologist's answer is yes:

> Unless the aging process differs in some mysterious and totally unforeseen way from other puzzles man has solved in the past, it is essentially inevitable that he will, before long, understand aging's sources, and with that understanding will come a considerable measure of control.[27]

This could result in the possibility of retirement, even at age 65, followed by 40 to 140 years of nonwork.[28] Conversely, such lengthened lifetimes and the vitality that would go with them might result in tremendous pressure on the labor market to absorb millions of people who would choose not to retire. In either case, the implications of enormously increased, rather than normally increasing, numbers of the aged, in terms of social problems, structures, and attitudes are staggering.

There are other possibilities to take into account. With rising costs of a university education, the graduate no longer recoups his or her investment through better income in a number of fields. Were this to lead to a general disaffection with higher education among the 35 percent of Americans of college age who attend universities, this addition to the labor force would increase the present pressure for jobs considerably.

Technology. Moving from the demographic to the technological possibilities, the range of opinions is wide, but all in one direction: The growth of technology is not only irreversible but synergistic. Despite the counter-pressure of neo-Luddites, foot-dragging caused by fear of job losses, cushioning which promises that no employee will lose a job because of new machines or methods, and the necessity to pay for the nonwork occasioned by machines, the image of home industries and hand craftsmen replacing modern production methods is more a hope or a dream than a projection into the probable future.

Even if the current energy difficulty were to become a drastic emergency, the result is much more likely to be widespread unemployment than a return to human labor. No conceivable amount of muscle can turn a giant turbine, continuously power computers, or air condition a building. On the contrary, some predictions which seem unlikely, but which are no more improbable than a computer would have seemed to a turn-of-the-century arithmetic teacher, or the moon landing to the Wright brothers' contemporaries, are at least possible:

Teaching machines will become the norm, and in time information will be directly transmitted to the human brain electronically. . . . Routine labor will be taken over by robot household servants (though many see as an alternative the breeding of intelligent animals, particularly primates, for low grade labor).[29]

A more conventional forecast is for robot machines, rather than animals. More and more uses are being found for such robots, in addition to those they now perform—i.e., jobs that are too dirty and too dangerous for human beings, such as arc welding of heavier parts, painting inaccessible places, and handling hot foundry parts. Although robots are said to need better fingers and keener intelligence and senses before there is a major takeover of jobs presently being performed by human beings, such robots are reportedly in the works, especially in Japan and the Soviet Union, and are only some few years off.[30]

The development of microprocessors, and in particular the use of silicon chips, is a different kind of technological change, but one which is said to have immense implications for the future of industry—especially for the communication/information areas.[31] One estimate has it that silicon chips will make redundant one-third of the workers in Britain's large electrical concerns.[32]

It should be noted, again, that not everyone agrees that technological advances necessarily result in diminution of human labor. In this view, technology results in new goods and services and creates new jobs. Certainly one result of technology has been new products and new services, but this does not negate the fact, observable in all directions, that people have more leisure than in the past and that the amount is growing. In fact, a current synonym for postindustrial society is "the leisure society." What this means is that technology is able to create new goods and services while simultaneously making possible less and less human work—i.e., an evidence of the strength of the technological thrust, rather than a weakness. Consequently, modern Western society has already arrived at the beginning of what has been termed the long-promised, much-worked-for day when machines could replace human labor in the production of goods and supply of services.[33]

These projections concerning the future of work can be summarized in a deliberately conservative manner:

(1) There is little evidence that the amount and proportion of unem-

ployment will decrease substantially over that which has existed in the Western industrialized countries for the last twenty years.

(2) There are almost no data which indicate that the number and proportion of the aged will not continue to increase, probably substantially.

(3) There is no reason to believe that the number of new groups entering the labor force—e.g., women—will diminish or cease.

(4) Technological progress will neither cease nor reverse.

(5) There is no reason to believe that per-person productivity will not continue to grow, regardless of its rate.

(6) No foreseeable situations indicate that the amount of human labor necessary, per person or as a total, will not continue to diminish as it has for the last hundred years at least.

Deriving from these cautious propositions

There is every reason to believe that future inventions, both mechanical and structural, will radically reduce the amount of human labor needed, including the human service professions. This is bound to have profound effects upon the social welfare system, linked as it is to work as a necessity, instrument, goal, and value.

The Future of Welfare

Some straight-line extrapolations

Costs. In the broad sense outlined in the second chapter, social welfare consists of the support of all those people who are not personally and directly engaging in activities designed to secure material necessities and luxuries. The more of the former there are, the greater the burden on the latter. That burden is already causing resistance and resentment. In many countries and subdivisions, social welfare costs more than any other single service of the government, and in some places more than all of them together.

In the United States, state and federal social welfare services cost $4 billion in 1928, but $112 billion in 1968,[34] and rose from 13.5 percent of the gross national product in 1968[35] to

23 percent by 1971.[36] Since 1950, social welfare costs in the United States have grown about seventeen times at current prices, or four times in real terms.[37] Take military pensions alone (which are not even usually included in social welfare computations): The U.S. Army pays out in military pensions more than it pays its active soldiers every year, more than the Air Force spends annually to buy missiles and planes, and more than the Navy spends in a year to buy ships.[38]

In Australia, federal welfare expenditures increased by almost 92 percent from 1974 to 1976.[39] In the German Federal Republic the rise was from 37 percent of the gross national product in 1970 to over 47 percent in 1975.[40] In England, social security is by far the most costly service and the largest single item of all general government expenditure. It costs more than defense, education, health and personal social services, and housing.[41]

The recent and continuing financial crisis in New York City is in large measure due to the costs of social welfare and pensions. One of the reasons for "revenue sharing" by the U.S. federal government with the state governments was the inability of some of the latter to maintain their social welfare programs. Part of the reason for this phenomenon is that once social welfare programs are set into motion, they are almost never reduced or phased out. Wilensky, reanalyzing Cutright's study of 76 countries, found that the age of social insurance programs is the strongest predictor concerning their extent and benefits.[42] Further, many programs establish categories of recipients and schedules of payments. Thus benefits become mandatory, and programs grow almost automatically. This is what has been termed "uncontrollable spending,"[43] and it is virtually limitless.

One result of such increases in social welfare costs is growing resentment on the part of those who pay the costs against those who reap the benefits. It has been noted, for example, that in a period of increasing unemployment those who are working become increasingly defensive about keeping their jobs and maintaining their incomes.[44] There is real danger that the resistance to higher taxes as such will spill over into the social contract implied in the current obligation of the employed to provide income for the unemployed and older population.[45] Another possibility is the actual bankruptcy of social insurance programs. In Germany, the extension of the welfare state is said to have reached a point not very far from that at which people will be unwilling to pay for social benefits.[46] Such rumblings have been heard from Scandinavia for some time now.

Although votes to increase coverage and benefits in American social security have been rather easily given in the past—indeed, it was considered political suicide to vote against such measures—the financial difficulties of the program as envisioned create dilemmas for the politicians.[47] There may be no alternative in the future to cutting social security benefits, although this entails "breaking faith" with those who contributed during their working lives. However, as pointed out previously, social security is not really an enforceable insurance contract, and lack of funds to cover benefits—and drying up of new sources of such funds—may result in partial or complete repudiation of its contract on the part of the government. With growing costs, this may become necessary. In other words, it may be necessary to break the link between work and welfare before that link breaks society.

Demography. Similarly, demographic changes and inflation have caused financial havoc among some insurance-type programs. The fiction of a trust fund has had to be abandoned, as the amounts paid into such funds at the rates of twenty to thirty years ago are insufficient for payments at current rates. Nor do current premiums suffice for current payments, in many cases. As the retired population continues to grow in relation to the working population, this problem can only become more acute.

The same situation will obtain concerning unemployment. Not only will the number and proportion of the aged grow, but as population increases and per-person productivity continues to grow the number of employable persons who cannot find work will also become a larger and larger problem. Already "we are confronted with the awesome task of creating millions of new jobs in addition to those that will be created by normal or even superheated growth in the economy."[48] The present insurance-type plans will not be able to cope with this change. More and more people will not be able to find enough work to acquire vestedness in such programs, and more and more people will exhaust their rights without finding new work.

Personal problems. Nor should social workers view this only as a financial problem. Since social-psychological factors can acquire a functional autonomy of their own, people having long-term difficulty in finding a job can develop attitudes of resignation and hopelessness which, on the one hand, can become real obstacles to active job-seeking,[49] and on the other can develop into a toxic condition,[50] or the assumption of a sick role.[51]

Riskier, but very possible, predictions

There is no reason to believe that the growth in social welfare costs will end, or even slow down.[52] On the contrary, the number of economically active persons is going to fall considerably after the year 2000. The number of pensionable people in 2035 will be 1.5 million higher than in 1970, with the basis of the population pyramid growing ever narrower.[53] Whereas the ratio of active earners to retired pensioners, for example, is 4 : 1 today, by the year 2025 it is expected to be 3 : 1 or 2 : 1.[54] However, given the increases in longevity mentioned previously, the lowering of retirement age, or a decided swing toward early retirement, there is no reason why this should not reach parity, with one working person for every retired person, or even an inverse ratio.

Similarly, with one person producing enough for 1.3 persons—expected to become 1.45 soon—there is no reason why continuing technological progress, resulting in greatly increased per-person productivity, cannot increase that ratio to parity or beyond. Indeed, one agricultural worker produces enough to feed another 57 people. There is nothing inherent in industry and services which makes them less susceptible to productivity increases than is agriculture.

It is impossible to predict at what point the rising ratio of nonworkers to workers will either bankrupt the social welfare system, cause violent resistance among workers, or both. But there must come a time when the sheer number or proportion of people living on social welfare will not allow that condition to be looked at or treated as undeserving. They will not be content with incomes below the poverty line, however that may be defined, or with living standards below that which they were accustomed to or below that of others. They will demand the right to a decent, dignified life simply because they are alive.[55]

The growth of the welfare rights movement, as manifested in a number of organizations,[56] indicates some stirrings in this direction. Recent history indicates how strong such a movement may become. If there is, as some hold, too much resistance to increasing the shares of the elderly by reducing the "slice of the pie" that goes to the working population,[57] we may see a repetition of the Townsend Movement, albeit in a somewhat different form: When the elderly felt themselves to be victims, rather than partners, during the Great Depression, they organized. At one time there were estimated to be 10 million adherents in 1200 clubs. Their newspaper had a circulation of over 200,000. Their political potential was greatly responsible for the adoption of American Social Security, and, as late as 1939, an amendment supported by the movement brought favorable testimony from 50 congressmen and 2 senators.[58] It is unlikely that large numbers of the current and future elderly will rest content in a condition of gross inequality relative to the working population.

Thus, whether based upon straight-line extrapolations or riskier predictions, the future of social welfare appears to be a no-win game. If the birth rate drops, as proponents of Zero Population Growth hope, then there will be proportionately fewer young working people in the future, supporting growing numbers of the elderly. If the birth rate grows, increasing per-person productivity will ensure growing unemployment. If jobs are redivided into smaller and smaller segments, feelings of uselessness, alienation, boredom, anomie, and resentment will grow. If large numbers of jobs are abolished, those who work will resent that fact and resist the support they are forced to provide nonworkers, and those without jobs will envy the income of the workers.

Leisure

Whether hours are shortened but jobs retained or many jobs are abolished, the result will be massive increases in leisure time. The role of social workers in dealing with the problems and possibilities of leisure has been and is almost insignificant except during the heyday of group work in the fifties,[59] and a return to this field can be expected. However, with the growth of leisure to date, other professions have entered the field, and there are those who define themselves as leisure experts, professionals, and academics.[60]

As work becomes quantitatively and qualitatively less and less important in people's lives—less time at work and less interest in or satisfaction from work—leisure pursuits will grow in importance. Increasingly, people are defining themselves in terms of their leisure, rather than their work, activities.[61] Indeed, the growth of leisure-oriented industries is a phenomenon of our times. Recreation vehicles, tennis shops, motels, cruise agents and ships, television—the list is virtually endless. The U.S. Department of Commerce estimates that about 60 percent of passenger car costs and maintenance can be attributed to pleasure.[62]

In fact, a qualifier sometimes offered against the anticipated growth of leisure is that leisure industries will require so much manpower that there will be no appreciable growth in leisure available—an argument fascinating in its logic.

Some very risky predictions

To this point, this chapter has dealt with straight-line extrapolations and some more venturesome predictions as regards the future of work and of welfare. What would happen, however, if present trends were to accelerate enormously or if new situations create quantum jumps in the direction being discussed? For example, suppose Cunningham's prediction comes true, and 10 percent of the people do all the work needed in society? How will the others be supported? How will they be viewed? How will they feel about themselves? How will they spend their time? The numbers alone will have a tremendous impact on thinking and values: "Shall we continue to regard the other 90 per cent in the same light in which we viewed yesterday's 4 per cent or 5 per cent unemployed? The question answers itself."[63]

The answer is that in the long run we will have to adopt a method of distributing society's resources other than through job-holding, because that is the only way we can break the present necessity to ensure that supply and demand remain in balance—"a necessity that... is incompatible with the continued development of the individual and the continued survival of the world."[64] In other words, since the values which undergird the present welfare system have been grafted onto an economic system which has been termed intrinsically hostile to the welfare ethic,[65] a new set of values which do not place work at the center of human existence is required. Some possible futures based on this conception are the subject of the next chapter, but it might be wise to first take a look at the transitional period which would be required to arrive at such a completely new situation.

The Transitional Stage

Whether one uses straight-line extrapolations, probable or possible future events, logic, or hunches, it is almost certain that eventually most human labor will be replaced by mechanical means. These may be called, and may include, mechanization, microprocessors, cybernetics, robots, or names yet to be invented, but the result will be the same—a world in which mechanical slaves work full time, all the time, with no psychological or sociological problems, and do the great majority of all the work needed.

For people to adapt to such a world will require a fundamental reconsideration concerning human values, and, indeed,
the meaning of life itself. Such a reconsideration will probably
flow from the march of events, rather than preceding it, and
will require and engage all the means of socialization now
extolling the virtues and rewards of work. The change to be
experienced will not be a change *within* the system, which is
somewhat easier to adapt to, but rather a change *of* the
system,[66] with all its threat to established modes of thinking
and doing. After all, the automatic machine is the precise
equivalent of slave labor, and anyone who attempts to compete
with slave labor must accept the same conditions of pay, hours,
fringe benefits, pace, and so on. Such conditions applied to
current labor would create an economic situation, not to mention the personal situations, which would make the Depression
of the 1930s seem a "pleasant joke."[67] Consequently, the more
current society emphasizes, defends, and reinforces the present
system of income distribution, the greater will be the wrench
and dislocation when it becomes necessary to change.

There are, it seems, at least three kinds of transitional periods
possible.

The cataclysm scenario

Ferkiss describes the underlying basis of this scenario:

Industrial society is not so much being transformed into a postindustrial, technological society as it is breaking down—economically, politically, and culturally. Rigidities in social institutions and
attitudes create a society comparable to a geological formation with
fault lines where slippage is inhibited and great earthquakes therefore necessarily build up. The existential revolution is building up
pressures that can lead to cataclysm, or it can be converted into . . .
a 'cultural shock-front' after the passage of which man will enter
upon a new and stable plateau of existence.[68]

The "cataclysm" scenario implies that reduction in human
labor will occur quite rapidly, and efforts to spread the remain-

ing work will reach the point of uselessness. Although, as in Zeno's paradox, there may be no logical limit as to how small units of work may become, in practice the limit can be analyzed and described.

Consequently, in this version of the transition, those who are working will attempt to safeguard their jobs, their values, and their incomes against a constantly growing group which attempts to usurp them. They will be supported by society which, despite its failure to provide everyone with jobs, will nevertheless continue to maintain and defend the job-income structure. In order that nonworkers should *want* to work—that is, to continue to subscribe to the existing values and structure—work will be further glorified. In a sense, this is a societal denial of reality, followed by a type of reaction-formation. The more work becomes mere time-filling and devoid of meaning,[69] the more numerous and stronger will become efforts to prove that work is both necessary and satisfying. This, indeed, is the raison d'etre of the recently emerged Quality of Working Life movement—an attempt to breathe satisfaction back into that work which exists,[70] rather than as a quality of life movement that would help people leave the unsatisfying world of work.

With the further glorification of work will come its corollary—that welfare is to be denigrated. This is the basis for what has been called the "welfare bind"[71]—hostility toward and derogation of the assisted poor in a society which creates and maintains the conditions causing poverty.

Although it is impossible to predict precisely when or under what conditions the flash point will occur, the essence of the cataclysm scenario is that the change, when it comes, will be extremely difficult, stressful, and possibly violent. This kind of transition will not only be difficult to make, but is sure to produce many casualties.[72] The reason for such a development will be society's stubborn refusal to plan for or even to consider the postindustrial, leisure, almost workless society which lies in the future.

The peace scenario

Another scenario is that, with the handwriting quite clear on the wall, the steps toward an almost workless society will be planned, paced, and supported. One possibility is that as jobs are taken over by technology, displaced workers will continue to receive their full salaries and perhaps even benefit by raises given other workers in the future, rather than to be paid an unemployment benefit, for a limited period of time, at a level considerably lower than that of the last salary. There is already precedent for such a step—namely, the previously mentioned guaranteed annual salary of longshoremen. Guaranteeing lifetime, rather than annual, salaries to displaced employees presents no insurmountable economic problem. Even given the costs of amortization, fuel, and repairs, the fact that a machine requires no salary or social benefit, works day and night, needs no vacations or sick time, does not gossip or dawdle, does not show up late or take Mondays off, and thus can produce many times what the worker could, makes payment of even several salaries as profitable as the previous situation.

Another peaceful possibility is the extension of universal income-maintenance programs. Thus, where family allowances pay benefits based upon the number of children, this could easily be expanded to include all family members. Or the resources made available by almost complete mechanization could be distributed through a reverse income tax, with supplements for special needs, payable to every person, or every adult, or every family head, with no vestedness requirements and in amounts sufficient for a satisfying life-style.

For this peaceful scenario to be workable, reductions in human labor should not be translated solely into more profits, or more goods and services, but should also result in maintaining the incomes of displaced workers. As technology advances, the number of nonworkers would grow, but not at the expense of workers. Value shifts would nevertheless be required if nonworkers are not to be looked down upon and are not to view themselves as deprived. Leisure activities would need to acquire social approbation. The competent tennis player, sailor, or chess player would probably require no special arrangements, but equating television viewing with reading the classics, or spectator sports with activity, or doing nothing discernible with being busily engaged will take a great deal of resocialization of the public. In particular, the concepts of normalcy and morality, as they have extended to work in the past, will have to be revised.

The passion scenario

The third possible scenario involves neither conflict nor passive acceptance of the inevitable, but rather an active, passionate attempt to achieve a workless world as a societal goal of overriding importance. In this situation, every effort would be made to invent and use labor-saving devices. Inventors, scientists, and workers would be offered large bonuses, in addition to guarantees of salary continuation, for labor-saving methods and machines. R and D funds would be enormously enlarged. Rather than fear of job loss, workers would enthusiastically try to figure out reasons why they are not needed.

The goal of a workless society would be supported in every way that work is glorified today. The release of human creativity and the increase of human happiness, which would come from freedom from the need to work, would become a societal goal of the highest importance. Mechanization and the desire for efficiency would not be stifled by fear of job losses.

There is no question but that a passionate desire to reduce human labor as much as possible would release a flood of creativity and inventiveness concerning labor-saving devices. For example, it was once dogma in the U.S. South that no machine could pick cotton. Separating the bolls from the leaves required human hands and intelligence. Once the exodus of southern Black farmers and farm hands to the cities and to the North took on sizable proportions, however, a mechanical cotton picker immediately hove into sight. Similarly, in other fields, the philosophy of mechanization has followed the fact of labor shortages. There is no reason to believe that it will not continue to do so, unless a deliberate effort is made to anticipate the future by consciously and deliberately seeking to reduce human labor to the smallest amount possible.

Even in the most benign of these scenarios there will certainly be many difficulties. So socialized are we all to view work as both necessary and desirable that a long period of reeducation may be necessary.[7 3] There is considerable danger that the required value change may not take place at the pace desired,[7 4] and that compulsive work may last longer than compulsory work.[7 5] Gabor, using the Exodus as an example, speaks of forty years as the time that might be required for educating a new generation which can live in leisure, and advocates "make-work" as necessary during the transitional period.[7 6] That a transitional period is necessary, however, seems to be generally agreed.

Once the basic facts and the probable future of the work-welfare link are understood, and the various ways in which the needed changes can come about are analyzed, it would seem axiomatic that society, social planners, or especially social welfare planners would begin to take conscious steps to reduce human labor and to arrive at a different basis for work, for leisure, and for welfare, as well preparing society to absorb these changes. Unfortunately, life is not that simple.

The views and values which have become attached to the subject of work are so deeply rooted that they often make objective discussion of the subject impossible. Most people simply *do not want to hear* the idea that work may become less important to people or that jobs may not be a central life interest. The very thought of people living a good life without (much) work bothers many people. It has been remarked that even a picture of "men at ease and in the middle of plenty" makes people observing it nervous and abusive.[7 7] Further, there is even a feeling that pain, including that derived from the necessity of work, is really an ennobling experience, of which people should not be deprived. Some people feel that the world needs pain in it, and they have become incapable of imagining that there could come a time when pain could cease to be. In short, pain (work) becomes a bad habit.[7 8]

A prerequisite, then, for a world without work is that there should be some other dominant value—that people should strive for, judge themselves and others by, and get psychic and material rewards from some value other than work. Some possibilities in this direction are the subject of the next chapter.

NOTES

1. H. E. Striner, *1984 and Beyond: The World of Work* (Kalamazoo: Upjohn Institute, 1967), p. 1.

2. Ibid.

3. Sheppard and Rix, op. cit., pp. 36-37.

4. V. C. Ferkiss, "Technological Man," in J. A. Inciardi and H. A. Siegel, *Emerging Social Issues: A Sociological Perspective* (New York: Praeger, 1975), pp. 157-193.

5. This is the method used by the United Nations in their population projections. *Concise Report on the World Population in 1970-75 and Its Long-Range Implications* (New York: United Nations, Department of Economic and Social Affairs, 1974), ST/ESA/SER.A/56.

6. F. Emery, *Futures We Are In* (Leiden: Martinus Nijhoff Social Sciences Division, 1977), p. 81.

7. M. Polanyi, "Tacit Knowing: Its Bearing on Some Problems of Philosophy," *Reviews of Modern Physics* 34 (1962): 601-616.

8. F. C. Ikle, "Can Social Predictions be Evaluated?" in D. Bell, *Toward the Year 2000: Work in Progress* (Boston: Beacon, 1967), p. 109.

9. Weiner et al., op. cit., p. 7.

10. K. Newton, "Some Socio-Economic Perspectives on the Quality of Working Life." *International Journal of Social Economics* 5 (1978): 179-187.

11. *Concise Report,* op. cit.

12. Bell, op. cit., p. 331.

13. Ibid.

14. Emery, op. cit.

15. Sheppard and Rix, op. cit., pp. 1-3; in addition, life expectancy at birth will have risen from 71 (in 1976) to about 75, beginning about 2050. P. Myers, *1976*

World Population Data Sheet (Washington, DC: Population Reference Bureau, 1976); *Concise Report,* op. cit.

16. Ibid., p. 4.

17. S. S. Tobin, "The Future Elderly: Needs and Services," *Aging* 279/280 (January/February 1978): 22-26.

18. Ibid.

19. Sheppard and Rix, op. cit., p. 48.

20. *Concise Report,* op. cit.

21. Sheppard and Rix., op. cit., p. 3.

22. D. Schafer, "Population, Age Structure, and Wealth," in *Human Well-Being: The Challenge of Continuity and Change* (New York: International Conference on Social Welfare, 1978), pp. 154-169.

23. Bale, op. cit.

24. T. Roszak, "Technocracy's Children," in J. A. Inciardi and H. A. Siegel, *Emerging Social Issues: A Sociological Perspective* (New York: Praeger, 1975), p. 90.

25. M. D. Dymmel, "Technology in Telecommunications: Its Effect on Labor and Skills." *Monthly Labor Review* 102 (January 1979): 13-19.

26. Shimmin, "The Future of Work," op. cit.

27. B. Strehler, "Implications of Aging Research for Society." *Proceedings of 58th Annual Meeting of Federation of American Societies for Experimental Biology, 1974* 34 (January 1975): 7.

28. Ibid., p. 6.

29. Ferkiss, op. cit., p. 164.

30. *World of Work Report* 4 (July 1979): 56.

31. A. Cherns, "Work and Work Organizations in the Age of the Microprocessor." Paper delivered at the NATO Conference on *Changes in the Nature and Quality of Working Life,* Thessaloniki, Greece, August 1979; to be published in K. D. Duncan, D. Wallis, and M. M. Gruneberg, *Changes in Working Life* (Chichester: John Wiley, forthcoming.)

32. British Broadcasting Corporation, *The Chips Are Down,* television documentary film, 1979.

33. Scott, op. cit.

34. March and Newman, op. cit.

35. Ibid.

36. Galper, op. cit.; and A. J. Kahn, *Social Policy and Social Services* (New York: Random House, 1973).

37. Chester, op. cit.

38. New York *Times,* January 30, 1977.

39. A. Graycar, *Social Policy: An Australian Introduction* (Melbourne: Macmillan, 1976).

40. A. Rauscher, "The Necessity for, and the Limits of, the Social Welfare State." *Review of Social Economy* 36 (December 1978): 333-347.

41. Chester, op. cit.

42. Wilensky, op. cit.

43. M. Derthick, *Uncontrollable Spending for Social Service Grants* (Washington, DC: Brookings Institution, 1975).

44. Scott, op. cit.

45. Sheppard and Rix, op. cit., p. 91.

46. Rauscher, op. cit., p. 343.

47. M. Derthick, "How Easy Votes on Social Security Came to an End," *Public Interest* 54 (1979): 94-105.

48. Yankelovich, op. cit.

49. H. L. Sheppard and A. H. Belitsky, *The Job Hunt: Job-Seeking Behavior of Unemployed Workers in a Local Economy* (Baltimore: Johns Hopkins Press, 1966), p. 150.

50. Friedmann, op. cit.

51. M. G. Field, "Structured Strain in the Role of the Soviet Physician." *American Journal of Sociology* 63 (1953): 493.

52. Chester, op. cit., p. 39.

53. Schafer, op. cit., p. 165.

54. Olmsted, op. cit.

55. This is what Smith refers to as the right to life. A. D. Smith, *The Right to Life* (Chapel Hill: University of North Carolina Press, 1955).

56. See, for example, J. F. Handler and E. J. Hollingsworth, *The 'Deserving Poor': A Study of Welfare Administration* (New York: Academic Press, 1971), p. 176: and *Welfare Mothers Speak Out,* op. cit.; and the Brotherhood of St. Laurence, in Melbourne.

57. P. Drucker, *The Unseen Revolution: How Pension Fund Socialism Came to America* (New York: Basic Books, 1976).

58. Macarov, *Incentives to Work,* op. cit.

59. The only place social workers seem to deal with leisure is in community centers—notably the Jewish Community Centers, which require a degree in social group work for career advancement.

60. At the International Seminar on Molding Leisure Policies for Educational, Communal, and Labor Frameworks (Jerusalem: Israel Leisure and Recreation Association, 1979), participants included those from recreation, communication, physical education, health, law, psychology, work, education, gerontology, philanthropy, community centers, mental health, and government. Only one social worker participated.

61. Kaplan, *Leisure in America,* op. cit.

62. Kaplan, *Leisure: Theory and Policy,* op. cit., p. 5.

63. Cunningham, op. cit.

64. R. Theobold, "Guaranteed Income Tomorrow: Toward Post-Economic Motivation," in F. Best, *The Future of Work* (Englewood Cliffs: Prentice-Hall, 1973), pp. 132-138.

65. The wording is that of L. Lowy, review of G. Vic and P. Wilding, *Ideology and Social Welfare* (London: Routledge & Kegan Paul, 1975), in *Administration in Social Work* 2 (Fall 1978): 374-376.

66. D. Coburn, "Work and General Psychological and Physical Well-Being." *International Journal of Health Services* 8 (1978): 415-435.

67. N. Wiener's *The Human Use of Human Beings,* quoted in Gabor, op. cit., p. 124.

68. Ferkiss, op. cit., p. 188.

69. Braude, op. cit., p. 190.

70. For example, "The only way government can increase production is by making work more attractive than non-work." J. Wanniski, *The Way the World Works* (New York: Basic Books, 1978).

71. Gottlieb, op. cit., p. 164.

72. L. Klein, *New Forms of Work Organisation* (Cambridge: Cambridge University Press, 1976).

73. One is reminded of Skidell's dictum: If you are for it, it is education; if you are against it, it is indoctrination.

74. E. Trist, "Toward a Postindustrial Culture," in R. Dubin, *Handbook of Work, Organization, and Society* (Chicago: Rand McNally, 1976), p. 1020.

75. Gabor, op. cit., p. 119.

76. Ibid.

77. G. Kateb, *Utopia and Its Enemies* (New York: Schocken, 1972), p. 126.

78. Ibid., pp. 126-127.

Chapter 10

THE PARAMETERS OF AN (ALMOST) WORKLESS WORLD: Some Scenarios

"Grow old along with me! The best is yet to be."
—Robert Browning,
Rabbi Ben Ezra

That a society in which there is very little need for human labor will be very different in many ways from that of the present is beyond question. There will necessarily be major changes in the income-distribution system, and therefore in social welfare. There will also be significant changes in (at least the content of) the educational system, health and mental health services (particularly in rehabilitation), corrections, and—most strikingly—in the leisure services. Individual life-styles, too, will change drastically. All such changes, however, will be based upon and conditioned by the underlying value-change which will be made necessary by and will therefore flow from the minimization of work. Consequently, some of the possibilities of changes in societal values will be examined first, moving from the most probable to riskier predictions as before, followed by some projections concerning structures and processes.

Value Changes

Work plays such a central role in the world today, structuring the day, offering contact with others, providing identification, and resulting in rewards, that it requires an effort of the imagination for most people to picture work as nonexistent. The removal of work as a value would seem, to many people, as the creation of an immoral world. Yet, if work is the source of alienation, anomie, and frustration for an enormous number of people, as it seems to be, then the removal of work should result in more happiness and mental and physical health—provided something more satisfying replaces it.

The simplest way to predict future value changes is to extrapolate from the present situation, using a logical construct. This is the method used by Mitchell, who has examined alternative futures based upon Maslow's hierarchy of human needs.[1] In each of Mitchell's three projections physiological and security needs are assumed to have been, in large measure, met. In our terms, this would stem from a sufficient income and from guarantees that this income would continue for life.

In Mitchell's "momentum" scenario (presumably so-called because it involves a continuation of present trends), the need for self-esteem would be dominant. Emphasis will be placed upon doing well whatever one chooses to do, to be successful at it and proud of the results, and thus to gain self-esteem. This does not necessarily require the approbation of others, but rather "doing one's own thing"—whatever one thinks interesting to, promising for, or important to, oneself. This would be an individualistically oriented society. However, Mitchell also posits a strong subordinate value in this society, which is belongingness. Thus, one might do one's own thing in company with others doing the same thing, and the resultant structure might be termed "individualistic groups." The roots of this type of society might be found in the counter-culture which began in the sixties, in which young people joined or founded groups in which they could do their "own thing" without the restrictions or pressures of the larger culture. Although there undoubtedly were and are abuses by and within such groups (and some cynical exploitation of them, as in some cults), their contribution to society included a heightened awareness of ecology, a deeper concern for human relations, and a rejection of societal sham, pretense, and hypocrisy. With not-working as the norm, the search for self-esteem might continue to emphasize these areas, while going on to become the cutting edge of new concerns.

Mitchell's second possibility is that society will move toward a more collective mode of life—the "belongingness" society. In this type of society emphasis will be placed on doing things together, on creating the type of interpersonal relationships which lead to acceptance by others. Undistracted by the need to work, with time not structured by job demands, group activities will proliferate. Being a good group member, loyal to the others, and contributing to the maintenance of the group, regardless of its aims or activities, will result in approbation. Being a "good member" will be an accolade, while being a "fringe" member, or even worse an "outsider," will be declassé. This pattern has its modern parallel in the more than two thousand communes said to exist in the United States and, with a longer and more stable history, in the Israeli kibbutz.

Indeed, the kibbutz, which has been described in detail in numerous places,[2] was established as the prototype of the ideal future society. The founders, as well as present-day members, view the kibbutz as the best and proper way of life, and at least hope—if not more than that—that its pattern will spread to the rest of the world. Although work in the kibbutz, as in the larger society, is a fundamental value, membership in the group itself is at least of equal importance. That is, people are voted into membership in the kibbutz on the basis of the sincerity of their belief in the kibbutz way of life, their ability to fit in with the rest of the members, and the promise they represent in terms of strengthening the group as such. The highest compliment in the kibbutz is to be called a "chevraman"—literally, a social person, or a group person—meaning that one pitches in wherever needed, is understanding and supportive, and represents the ideals of the group in everything one does.

The belongingness society would place less stress on achievement and more on relationships. We should find family ties strengthened, neighborhoods more meaningful, and organizational life proliferating.[3]

The third of Mitchell's projections to be discussed here is the mature growth society—the growth referred to being individual, not national economic, growth. This model stems from Maslow's self-actualization need. In this model, people would attempt to achieve maximum individual growth, to use all of their potential to the utmost, to be and become everything they are capable of being or becoming. Self-actualization differs from self-esteem, because in the latter one strives to excel, even though the activity itself may be marginal or even meaningless, and may not require all of one's effort. The "thing" that one does may be a matter of momentary inclination or passing interest. In the self-actualization frame, however, one attempts to identify and use all of one's powers to the utmost.

In this society we might expect to find a growth in "know thyself" groups or services—psychiatry and psychoanalysis, consciousness-raising attempts, and preoccupational guidance—as well as expanded formal and informal education efforts, ranging from crafts to the classics.

It should be noted that Mitchell sees the mature growth society as the hardest to achieve, not because of economic difficulties or societal structures, but because of "the paucity of off-the-shelf, proven knowledge of how to produce self-actualizing people."[4] Yet, given the workless society, we may not have to achieve such a society so much as let it come into being.

If work as the dominant value in American life is replaced by another, equally dominant value, it will not be confined to the needs identified by Maslow. In describing possible ascendant values which will come into being in an almost workless society, there are a number of good candidates. Given the American free education system, and the prestige (if not always the money) accorded the well-educated, it is quite possible that education will replace work as the central value in a workless society. In such a situation, persons with double doctorates might become the top elite, with university faculty—especially those teaching exclusively in doctoral programs—making up the upper stratum of society. Below the middle classes of those with master's and bachelor's degrees would be the equivalent of today's bluecollar workers—those who did not go to university. "Poor people," to be pitied and help, or despised and punished, will be those who did not go to school or dropped out of their own volition. People unable to compete intellectually will be seen as disabled, entitled to help and protection. But those who have the intelligence and refuse to enroll will be the deviants, to be scorned and avoided. If, in this scenario, material goods are not divided equally or according to need, then differential rewards will accompany educational accomplishments, and getting ahead financially will be dependent upon one's grades.

Somewhat more fantastic values can easily be imagined. If music were to become a dominant value, then prima donnas and maestros would make up the elite, followed perhaps by performers, manufacturers of musical instruments, purveyors of sheet music, and so on. The tone deaf might become the pathological, and lovers of silence, the deviants.

In a steady-income society, however, values would not necessarily be utilitarian. The way in which one used one's time would be judged by society. In this situation, a number of other values might come to the fore. Volunteering to help others in a number of ways might be the focus of leisure for many people. This does not necessarily have to be in place of or as a supplement to work in the usual sense. Gidron's study of volunteers indicates little desire on the part of volunteers that what they do be similar to paid work, but rather that there be opportunity for contact with others, an opportunity to do something interesting, and an opportunity to be of service to others.[5]

The number of additional values which might become important are legion. There might be a return to religious belief and manifestation, or even the creation of a syncretic or new religion, which will become the core of societal striving.

Finally, it is also possible that there will be no dominant value in future society. People will be free to use their free time as they see fit, within the limits of law. This will not have to be "constructive," "productive," or "positive." Those who like to sit and watch the grass grow will do so, and those who want to learn skills or participate in activities will have ample opportunity, provided by society, to do so. The latter might become a focus of the volunteering mentioned previously. However, leisure will no longer be seen as useful only because it helps people become better workers.[6]

If some of these scenarios seem fantastic, they have their precedents and even current examples. Education as a central value has always marked traditional Jewish life. Only recently has this been formalized into university education. For centuries this tradition was carried on with the rabbi, sage, or learned man instructing others in small groups, or in one-to-one relationship, in the chavura, or peer-instruction groups, or in self-study. The scholars were supported by the nonscholars and, as Rotenberg has pointed out, equal status accrued to each. Honor was paid those supporting students, and honor was paid to students.[7] In some areas of Jewish life today this symbiotic relationship continues.

Similarly, there are religious orders in which the central value is service to others—through nursing, care of orphans, social action—and in which the members are supported through taxes on or gifts of others. The existence of such a symbiotic relationship does not require that there be more, or an equal number of, "others" who work; given sufficient resources, which our basic scenario calls for, other values can be supported or enlarged.

Unfortunately, so many people have been conditioned to consider as ideal a hierarchy in which all other values are determined in respect to their relation to the economic[8] that value change seems not only threatening, but distinctly malevolent. The utopian novels and science fiction of the past,[9] most of which were intended to really portray a utopia, were read as horror stories by many. Today the world's literary visions of the future have been termed "almost a nightmare."[10]

And yet a society based upon education as the dominant value, on service to others, on self-fulfillment, even on the freedom to do what one most enjoys is hardly a future from which one must recoil in horror. To do those things which a robot cannot do: "To build, carve, write, act, design, to recover the charm of craftsmanship in an atmosphere of freedom. Is this prospect so alarming?"[11]

Take, for example, the most completely workless civilization the world has ever known—that of ancient Greece. As outlined in Chapter 2, work was seen as a threat to the important aspects of life. It was possible in those circumstances not only to talk about a life not based on the need to work, but to practice such a life. The presence of slaves to do the work made such application possible, of course. In the fourth century all full citizens were in receipt of a sufficient amount of food and money to secure them their livelihood.[12] Leaving out of consideration the feelings of the slaves (since in the future these will be mechanical, not human, slaves), what was the result of a society in which work as we know it was virtually nonexistent? We owe to the ancient Greeks the beginnings of modern drama, dance, philosophy, mathematics, and other arts and sciences too numerous to list. Freed from the day-to-day exigencies of making a living, they were able to create in widely different fields, as well as enjoying life as they did so. There is no valid reason to believe that modern humanity will, or will be able to, do less.

Nor is the Puritan ethic that the devil finds work for idle hands supported by the evidence. A study of the effect of leisure on family life concludes that time spent at home is an extraordinarily strong factor toward marital cohesion.[13] In fact, it is the constant preoccupation with work and economic questions which obscures concern for even more important implications of life.[14]

The Distribution of Resources

If work is to be disassociated from income, or income from work, then another method of distributing the resources of society—i.e., the fruits of work—must be devised. Many of the futuristic scenarios, realistic as well as fantastic, assume that this will be done on an equal-shares basis. In this view, since (practically) no one will work, there will be no basis for differential rewards.

It is possible that it is this vision of everyone sharing equally, regardless of differences in motivation, effort, ability, behavior, and morals, which causes the unwillingness or inability of many people to contemplate a future almost without work. The very prospect seems immoral and is often flagellated with scare words like "socialism," "communism," and "collectivism." But there are models of partial or complete division of resources without a basis in differential amounts of labor.

Australia, Canada, Denmark, and Israel, among others, have univeral children's or family allowances. Payments are made to every family with children, regardless of attachment to the labor force or any other condition except, in some cases, some residency or citizenship requirements. These programs are based upon a philosophy that children—all children—deserve the right to grow up healthy and happy, regardless of their parents' work record, criminal record, education, or anything else. This is in contrast to the situation in which "children . . . suffer from poverty and malnutrition on the grounds that the parents ought not to have had them."[15]

An extension of the principle that everyone has a right to a decent life, regardless of any other consideration, is found in the various plans for a guaranteed minimum income, through the medium of a reverse income tax or through some other means, now being contemplated in a number of countries.[16] Being devised in a work-centered world, the problem with most of the current proposals is that they contemplate different rates for those in the labor force and those outside, and they do not pay enough to bring everyone out of poverty. In a workless society, there is no reason why these restrictions should continue.

Scott uses a pragmatic explanation as to why the gains from productivity growth have not already resulted in a more egalitarian society:

> The economic and in some cases social benefits that could derive from some technology are not shared by the community or by the victims of displacement. They are appropriated by the people who

make the technology, those who own it and the skilled and highly paid workers who operate it.

The Utopias of the past all assumed a sharing of the benefits. The fortunate few for whom there was no work would be entitled to a standard of living, generated by surplus created by the machines and the men and women who worked them. This living standard could, and would, be high enough to allow a useful creative existence for all. The machines and the productive capacity exist, but the sharing ideal has not eventuated.[17]

The proposed equal division of income or resources, or even flat-rate payments as in most children's and family allowances, is based upon the principle of equality. There is another possibility, however, and that consists of sharing on the basis of equity—to each according to his or her needs. Means-tested programs, currently in use in Australia, are examples.

Perhaps the best example of a complete social system based upon the principle of equity is in the aforementioned kibbutz. Although it is basically a work-centered society, in which everyone is expected to contribute according to his or her ability, there are no differential material rewards for amount of work, type of work, or quality of work. Every member receives the necessities and luxuries of life, with allowances made for special needs. Thus, some kibbutzim not only have television and telephones in each member's apartment, and kibbutz-owned cars that members may use, but provide for trips abroad. The aged are provided for, as are the disabled. Care in the kibbutz has been said to extend beyond "from the cradle to the grave," which was the concern of the original welfare state proposal, to care "from the womb to the tomb," which is literally true. The results of this egalitarian society, as judged by observation, experience, and research are—to state it conservatively—no worse than those of competitive society, and in a number of significant ways much better.

Although the work requirement has always been strong in the kibbutz, there are marked differences in patterns of work. Asked to rate all other members of the kibbutz as exceptionally good workers, above average workers, average workers, or poor workers, 218 respondents created a range which extended from 177 votes for one member as an exceptional worker to 119 votes for another as a poor worker. By use of the standard deviation 38 overworkers and 39 underworkers were identified. Nevertheless, every member received his or her share of resources, regardless of work pattern.[18]

With the passage of time, prosperity and mechanization have led to decreased need for human labor in the kibbutz. Enormous hothouses, furnishing some kibbutzim with the major part of their income through flowers flown to European markets every morning, are automated to the point that two workers are assigned to them. In fact, some predictions of the future of the kibbutz envision a workless society in which the fruits of automation allow the members to live in veritable mansions, travel abroad quite often, and participate full time in politics, education, defense, and other areas.

Another possibility is that the distribution of income will not be on equal or equitable bases, but will be tied to whatever dominant value replaces that of work. For example, in an education-centered society, not only status and prestige would extend to the educators, but material rewards as well. Then students would be paid in accordance with their grades, and those unable or unwilling to study would not only be shunned, but condemned to poverty. One could make similar projections for music, physical strength, military prowess, or religiosity as the yardstick against which income would be determined. Somewhat more difficult, but not impossible, would be the transformation of neighborliness, altruism, good citizenship, successful parenting, and other attributes which defy easy quantification.

Who Will Do the Work?

As reduction in work hours takes place in present-day society, the reduction is shared more or less equally among all workers. Everyone who works simply works fewer hours, days, or years. Most projections of diminishing work time assume a continuation of this pattern—i.e., it is assumed that everyone capable of it will work throughout his or her working life (however that is defined), but this will include fewer hours or days per week, and longer vacations. Whether the days drop to three, or two, or even one; whether the hours are twenty, ten, five, or one; everyone would be expected to work most of his or her lifetime. Under this arrangement, resource distribution would continue to be based on work, with differentials for type and amount of work.

However, this arrangement would not solve the problem of the nonworking population—the aged, the young, the disabled, and those who could not report to work even for such limited time periods. The distinction between the deserving and the undeserving poor would thus remain and, work incentives still being necessary, the nonworkers would be kept financially disadvantaged in relation to the workers.

Another possibility would be to concentrate the work during certain years. Whatever work required of an individual would be performed within a narrow span of years, whether this would involve full-time, overtime, half-time, or less. One proposal to this effect was made during the days of the Great Depression, in which everyone would work between the years of 18 and 26, after which they would be free to live on the level provided, or to work to achieve higher levels, if they so wished. [19]

More recently, there have been proposals that life consist of alternating sections of education, work, and free time, continuing until final retirement from work. [20] By increasing the education and free-time segments, society could arrive at an almost nonwork situation.

A third possibility is a variation on current flexitime arrangements, whereby a worker puts in his or her hours, but at individual convenience, within certain limits. People could work for two, three, or more years, depending upon society's needs, but could pick their own time to do it. Some might want to work while young and get it over with; others might want to wait until their children are all on their own; still others might want to put it off until they could not do other things they enjoyed. This arrangement could also be combined with the minimum hours required, so that some would elect to work 1000 hours in one year (or even less), while others would stretch it out—100 hours a year each of ten years. Or the years that one worked could be determined by outside forces—e.g., the government. Just as the selective service system determined who joined the army when and who was excused, so the years that one was to work could be decided by chance.

Another possibility, admittedly written with tongue in cheek, takes at face value the purported desire of most people to work, and their reported satisfactions from working. Let work be left to those who enjoy it,[21] and thus volunteer for it. If, as societal mythology has it, there would be too many people vying for the privilege, then a lottery might be arranged, or, better yet, people could bid for the right to work. Or, still based upon the supposition that people want to work or that some people want to work, the privilege of working could be a reward for attainment—educational excellence, for example, or musical talent, or athletic prowess.

The face-absurdity of the last two proposals is apparent, but they bring into sharp focus some of the equal absurdities in the generally accepted belief that most people enjoy their work, prefer to work, and are unhappy when not working. These are clearly artifacts of a work-centered society. Let the great majority not work, and it is very doubtful whether even an extremely curtailed amount of work would be accomplished voluntarily. The usual assumptions and reports concerning work motivations have been made in cultural settings where work is regarded as an important part of life. If leisure becomes a more important alternative to work, not working may become more socially acceptable.[22]

It would also be possible and make more sense to reverse the thrust of the last two proposals, and to regard work as punishment, as it is in some places today—e.g., prisons. Work could then be performed only by prisoners. If the number proved insufficient, work could become the punishment for more minor crimes, instead of fines, as for traffic offenses. The type of work could even fit the crime—hard work for serious crimes, light work for minor transgressions. Work could also become punishment in another way. Persons who did not attain society's minimum standards in certain areas might be required to work. The standards might be as various as personal behavior, interpersonal relations, educational attainments, or participation in civic activities.

Finally, it might be possible, and easier, to simply maintain the present system in which the workers are an elite, better supported than nonworkers. In this case the small percentage who work would be given incomes higher than all others. If the majority were living at a sufficient level—measured in absolute terms—then poverty would be relative, and the reference group of most people would be others more or less like themselves. The amount of resentment against the 10 percent who were the elite might not become serious. Choosing the 10 percent, however, would present the same problems mentioned previously and could be done through the same means—by rotation, by chance, or by attainments of various sorts.

In any case, decisions about who should work in an almost workless situation present interesting, but not insurmountable, problems. As long as there is no differential material reward attached to working and not working, or to different kinds or amounts of work, the division of work can be made on a number of different bases.

Summarizing: Work can either continue to dwindle so that people continue to work, but put in less and less time, leaving untouched the problems of those who cannot or should not work, or the necessary work can be concentrated in a relatively small minority. Incomes can continue to be based on work, perpetuating current inequalities and inequities, they can be based upon other valued activities, or they can be distributed more or less equally. In every case, the value of work will diminish, to be replaced by a number of other standards—education, talent, altruism, human relationships, volunteering, good citizenship, and others.

NOTES

1. A. Mitchell, "Human Needs and the Changing Goals of Life and Work," in F. Best, *The Future of Work* (Englewood Cliffs: Prentice-Hall, 1973), pp. 32-43.

2. There are a number of good books explaining the kibbutz. See, for example, Y. Criden and S. Gelb, *The Kibbutz Experience: Dialogue in Kfar Blum* (New York: Herzl Press, 1974).

3. "More sharing and more trust," in Trist's words. Trist, op. cit., p. 1011.

4. Mitchell, op. cit.

5. B. Gidron, "Volunteer Work and Its Rewards." *Volunteer Administration* 11 (1978): 3.

6. A. N. Pack, *The Challenge of Leisure* (New York: Macmillan, 1934), p. 17.

7. Rotenberg, op. cit., final chapter.

8. G. Negley and J. M. Patrick, *The Quest for Utopia* (Garden City, NY: Doubleday, 1964), p. 575.

9. Ibid.; H. B. Franklin, *Future Perfect* (London: Oxford University Press, 1966).

10. Franklin, op. cit., p. 391.

11. Kranzberg and Gies, op. cit., p. 218.

12. Hasebroek, op. cit., p. 35.

13. K. Varga, "Marital Cohesion as Reflected in Time-Budgets," in A. Szalai, *The Use of Time* (The Hague: Mouton, 1972), p. 360.

14. V. S. Lewis, op. cit.

15. Lalonde, op. cit., pp. 18-19.

16. At the moment of writing, such a proposal has been approved by an interministerial committee in Israel and is before the Government (Cabinet), after which, if approved, it will come before the Knesset (Parliament). Such a plan was narrowly defeated in America—liberals felt it was too stingy and conservatives felt it was too generous. See D. P. Moynihan, *The Politics of a Guaranteed Income: The Nixon Administration and the Family Assistance Plan* (New York: Free Press, 1969).

17. Scott, op. cit.

18. Macarov, "Work Without Pay," op. cit.

19. C. Bird, *The Invisible Scar* (New York: Pocket Books, 1967.

20. F. Best and B. Stern, *Lifetime Distribution of Education, Work and Leisure: Research, Speculations and Policy Implications of Changing Life Patterns* (Washington, DC: Washington University, 1976, unpublished. Quoted in M. Kaplan, *Leisure: Lifestyle and Lifespan*, op. cit. (Philadelphia: Saunders, 1979).

21. A. McLean, *Mental Health and Work Organizations* (Chicago: Rand-McNally, 1970), p. 20.

22. M. Argyle, *The Social Psychology of Work* (Harmondsworth: Penguin, 1974), p. 246.

Chapter 11

CONCLUSION (AND A PERSONAL NOTE)

"We must view with profound respect the infinite capacity of the human mind to resist the introduction of useful knowledge."

—Thomas Raynesford Lounsbury,
quoted by F. C. Lockwood, *The Freshman and His College,* 1913

"A man with a conviction is a hard man to change. Tell him you disagree and he turns away. Show him facts and figures and he questions your sources. Appeal to logic and he fails to see your point."

—L. Festinger, H. W. Riecken,
and S. Schachter, *When Prophecy Fails*

On Planning

Changes in basic societal values do not come about simply because someone decrees it. Only when facts and circumstances have brought people to a readiness for change, or when they require change, can such efforts bear fruit. I have no illusions, therefore, that this book—or any number of books like it—will bring about major changes in current values. Changes in the world of work, however, which are clearly coming sooner or later, will make such basic changes not only necessary, but welcome.

Most changes, too, are not man-made or the result of plans. The depletion of fossil fuels, for example, on the physical side, or the continuing demand for equality and/or equity by various minority groups, on the social side, are simply happening. The role of planning is to try to determine how the effects of such developments will be dealt with. In the same way, the changes which are taking place in the world of work require thought and effort if the result is not to be chaos.

It may be, of course, that the projections flowing from the previous chapters will be confounded by future events. There may not come into being a large and growing proportion of social welfare recipients (i.e., nonworkers), in relation to the number of workers. The amount of human labor required may not shrink to a problematic base. Workers may not refuse to maintain social welfare recipients at a much higher level than heretofore—a level of sufficiency-to-abundance—without complaint, resentment, and resistance. And it is possible that the large proportion of social welfare recipients will remain content with a poverty or near-poverty level of existence. However, there are certainly enough indicators in past and present trends to make it at least possible that any or all of these things will happen. It would be tragic for the future if our present values, emotions, or biases, or even pure inattention, kept us from acknowledging the possibility and attempting to plan for it.

Sheppard and Rix put this point of view well:

> It is valuable and practical—not merely interesting—to think about the future . . . such thinking should provide a basis for . . . decision making on the part of individuals, organizations, and the government. . . . Such "controlled speculation" allows us to formulate some options for controlling or influencing that future.[1]

Further:

> It is better to consider . . . arguments on their merits than to dismiss them out of hand, and better to prepare for the contingency that we

may be more correct than wrong. . . . In any event, the charge of crying wolf does not mean that there are no wolves.[2]

In the same vein, take the method of dealing with national defense. These are usually considered such important matters that plans are routinely drawn to cover even the most remote contingencies. There does not have to be consensus, nor even majority opinion, that the contingency will eventuate, to justify the drawing of plans. Together with such plans, indicators which would signify the onset of the contingency are identified. Social planning, unfortunately, does not follow the same model. And yet planning for future socioeconomic possibilities is as important in its own way as is planning for military security.

The indications of coming changes in the world of work, and therefore in the work-welfare link, are too clear to be ignored. It is also highly unlikely that these changes will be minor, and that they can be absorbed by some tinkering with the present system. Taking the present system as immutable, inevitable, or for granted, and not planning for an alternative system, has already shown itself bankrupt in the face of the problem.[3] It is not enough to try to predict the future. With all the alternatives before us, what is needed is an inventing of the future.[4]

There are at least four strong and interrelated reasons why we should plan for the future:

(1) There are real alternative futures before us.
(2) We can to a useful extent anticipate and picture what those futures may be.
(3) We have the means to chart a course among those alternative futures rather than just drift in a tide of time and events.
(4) We have the moral obligation to use these capabilities.[5]

As rational, intelligent persons, and as feeling, caring people, we need to consciously confront the future, with all its possibilities, with the intention not just to endure and not just to prevail, but to enjoy and help all others enjoy a fuller, happier life. If this book succeeds in stimulating thinking and debate as to how that is to be done, it will have served its purpose.

And a Personal Note

The author of a book learns more while writing than others do from reading it. Writing this book has been a difficult but rewarding experience. Some of my preconceptions were shaken and changed as I got deeper into the data, while others were confirmed and strengthened, and some ideas arose that were completely new to me.

However, the overwhelming impression that remains with me is the realization of the strength of the emotions with which most people regard the subject of work. I have had occasion to present some of the ideas in this book as they unfolded, as work in progress, at various classes, seminars, and colloquia as well as discussing them with colleagues, friends, and family. Almost without exception the initial reaction to my questions and doubts about the wisdom of linking welfare to work, and the necessity and desirability of work as such, has been one of amused disbelief. No one has believed on first hearing that I could be serious. Questioning the role of work seems to be so socially unacceptable, such a breach of manners and morals, that listeners did me the "favor" of assuming that I was pretending.

When finally convinced that *I* am serious in my contentions, the usual audience reaction is to become humorous—to crack jokes, to offer themselves as subjects for experimentation, and so on. One does not have to be deeply immersed in Freudian theory to recognize the role of humor in these cases as covering disquiet and unease. People are simply uncomfortable in the presence of such questions.

Further, as a teaching device, I have asked members of various groups from Pennsylvania to Jerusalem, from Garden City to Melbourne, whether anyone present would cease working if he or she were assured of an adequate income otherwise. Of the few brave souls who ventured to raise their hands, I have made the request that they put these feelings into a simple declaratory statement to the group present—e.g., "If I were assured continuation of my present salary for life, I would stop doing all work." After overcoming the obvious difficulty of summoning up courage enough to make such a statement, the person doing so has almost invariably accompanied it with a smile. Almost no one in my experience has made this statement with a straight face. Asked why the smile, they are usually unable to come up with a coherent explanation. The smile, of course, is metacommunication, saying, in effect, "I'm joking," or more precisely, "I know that what I am saying seems shocking or immoral, so if you find it so, please assume that I am only fooling."

After the amused responses have been overcome, and when it is clear that I really do believe that nonworkers should be paid what they need, even if it gives them much more than other people make as salaries, and after I answer the subsequent question as to why people would work with the comment that many of them should not and that much work is unnecessary, undesirable, or unsatisfying, the reaction turns to scorn and derision. Even members of academic faculties, presumably objective, open to new ideas, and judging proposals rationally, have been known to become defensive (and sometime offensive), irrational, and obviously upset at the thought that work might not be a completely positive phenomenon. Some become angry that such a heresy is voiced, while others persist in trying to laugh it off, assuming—despite repeated protestations to the contrary—that no more or less respected academician could seriously hold such a view. If I persist, the next reaction is, to nitpick the data: "How big was Goodwin's sample?" "Gans didn't use empirical data," and such.

The final type of reaction, and one which usually closes off further discussion, is resort to ad hominem arguments: "Well, you may not be happy in your work, but I love my work and put in lots of extra time at it."

These reactions are not confined to formal meeting situations. When, at a social gathering or visiting new acquaintances, I am asked, "What is your particular field?" I have learned to mumble "social welfare policy," which usually stifles further questions or interest. I am forbidden by my family, reinforced by an occasional raised eyebrow, to discuss the ideas outlined in this book in informal, friendly settings. We have seen too many evenings turned into debates and sometimes shouting matches; too many friends begin to eye me with the suspicion that I have been pulling their leg; and, conversely, too much mutual respect transmuted into a relationship where I am to be humored and kidded because I dare question the nobility, righteousness, and usefulness of hard work as a central societal value.

These reactions have only served to confirm for me—not that I am necessarily correct in my predictions, but that if I am even partially correct—what an enormous task there is ahead of us in adapting to the new situation with as little disruption, conflict, and suffering as possible. If social workers and social welfare planners evade this responsibility, no other profession will undertake it.

"The task is difficult; the time is short; and the goals are urgent."

NOTES

1. Sheppard and Rix, op. cit., p. ix.
2. Ibid., p. vii.
3. B. Smoot, "Giving Up on the Problem: Life on the Job." *Nation* 225 (1977): 81-84.
4. Gabor, op. cit.
5. J. F. Coates, "Why Think About the Future: Some Administrative-Political Perspectives." *Public Administration Review* 36 (September/October 1976): 580-585.

SOURCES

Adams, L. P. *Public Attitudes Toward Unemployment Insurance: A Historical Account with Reference to Alleged Abuse.* Kalamazoo: Upjohn, 1971.

Allardt, E. *Dimensions of Welfare in a Comparative Scandinavian Study.* Helsinki: University of Helsinki, 1975.

Allen, V. L. "Personality Correlates of Poverty," in V. L. Allen, *Psychological Factors in Poverty.* Chicago: Markham, 1970.

――― *Psychological Factors in Poverty.* Chicago: Markham, 1970.

Alston, J. P. and K. I. Dean. "Socioeconomic Factors Associated with Attitudes toward Welfare Recipients and the Causes of Poverty." *Social Service Review* 40 (1972): 13-23.

Amendment to Family Law (Support) 1959. Jerusalem: Government of Israel, 1959. (Hebrew)

Anthony, P. D. *The Ideology of Work.* London: Social Science Paperback, 1978.

Arendt, H. *The Human Condition.* Chicago: University of Chicago Press, 1958.

Argyle, M. *The Social Psychology of Work.* Harmondsworth: Penguin, 1974.

Arnold, M. G. and G. Rosenbaum. *The Crime of Poverty: A Basic Overview of the Social Welfare Problem.* Skokie, IL: National Textbook, 1973.

Bale, M. D. "Worker Adjustment to Import Competition: The United States Experience." *International Journal of Social Economics* 5 (1978): 71-80.

Ball, R. M. *Social Security Today and Tomorrow.* New York: Columbia University Press, 1978.

Barfield, R. E. and J. N. Morgan. *Early Retirement: The Decision and the Experience and a Second Look.* Ann Arbor: University of Michigan, 1975.

Barth, M. C., G. J. Carcagno, and J. L. Palmer. *Toward an Effective Income Support System: Problems, Prospects, and Choices.* Madison: University of Wisconsin, 1974.

Beck, B. M. "Welfare as a Moral Category." *Social Problems* 14 (1967): 260-264.

Bell, D. "The Future That Never Was." *Public Interest* 51 (1978): 35-73.

――― *Toward the Year 2000: Work in Progress.* Boston: Beacon, 1967.

Bequele, A. and D. H. Freedman. "Employment and Basic Needs: An Overview." *International Labour Review* 118 (May/June 1979): 315-329.

Bernardo, R. M. *The Theory of Moral Incentives in Cuba.* University: University of Alabama Press, 1971.

Bernfield, A. "Structural Improvements with a View to Employment Maintenance." *International Social Service Review* 31 (1978): 123-143.

Best, F. *The Future of Work.* Englewood Cliffs: Prentice-Hall, 1973.

——— and B. Stern. *Lifetime Distribution of Education, Work and Leisure: Research, Speculations and Policy Implications of Changing Life Patterns.* Washington, DC: Washington University, 1976. (Unpublished)

Beveridge, W. H. *Social Insurance and Allied Services.* New York: Macmillan, 1942.

Bird, C. *The Invisible Scar.* New York: Pocket Books, 1967.

Bishop, J. "The Welfare Brief." *Public Interest* 53 (Fall 1978): 169-175.

Black, B. J. *Industrial Therapy for the Mentally Ill in Western Europe.* New York: Altro Health and Rehabilitation Services, 1965.

——— "Vocational Rehabilitation." *Encyclopedia of Social Work.* New York: National Association of Social Workers, 1965.

Blauner, R. "Work Satisfaction and Industrial Trends in Modern Society," in W. Galenson and S. Lipset, *Labor and Trade Unionism.* New York: John Wiley, 1960.

Bluestone, B. "Low Wage Industries and the Working Poor." *Poverty and Human Resources Abstracts* 3 (1968): 1-14.

Boulet, J. and A. Bell. *Unemployment and Inflation.* London: Economic Research Council, 1973.

Braude, L. *Work and Workers: A Sociological Analysis.* New York: Praeger, 1975.

Bregger, J. E. "Unemployment Statistics and What They Mean," *Monthly Labor Review Reader.* Washington, DC: Government Printing Office, 1975.

Brinker, P. A. *Economic Insecurity and Social Security.* New York: Appleton-Century-Crofts, 1968.

British Broadcasting Corporation. *The Chips Are Down.* Television documentary film, 1979.

Brown, M. *Poor Families and Inflation.* London: Her Majesty's Stationery Office, 1967.

Bruce, M. "Thirty Years on the Politics of Welfare." *Social Service Quarterly* 52 (September 1978): 5-8.

Buchholz, R. A. "The Work Ethic Reconsidered." *Industrial and Labor Relations Review* 31 (July 1978): 450-459.

Buck, T. "Experiments with Job Creation Subsidies." *Industrial Relations* 8 (Winter 1977/78): 12-18.

Buckingham, W. *Automation.* New York: Mentor, 1961.

Burghes, L. "Who Are the Unemployed?" in F. Field, *The Conscript Army.* London: Routledge & Kegan Paul, 1977.

Busse, G. W. "Psychoneurotic Reactions and Defense Mechanisms in the Aged," in P. H. Hock and J. Zabin, *Psychopathology of Aging.* New York: Grune & Stratton, 1961.

Caplovitz, D. "Economic Aspects of Poverty," in V. L. Allen, *Psychological Factors in Poverty.* Chicago: Markham, 1970.

Carter, G. W. and L. H. Fifield. *Welfare Concepts and Welfare Services: Results of an Opinion Poll of Public Attitudes.* Los Angeles: University of Southern California, 1973.

Charnow, J. *Work Relief Experience in the United States.* Washington, DC: Social Science Research Council, 1943.

Cherns, A., "Work and Work Organizations in the Age of the Microprocessor." Paper delivered at the Nato Conference on *Changes in the Nature and Quality of Working Life*, Thessaloniki, Greece, August 1979; to be published in K. D. Duncan, D. Wallis, and M. M. Gruneberg, *Changes in Working Life*. Chichester: John Wiley, forthcoming.

Chester, T. E. "Social Security, Work and Poverty." *National Westminister Bank Quarterly Review* (November 1977): 38-46.

Clayre, A. *Work and Play: Ideas of Experience of Work and Leisure*. New York: Harper & Row, 1974.

Cleveland, H. G., J. Mangone, and J. C. Adams. *The Overseas Americans*. New York: McGraw-Hill, 1960.

Coates, J. F. "Why Think About the Future: Some Administrative-Political Perspectives." *Public Administration Review* 36 (September/October 1976): 580-585.

Coburn, D. "Job-Worker Incongruence: Consequences for Health." *Journal of Health and Social Behavior* 16 (1975): 198-212.

――― "Job Alienation and Well-Being." *International Journal of Health Services* 9 (1979): 41-59.

――― "Work and General Psychological and Physical Well-Being." *International Journal of Health Services* 8 (1978): 415-435.

Concise Report on the World Population in 1970-75 and Its Long-Range Implications. New York: United Nations, Department of Economic and Social Affairs, 1974, ST/ESA/SER.A/56.

Constitution of the Union of Soviet Socialist Republics (1936).

Criden, Y. and S. Gelb. *The Kibbutz Experience: Dialogue in Kfar Blum*. New York: Herzl Press, 1974.

Csikszentmihalyi, M. *Beyond Boredom and Anxiety*. San Francisco: Jossey-Bass, 1975.

Cunningham, R. L. *The Philosophy of Work*. New York: National Association of Manufacturers, 1964.

"Current Information: France—Recent Developments in Social Security Legislation." *International Labour Review* 106 (1972): 367-372.

Current Population Reports, P-60, No. 86.

Cutright, P. "Political Structure, Economic Development, and National Social Security Programs." *American Journal of Sociology* 70 (1965): 537-549.

van Dam, A. "The Future Role of Man in Enterprise." *Personnel Journal* 56 (January 1977): 32-33, 42-43.

Daniel, W. W., "Industrial Behaviour and Orientation to Work: A Critique." *Journal of Management Studies* 8 (1969): 366-375.

Dasgupta, S. "Facing the New Era: A Plea for a New Approach to Human Well-Being," in *Human Well-Being: The Challenge of Continuity and Change*. New York: International Council on Social Welfare, 1978.

Davis, L. E. "Changes in the Working Environments: The Next 20 Years." Paper delivered at NATO Conference on *Changes in the Nature and Quality of Working Life*, Thessaloniki, Greece, August 1979; to be published in K. D. Duncan, D. Wallis, and M. M. Gruneberg, *Changes in Working Life*. Chichester: John Wiley, forthcoming.

Derthick, M. *Uncontrollable Spending for Social Service Grants*. Washington, DC: Brookings Institution, 1975.

––– "How Easy Votes on Social Security Came to an End." *Public Interest* 54 (1979): 94-105.

"Development and Trends in Social Security." *International Social Security Review* 30 (1977): 271-313.

Downing, R. I. "Economic and Social Background to Poverty in Melbourne," in R. F. Henderson, A. Harcourt, and R.J.A. Harper. *People in Poverty: A Melbourne Survey.* Melbourne: University of Melbourne, 1970.

Drucker, P. *The Unseen Revolution: How Pension Fund Socialism Came to America.* New York: Basic Books, 1976.

Dubin, R. "Industrial Workers' Worlds: A Study of the Central Life Interests of Industrial Workers," in A. M. Rose, *Human Behavior and Social Processes.* London: Routledge & Kegan Paul, 1967.

––– *Handbook of Work, Organization, and Society.* Chicago: Rand McNally, 1976.

––– F. A. Hedley, and T. C. Taveggia. "Attachment to Work," in R. Dubin, *Handbook of Work, Organization, and Society.* Chicago: Rand McNally, 1976.

Duncan, K. D., D. Wallis, and M. M. Gruneberg. *Changes in Working Life.* New York: John Wiley, forthcoming.

Dymmel, M. D. "Technology in Telecommunications: Its Effect on Labor and Skills." *Monthly Labor Review* 102 (January 1979): 13-19.

Eagle, E. "Charges for Care and Maintenance in State Institutions for the Mentally Retarded." *American Journal of Mental Deficiency* 65 (September 1960): 199.

Economic Outlook 22 (1977): 4.

Elman, R. M. *The Poorhouse State.* New York: Random House, 1966.

Emery, F. *Futures We Are In.* Leiden: Martinus Nijhoff Social Sciences Division, 1977.

Employment and Unemployment, May, 1977. Canberra: Bureau of Statistics, 1977.

Employment Security Review 22 (1955): 57-58.

Encyclopedia Britannica. Chicago: Benton, 1965.

Encyclopedia Britannica Yearbook 1967. Chicago: Benton, 1967.

Encyclopedia of Social Work. New York: National Association of Social Workers, 1965, 1971.

European Industrial Relations Review 56 (September 1978): 6.

Feagin, J. R. "American's Welfare Stereotypes." *Social Science Quarterly* 52 (1972): 921-933.

Fein, M. "Motivation to Work," in R. Dubin, *Handbook of Work, Organizations, and Society.* Chicago: Rand McNally, 1978.

Ferkiss, V. C. "Technological Man," in J. A. Inciardi and H. A. Siegel, *Emerging Social Issues: A Sociological Perspective.* New York: Praeger, 1975.

Festinger, L. *A Theory of Cognitive Dissonance.* Evanston, IL: Row Peterson, 1957.

Field, F. "The Need for a Family Lobby." *Poverty* 38 (1977): 3-7.

––– "Making Sense of the Unemployment Figures," in F. Field, *The Conscript Army.* London: Routledge & Kegan Paul, 1977.

––– *The Conscript Army: A Study of Britain's Unemployed.* London: Routledge & Kegan Paul, 1977.

Field, M. G. "Structured Strain in the Role of the Soviet Physician." *American Journal of Sociology* 63 (1953): 493.

Fox, A. *A Sociology of Work in Industry.* London: Macmillan, 1971.

Franklin, H. B. *Future Perfect.* London: Oxford University Press, 1966.

Freud, S. *Civilization and Its Discontents.* New York: Paperback, 1958.

Friedmann, G. *The Anatomy of Work.* New York: Free Press, 1964.

Gabor, D. *Inventing the Future.* New York: Knopf, 1971.

Galenson, W. and S. Lipset, *Labor and Trade Unionism.* New York: John Wiley, 1960.

Galper, J. "Private Pensions and Public Policy." *Social Work* 18 (1973): 5-22.

——— *The Politics of Social Services.* Englewood Cliffs: Prentice-Hall, 1975.

Gans, H. "Income Grants and 'Dirty Work'." *Public Interest* 6 (1967): 110.

——— *More Equality.* New York: Vintage, 1974.

Gartner, A. and F. Riessman. *The Service Society and the Consumer Vanguard.* New York: Harper & Row, 1974.

Gavin, J. F. "Occupational Mental Health: Forces and Trends." *Personnel Psychology* 56 (1977): 198-201.

George, V. and P. Wilding. *Ideology and Social Welfare.* London: Routledge & Kegan Paul, 1976.

Gerard, D. "Democracy—A Fiction?" *Social Service Quarterly* 52 (September 1978): 24-27.

Gersuny, C. and W. R. Rosengren. *The Service Society.* Cambridge, MA: Schenkman, 1973.

Ghez, G. R. and G. S. Becker. *The Allocation of Time and Goods Over the Life Cycle.* New York: Columbia University Press, 1975.

Gidron, B. "Volunteer Work and Its Rewards." *Volunteer Administration* 11 (1978): 3.

Gil, D. G. *Unravelling Social Policy.* Cambridge, MA: Schenkman, 1973.

Ginzberg, E. *Jobs for Americans.* Englewood Cliffs: Prentice-Hall, 1976.

Glickman, A. S. and Z. H. Brown. *Changing Schedules of Work: Patterns and Implications.* Kalamazoo: Upjohn, 1974.

Goedhart, T., V. Halderstadt, A. Kapteya, and B. van Prang. "The Poverty Line: Concept and Measurement." *Journal of Human Resources* 12 (1977): 503-520.

Goldstein, J. H. *The Effectiveness of Manpower Training Programs: A Review of Research on the Impact on the Poor.* Washington, DC: Government Printing Office, 1972.

Goodwin, L. *Do the Poor Want to Work? A Social-Psychological Study of Work Orientations.* Washington, DC: Brookings Institution, 1972.

Gordon, M. S. *Poverty in America.* San Francisco: Chandler, 1965.

Gottlieb, N. *The Welfare Bind.* New York: Columbia, 1974.

Gouldner, A. W. *The Hellenic World: A Sociological Analysis.* New York: Harper & Row, 1969.

Grad, S. "New Retirees and the Stability of the Retirement Decision." *Social Security Bulletin* 40 (1977): 3-12.

Graycar, A. *Social Policy: An Australian Introduction.* Melbourne: Macmillan, 1976.

Griffiths, D. *The Waiting Poor: An Argument for Abolition of the Waiting Period on Unemployment and Sickness Benefits.* Fitzroy, Victoria, Australia: Brotherhood of St. Laurence, 1974.

Grimaldi, D. L. "Distributive and Fiscal Impacts of the Supplementary Security Income Program." *Review of Social Economy* 26 (October 1978): 175-196.

Grimm, J. W. and J. D. Orten. "Student Attitudes Toward the Poor." *Social Work* 18 (1973): 94-100.

Gutek, B. A., "The Relative Importance of Intrapsychic Determinants of Job Satisfaction." Paper delivered at the NATO conference on *Changes in the Nature and Quality of Working Life,* Thessaloniki, Greece, August 1979; to be published in K. D. Duncan, D. Wallis, and M. M. Gruneberg, *Changes in Working Life.* Chichester: John Wiley, forthcoming.

Gutman, H. G. *Work, Culture and Society in Industrializing America.* New York: Knopf, 1976.

Habib, J., and R. Lerman. *Alternative Benefit Formulas in Income Support Programs for the Aged.* Jerusalem: Brookdale Institute, 1976.

Hamalian, L. and F. R. Karl. *The Fourth World: The Imprisoned, the Poor, the Sick, the Elderly and Underaged in America.* New York: Dell, 1976.

Hampden-Turner, C. *From Poverty to Dignity.* Garden City, NY: Doubleday Anchor, 1975.

Hanby, U. J. and M. P. Jackson. "An Evaluation of Job Creation in Germany." *International Journal of Social Economics* 6 (1979): 79-117.

Handler, J. F. and E. J. Hollingsworth. *The 'Deserving Poor': A Study of Welfare Administration.* New York: Academic, 1971.

Hanlon, A. and S. Jacobs. "Social Work and Private Industry." *Social Casework* 50 (1969): 152-156.

Hardwick, E. "Domestic Manners." *Daedalus* 107 (1978): 1-11.

Harrington, M. *The Other America.* New York: Macmillan, 1963.

Hasebroek, J. *Trade and Politics in Ancient Greece.* London: Bell, 1933.

Hayghe, H. F. and K. Michelotti. "Multiple Jobholding in 1970 and 1971," in *Monthly Labor Review Reader.* Washington, DC: Government Printing Office, 1975.

Heap, K. "The Scapegoat Role in Youth Groups." *Case Conference* 12 (1966): 215.

Heise, K. "Changing Perceptions of the Poor." *Public Welfare* 35 (1977): 640.

Henderson, R. F. *Poverty in Australia.* Canberra: Australian Government Printing Service, 1975.

――― A. Harcourt, and R.J.A. Harper. *People in Poverty: A Melbourne Survey.* Melbourne: University of Melbourne, 1975.

Herzog, B. R. *Aging and Income: Programs and Prospects for the Elderly.* New York: Human Sciences Press, 1978.

Hock, P. C. and J. Zabin. *Psychopathology of Aging.* New York: Grune & Stratton, 1961.

Hoffman, M. L. and L. W. Hoffman. *Review of Child Development Research,* Volume One. New York: Russell Sage, 1964.

House Committee Print Number 291. Washington, DC: Government Printing Office, 1956.

Ikle, F. C. "Can Social Predictions Be Evaluated?" in D. Bell, *Toward the Year 2000: Work in Progress.* Boston: Beacon, 1967.

Inciardi, J. A. and H. A. Siegel. *Emerging Social Issues: A Sociological Perspective.* New York: Praeger, 1975.

Jackson, D. *Poverty.* London: Macmillan, 1972.

Jaques, E. *Work, Creativity, and Social Justice.* London: Heineman, 1970.

Jenkins, D. *Job Power: Blue and White Collar Democracy.* Baltimore: Penguin, 1973.

Johnston, D. F. "The Future of Work: Three Possible Alternatives," in *Monthly Labor Review Reader.* Washington, DC: Government Printing Office, 1975.

Kahn, A. J. *Social Policy and Social Services.* New York: Random House, 1973.

Kallen, D. J. and D. Miller. "Public Attitudes Toward Welfare." *Social Work* 16 (1971): 89-95.

Kaplan, M. *Leisure in America: A Social Inquiry.* New York: John Wiley, 1960.

――― *Leisure: Lifestyle and Lifespan.* Philadelphia: Saunders, 1979.

――― *Leisure: Theory and Policy.* New York: John Wiley, 1975.

――― and P. Bosserman. *Technology, Human Values, and Leisure.* Nashville: Abingdon, 1971.

Kateb, G. *Utopia and Its Enemies.* New York: Schocken, 1972.

Kershaw, J. A. "The Attack on Poverty," in M. S. Gordon, *Poverty in America.* San Francisco: Chandler, 1965.

Killingsworth, C. C. "The Role of Public-Service Employment," in J. L. Stern and B. D. Dennis, *Proceedings of the 1977 Annual Spring Meeting.* Madison: Industrial Relations Research Association, 1977.

――― "The Fall and Rise of the Idea of Structural Unemployment," in *Proceedings of the Thirty-First Annual Meeting.* Madison: Industrial Relations Research Association, 1978.

Kimmel, P. "Research on Work and the Worker in the United States," in J. P. Robinson, R. Athanasiou, and K. B. Head, *Measures of Occupational Attitudes and Occupational Characteristics.* Ann Arbor: University of Michigan, 1969.

Klein, L. *New Forms of Work Organisation.* Cambridge: Cambridge University Press, 1976.

Kohak, E. V. "Being Young in a Postindustrial Society." *Dissent* (February 1971): 30-40.

Kohlberg, L. "Development of Moral Character and Moral Ideology," in M. L. Hoffman and L. W. Hoffman, *Review of Child Development Research,* Volume One. New York: Russell Sage, 1964.

Kornhauser, A. *Mental Health of the Industrial Worker.* New York: John Wiley, 1965.

Korsching, P. F. and S. G. Sapp. "Unemployment Estimation in Rural Areas: A Critique of Official Procedures and a Comparison with Survey Data." *Rural Sociology* 43 (Spring 1978): 102-112.

Kranzberg, M. and J. Gies. *By the Sweat of Thy Brow.* New York: Putnam, 1975.

Kreps, J. M. "The Allocation of Leisure to Retirement," in Kaplan, M. and P. Bosserman, *Technology, Human Values, and Leisure.* Nashville: Abingdon, 1971.

Krickus, R. J. "White Working-Class Youth," in L. Zimpel, *Man Against Work.* Grand Rapids, MI: Eerdsman, 1974.

Kutscher, R. E., J. A. Mark, and J. R. Norsworthy. "The Productivity Slowdown and the Outlook to 1985." *Monthly Labor Review* 100 (May 1977): 3-8.

Lalonde, M. *Working Paper on Social Security in Canada.* Ottawa: Government of Canada, 1973.

Lampman, R. L. "Employment Versus Income Maintenance," in E. Ginzberg, *Jobs for Americans*. Englewood Cliffs: Prentice-Hall, 1976.

Lasson, K. *The Workers*. New York: Grossman, 1971.

LeMasters, E. E. *Bluecollar Aristocrats: Life-Styles at a Working-Class Tavern*. Madison: University of Wisconsin Press, 1975.

Leontiff, W. "The Future of the World Economy." *Socio-Economic Planning Sciences* 2 (1977): 171-182.

Levitan, S. A. and R. S. Belous. *Shorter Hours, Shorter Weeks: Spreading the Work to Reduce Unemployment*. Baltimore: Johns Hopkins Press, 1974.

——— "Reduced Worktime: Tool to Fight Unemployment." *Worklife* 3 (April 1978): 22-26.

——— M. Rein, and D. Marwick. *Work and Welfare Go Together*. Baltimore: Johns Hopkins Press, 1972.

Leviticus II : 10, VI : 9.

Lewis, O. *The Children of Sanchez*. Harmondsworth: Penguin, 1961.

Lewis, V. S. "Historical Studies and Social Policy Analysis." *Contemporary Social Work Education* 1 (1977): 36-42.

Liebow, E. "No Man Can Live with the Terrible Knowledge That He is Not Needed." *New York Times Magazine* (April 5, 1970).

Lowy, L. "Book Review." *Administration in Social Work* 2 (Fall 1978): 374-376.

Lurie, I. "Work Requirements in Income-Conditioned Transfer Programs." *Social Security Review* 52 (December 1978): 551-566.

Macarov, D. *Incentives to Work*. San Francisco: Jossey-Bass, 1970.

——— *Work Incentives in an Israeli Kibbutz*. Jerusalem: Hebrew University, 1973.

——— *Attitudes Toward Poverty in Jerusalem*. Jerusalem: Hebrew University, 1974.

——— "Work Without Pay: Work Incentives and Patterns in a Salaryless Environment." *International Journal of Social Economics* 2 (1975): 106-114.

——— "Social Welfare as a By-Product: The Effect of Neo-Mercantilism." *Journal of Sociology and Social Welfare* 4 (1977): 1135-1144.

——— "Reciprocity Between Self-Actualization and Hard Work." *International Journal of Social Economics* 3 (1976): 39-44.

——— "Management in the Social Work Curriculum." *Administration in Social Work* 1 (1977): 135-148.

——— *The Design of Social Welfare*. New York: Holt, Rinehart & Winston, 1978.

——— *The Roots of Hard Work: A Preliminary Investigation*. Jerusalem: The Hebrew University, 1978. (mimeographed)

——— and G. Fradkin. *The Short Course in Development Training*. Ramat Gan: Massada, 1973.

——— and U. Yannai. *A Study of Centers for Discharged Reservists*. Jerusalem: Ministry of Labor, 1974. (Hebrew)

Machlowitz, M. M. *The Workaholic*. New Haven: Yale University, 1976. (mimeographed)

McGregor, D. *The Human Side of Enterprise*. New York: McGraw-Hill, 1960.

McLean, A. "Work and Mental Health: Summary and Recommendations," in A. McLean, *Mental Health and Work Organizations*. Chicago: Rand McNally, 1970.

——— *Mental Health and Work Organizations*. Chicago: Rand McNally, 1970.

McLuhan, M. *Understanding Media*. London: Routledge & Kegan Paul, 1964.

Main Economic Indicators: Historical Statistics, 1955-1971, and *Supplement 1, 2, & 3.* Paris: Organisation for Economic Co-operation and Development, 1973, 1977.

March, M. S. and E. Newman. "Financing Social Welfare: Governmental Allocation Procedures," in *Encyclopedia of Social Work.* New York: National Association of Social Workers, 1971.

Markus, E. J. *Post-Relocation Mortality Among Institutionalized Aged.* Cleveland: Benjamin Rose Institute, 1970.

Marrus, M. R. *The Emergence of Leisure.* New York: Harper & Row, 1974.

The Measurement of Poverty. Ottawa: Research and Statistics Directorate, Government of Canada, 1970.

Miller, G. W. *Use of and Attitude Toward the Ohio Bureau of Unemployment Compensation: A Research Report.* Columbus: Ohio State University, 1963.

Mills, C. W. "The Meanings of Work Throughout History," in F. Best, *The Future of Work.* Englewood Cliffs: Prentice-Hall, 1973.

Milwaukee County Welfare Rights Organization. *Welfare Mothers Speak Out.* New York: Norton, 1972.

Mitchell, A. "Human Needs and the Changing Goals of Life and Work," in F. Best, *The Future of Work.* Englewood Cliffs: Prentice-Hall, 1973.

Monthly Labor Review 102 (March 1979): 91, 107.

Moynihan, D. P. *The Politics of a Guaranteed Income: The Nixon Administration and the Family Assistance Plan.* New York: Free Press, 1969.

Myers, P. *World Population Data Report 1976.* Washington, DC: Population Reference Bureau, 1976.

Neff, W. S. *Work and Human Behavior.* New York: Atherton, 1968.

Negative Income Tax. Paris: Organisation for Economic Co-operation and Development, 1974.

Negley, G. and J. M. Patrick. *The Quest for Utopia.* Garden City, NY: Doubleday, 1964.

Neulinger, J. *The Psychology of Leisure.* Springfield, IL: Charles C. Thomas, 1974.

――― "The Need for and the Implications of a Psychological Conception of Leisure." *Ontario Psychologist* 8 (June 1976): 13-20.

Newton, K. "Some Socio-Economic Perspectives on the Quality of Working Life." *International Journal of Social Economics* 5 (1978): 179-187.

New York Times. October 3, 1976, October 24, 1976, January 30, 1977.

New Zealand Official Yearbook 1972. Wellington: Government Printer, 1973.

Oechslin, J. J. "The Role of Employers' Organisations in France." *International Labour Review* 106 (1972): 391-413.

Ogren, E. H. "Public Opinions About Public Welfare." *Social Work* 18 (1973): 101-107.

Olmsted, B. "Job Sharing: An Emerging Work Style." *International Labour Review* 118 (May/June 1979): 283-297.

Orshansky, M. "Who's Who Among the Poor." *Social Security Bulletin* 28 (1965): 3.

Osborne, J. S. *The Silent Revolution: The Industrial Revolution in England as a Source of Cultural Change.* New York: Scribners, 1970.

Ostow, M. and A. B. Dutka. *Work and Welfare in New York City*. Baltimore: Johns Hopkins Press, 1975.

Ozawa, M. N. "Anatomy of President Carter's Welfare Reform Proposal." *Social Casework* 58 (December 1977): 615-620.

——— "Issues in Welfare Reform." *Social Security Review* 52 (1978): 37.

Pack, A. N. *The Challenge of Leisure*. New York: Macmillan, 1934.

Palmore, E. B. "Physical, Mental and Social Factors in Predicting Longevity." *Gerontologist* 9 (1969): 103-108.

Parker, S. *The Future of Work and Leisure*. New York: Praeger, 1974.

Pasamanick, B., D. W. Roberts, P. W. Lemkau, and D. B. Krueger. "A Survey of Mental Disease in an Urban Population: Prevalence by Race and Income," in F. Reissman, J. Cohen, and A. Pearl, *Mental Health of the Poor: New Treatment Approaches for Low-Income People*. New York: Free Press, 1964.

Patchen, M. *Some Questionnaire Measures of Employee Motivation and Morale: A Report on Their Reliability and Validity*. Ann Arbor: University of Michigan, 1965.

Plattner, M. F. "The Welfare State *vs.* the Redistributive State." *Public Interest* 55 (Spring 1979): 28-48.

Podell, L. *Families on Welfare in New York City*. New York: Center for the Study of Urban Problems, The City University of New York, n.d.

Polanyi, M. "Tacit Knowing: Its Bearings on Some Problem of Philosophy." *Reviews of Modern Physics* 34 (1962): 601-616.

Poverty 39 (1978).

Poverty Fact Sheet. London: Child Poverty Action Group, n.d.

Price, C. R. *New Directions in the World of Work: A Conference Report*. Kalamazoo: Upjohn, 1971.

Prigmore, C. J. *Social Work in Iran Since the White Revolution*. University: University of Alabama Press, 1976.

Productivity and the Quality of Working Life. Scarsdale, NY: Work in America Institute, 1978.

Query, W. T. *Illness, Work, and Poverty*. San Francisco: Jossey-Bass, 1968.

Quinn, R. P. et al. "Evaluating Working Conditions in America." *Monthly Labor Review* 96 (1973): 32-43.

Ragan, J. F. "Minimum Wages and the Youth Labor Market." *Review of Economics and Statistics* 59 (1977): 129-136.

Rauscher, A. "The Necessity for, and the Limits of, the Social Welfare State." *Review of Social Economy* 36 (December 1978): 333-347.

Reingold, J., R. L. Wolk, and S. Schwartz. "Attitudes of Adult Children Whose Aging Parents Are Members of a Sheltered Workshop." *Aging and Human Development* 3 (1972): 331-337.

Reissman, F., J. Cohen, and A. Pearl. *Mental Health of the Poor: New Treatment Approaches for Low-Income People*. New York: Free Press, 1964.

Reynolds, A. "Reality in One Lesson." *Public Interest* 53 (1978): 159-165.

Rhine, S. H. quote in *Newsday* (October 30, 1978): 2A.

Ritti, R. R. and D. W. Hyman. "The Administration of Poverty: Lessons from the 'Welfare Explosion' 1967-1973." *Social Problems* 25 (1977): 157-175.

Robinson, J. P. "Occupational Norms and Differences in Job Satisfaction: A Summary of Survey Research Evidence," in J. P. Robinson, R. Athanasiou, and K. B. Head, *Measures of Occupational Attitudes and Occupational Characteristics.* Ann Arbor: University of Michigan, 1969.

– – –, R. Athanasiou, and K. B. Head. *Measures of Occupational Attitudes and Occupational Characteristics.* Ann Arbor: University of Michigan, 1969.

Roby, P. *The Poverty Establishment.* Englewood Cliffs: Prentice-Hall, 1974.

Rose, A. M. *Human Behavior and Social Processes.* London: Routledge & Kegan Paul, 1967.

Rosow, J. M. *The Worker and the Job: Coping with Change.* Englewood Cliffs: Prentice-Hall, 1974.

Roszak, T. "Technocracy's Children," in J. A. Inciardi and H. A. Siegel, *Emerging Social Issues: A Sociological Perspective.* New York: Praeger, 1975.

Rotenberg, M. *Damnation and Deviance.* New York: Free Press, 1978.

Rubin, L. B. *Worlds of Pain: Life in the Working Class Family.* New York: Basic Books, 1976.

Ryan, W. "Blaming the Victim: Ideology Serves the Establishment," in P. Roby, *The Poverty Establishment.* Englewood Cliffs: Prentice-Hall, 1974.

Rytina, J. H., W. H. Form, and J. Pease. "Income and Stratification Ideology: Beliefs about the American Occupational Structure." *American Journal of Sociology* 75 (1970): 703-716.

Sanders, D. S. *The Impact of Reform Movements on Social Policy Change: The Case of Social Insurance.* Fairlawn: Burdick, 1973.

Sarason, S. B. *Work, Aging, and Social Change.* New York: Free Press, 1977.

Saxer, A. *Social Security in Switzerland.* Berne: Paul Haupt, 1965.

Schafer, D. "Population, Age Structure, and Wealth," in *Human Well-Being: The Challenge of Continuity and Change.* New York: International Conference on Social Welfare, 1978.

Schiltz, M. E. *Public Attitudes toward Social Security 1935-1965.* Washington, DC: Department of Health, Education, and Welfare, 1970.

Schottland, C. I. "The Changing Roles of Government and Family," in P. E. Weinberger, *Perspectives on Social Welfare: An Introductory Anthology.* New York: Macmillan, 1974.

Schrecker, P. *Work and History: An Essay on the Structure of Civilization.* Gloucester, MA: Peter Smith, 1967.

Schulz, J. H., T. D. Leavitte, and L. Kelly. "Private Pensions Fall Far Short of Preretirement Income Levels." *Monthly Labor Review* 102 (February 1979): 28-32.

Schweinitz, K. de. *England's Road to Social Security.* Philadelphia: University of Pennsylvania Press, 1943.

Scott, D. "A View of the XIXth International Conference on Social Welfare: The Discussions and the Organisation." Paper delivered in Jerusalem, August 27, 1978. (mimeographed)

The Secret of Affluence. Washington, DC: Department of Agriculture, 1976.

Shapiro v. *Thompson,* 394 U.S. 618 (1969).

Sheppard, H. L. and A. H. Belitsky. *The Job Hunt: Job-Seeking Behavior of Unemployed Workers in a Local Economy.* Baltimore: Johns Hopkins Press, 1966.

――― and S. E. Rix. *The Graying of Working America: The Coming Crisis of Retirement-Age Policy.* New York: Free Press, 1977.

Shimmin, S., "The Future of Work." Paper delivered at the NATO Conference on *Changes in the Nature and Quality of Working Life,* Thessaloniki, Greece, August 1979; to be published in K. D. Duncan, D. Wallis, and M. M. Gruneberg, *Changes in Working Life.* Chichester: John Wiley, forthcoming.

――― "Concepts of Work." *Occupational Psychology* 40 (1966): 195-201.

Shipman, C. T. *Stone-Age Cultures of the Australian Aboriginals.* Melbourne: Privately printed for the Israel Museum, Jerusalem, 1977.

Shostak, A. B. and W. Gomberg. *New Perspectives on Poverty.* Englewood Cliffs: Prentice-Hall, 1965.

Simmons, O. *Work and Mental Illness: Eight Case Studies.* New York: John Wiley, 1965.

Smith, A. D. *The Right to Life.* Chapel Hill: University of North Carolina Press, 1960.

Smith, W. T., II. "Public Welfare: The 'Impossible' Dream." Paper delivered at the County Officers Association of the State of New York, Rochester, N.Y., 1975. (mimeographed)

Smoot, B. "Giving Up on the Problem: Life on the Job." *Nation* 225 (1977): 81-84.

Social Security: 1976. Ottawa: Statistics Canada, 1976.

"Social Security Abroad: Earnings Index and Old Age Security in West Germany." *Social Security Bulletin* 40 (1977): 34-35.

Social Security Bulletin: Annual Statistical Supplement, 1975. Washington, DC: Department of Health, Education, and Welfare, 1975.

Social Security Bulletin 40 (1977): 15.

Social Security Hearings Before the Committee on Finance. Washington, DC: Government Printing Office, 1965.

Social Security Programs Throughout the World, 1975. Washington, DC: Department of Health, Education and Welfare, 1975.

Social Security Programs Throughout the World, 1977. Washington, DC: Department of Health, Education and Welfare, 1977.

Sommer, J. J. "Work as a Therapeutic Goal: Union-Management Clinical Contribution to a Mental Health Program." *Mental Hygiene* 53 (1969): 263-268.

Spilerman, S. and D. Elesh. "Alternative Conceptions of Poverty and Their Implications for Income Maintenance." *Social Problems* 18 (1971): 358-373.

Stagner, R. "The Affluent Society Versus Early Retirement." *Aging and Work* 1 (Winter 1978): 25-31.

Stanfield, J. R. "On Liberalism and Capitalism: A Reply to O'Boyle." *Review of Social Economy* 36 (October 1978): 209-211.

Stern, J. L. and B. D. Dennis. *Proceedings of the 1977 Annual Spring Meeting.* Madison: Industrial Relations Research Association, 1977.

Strauss, G. "Workers' Attitudes and Adjustments," in J. M. Rosow, *The Worker and the Job: Coping with Change.* Englewood Cliffs: Prentice-Hall, 1974.

――― "Job Satisfaction, Motivation, and Job Redesign," in *Organisational Behaviour: Research and Issues.* Madison: Industrial Relations Research Association, 1974.

Straussman, J. D. "The 'Reserve Army' of Unemployed Revisited." *Society* 14 (1977): 40-45.

Strehler, B. "Implications of Aging Research for Society." *Proceedings of 58th Annual Meeting of Federation of American Societies for Experimental Biology,*

1974 34 (January 1975): 7.

Striner, H. E. *1984 and Beyond: The World of Work.* Kalamazoo: Upjohn, 1967.

Supplementary Benefits Commission Annual Report 1975. London: Her Majesty's Stationery Office, 1976.

Szalai, A. *The Use of Time.* The Hague: Mouton, 1972.

Tannenbaum, A. S. and W. J. Kuleck, Jr. "The Effect on Organizational Members of Discrepancy Between Perceived and Preferred Rewards Implicit in Work." *Human Relations* 31 (1978): 809-822.

Terkel, S. *Working.* New York: Random House, 1972.

Theobold, R. "Guaranteed Income Tomorrow: Toward Post-Economic Motivation," in F. Best, *The Future of Work.* Englewood Cliffs: Prentice-Hall, 1977.

Thessalonians III : 10.

van Til, S. B. *Work and the Culture of Poverty: The Labor Force Activity of Poor Men.* San Francisco: R and E Research Associates, 1976.

Titmuss, R. N. *Essays on "The Welfare State."* New Haven: Yale University Press, 1959.

Tobin, S. S. "The Future Elderly: Needs and Services." *Aging* 279-280 (January/February 1978): 22-26.

Trist, E., "Toward a Postindustrial Culture," in R. Dubin, *Handbook of Work, Organization, and Society.* Chicago: Rand McNally, 1976.

Tropman, J. E. "The Image of Public Welfare: Reality or Projection?" *Public Welfare* 35 (1977): 17-23.

Varga, K. "Marital Cohesion as Reflected in Time-Budgets," in A. Szalai, *The Use of Time.* The Hague: Mouton, 1972.

Vic G. and P. Wilding. *Ideology and Social Welfare.* London: Routledge & Kegan Paul, 1975.

Vickery, C. "The Time-Poor: A New Look at Poverty." *Journal of Human Resources* 12 (1977): 27-48.

Walbank, M. "Effort in Motivated Work Behavior." Paper delivered at the NATO Conference on *Changes in the Nature and Quality of Working Life,* Thessaloniki, Greece, August 1979; to be published in K. D. Duncan, D. Wallis, and M. M. Gruneberg, *Changes in Working Life.* Chichester: John Wiley, forthcoming.

Walfish, B. "Job Satisfaction Declines in Major Aspects of Work, Says Michigan Study: All Occupational Groups Included." *World of Work Report* 4 (February 1979): 9.

Walinsky, A. "Keeping the Poor in Their Place: Notes on the Importance of Being One-Up," in A. B. Shostak and W. Gomberg, *New Perspectives on Poverty.* Englewood Cliffs: Prentice-Hall, 1965.

Waller, R. "Job Satisfaction: The Throw-Away Society." *Business Horizons* 16 (October 1973): 51-52.

Walters, J., K. B. Mellor, D. R. Cox, J. M. Taylor, and L. J. Tierney. *Cultures in Context.* Melbourne: Victorian Council of Social Services, n.d.

Wanniski, J. "Taxes, Revenues, and the 'Laffer Curve'." *Public Interest* 50 (Winter 1978): 3.

––– *The Way the World Works.* New York: Basic Books, 1978.

Warren, M. and S. Berkowitz. "The Employability of AFDC Mothers and Fathers." *Welfare in Review* 7 (1969): 1-7.

Weaver, C. N. "Relationships Among Pay, Race, Sex, Occupational Prestige, Supervision, Work Autonomy, and Job Satisfaction in a National Sample." *Personnel Psychology* 30 (1977): 437-444.

Weber, M. *The Protestant Ethic and the Spirit of Capitalism.* New York: Scribners, 1952.

Weinberger, P. E. *Perspectives on Social Welfare: An Introductory Anthology.* New York: Macmillan, 1974.

Weiner, H. J. and S. H. Akabas. *Work in America: The View from Industrial Social Welfare.* New York: Columbia University School of Social Work, 1974.

———, S. H. Akabas, E. Kremen, and J. J. Sommer. *The World of Work and Social Welfare Policy.* New York: Columbia University School of Social Work, 1971.

Welfare Mothers Speak Out. Milwaukee: Milwaukee County Welfare Rights Organization, 1972.

Wezel, J.A.M., van. "Re-entry into the Labour Process: A Research Among Unemployed." *Sociologia Neerlandica* 10 (1974): 162.

Whitten, E. B. "Disability and Physical Handicap: Vocational Rehabilitation," in *Encyclopedia of Social Work.* New York: National Association of Social Workers, 1965.

Wilensky, H. L. *The Welfare State and Equality: Structural and Ideological Roots of Public Expenditures.* Berkeley: University of California Press, 1975.

——— and C. N. Lebeaux. *Industrial Society and Social Welfare.* New York: Free Press, 1958.

Williamson, J. B. "Beliefs About the Motivation of the Poor and Attitudes Toward Poverty Policy." *Social Problems* 21 (1974): 634-648.

——— "Beliefs About the Welfare Poor." *Sociology and Social Research* 58 (1974): 163-175.

——— et al. *Strategies Against Poverty in America.* New York: John Wiley, 1975.

Winyard, S. *No Fault of Their Own: Poverty in Britain.* Liverpool: Liverpool Institute of Socio-Religious Studies, 1977.

Woodcock, L. "Changing World of Work: A Labor Viewpoint." Paper delivered to the American Assembly, November 1, 1973, New York City.

Woodrofe, K. *From Charity to Social Work in England and the United States.* Toronto: University of Toronto Press, 1962.

Work Disability in the United States: A Chartbook. Washington: Government Printing Office, 1978.

Work in a Changing Industrial Society. Paris: Organisation for Economic Cooperation and Development, 1975.

"Working the 100-Hour Week—and Loving It." New York Times (October 3, 1976).

World of Work Report 3 and 4.

Wright, S. R. and J. D. Wright. "Income Maintenance and Work Behavior." *Social Policy* 6 (1975): 24.

Yankelovich, D. "The New Psychological Contracts at Work." *Psychology Today* 11 (May 1978): 46-50.

Yearbook of Labor Statistics: Sixteenth Edition; Twenty-Sixth Edition; Thirty-Sixth Edition. Geneva: International Labour Organization, 1956; 1966; 1976.

Zimpel, L. *Man Against Work.* Grand Rapids, MI: Eerdsman, 1974.

AUTHOR INDEX

SUBJECT INDEX

ABOUT THE AUTHOR

DAVID MACAROV is Associate Professor at the Paul Baerwald School of Social Work at the Hebrew University of Jerusalem. He has investigated and written extensively about various aspects of social welfare and social work practice, as well as incentives to work and work patterns in Israeli kibbutzim. He was the organizer and first director of the J. J. Schwartz Graduate Program for Training Community Center Executives and has directed numerous seminars for teachers of social work in Europe, under the auspices of the United Nations and the IASSW. He holds a B.S. from the University of Pittsburgh, M.S. from Western Reserve University, and a Ph.D. from Brandeis University. His previous books include *Incentives to Work, The Short Course in Development Activities,* and *The Design of Social Welfare.*